The Greek Civil War

EDGAR O'BALLANCE

The Greek Civil War

1944–1949

WITH A FOREWORD BY
THE HON. C. M. WOODHOUSE

FREDERICK A. PRAEGER, *Publishers*

NEW YORK · WASHINGTON

BOOKS THAT MATTER

Published in the United States of America in 1966
by Frederick A. Praeger, Inc., Publishers
111 Fourth Avenue, New York 3, N.Y.

All rights reserved

Library of Congress Catalog Card Number: 66–12479

Printed in Great Britain

Contents

Maps

Foreword

by the Hon. C. M. Woodhouse, DSO, OBE, MA, MP

Greece is one of the few countries in the world, and the only one in Europe, where Communist attempts to seize power by armed force have been successfully confronted and defeated. (If Spain be regarded as another such case, which is controversial, then the qualification 'since the second world war' must be added.) There were in fact three successive attempts made by the Greek Communist party, the KKE. The first, and least well known, was made during the German occupation in 1943–44, in anticipation of an early end to the second world war. The second was made in Athens in December 1944. The third was made during the early stages of the so-called 'cold war', between 1946 and 1949.

There are two essential questions with which Major O'Ballance's expert study of *The Greek Civil War* is concerned. The first is: what made these ventures possible? The second is: why did they fail? In answering these two questions, Major O'Ballance has had the benefit not only of having studied the many sources on the recent history of Greece and the Balkans, but also of having devoted his own professional attention to other wars which originated in not dissimilar political circumstances.

The three attempts to seize power in Greece took place in circumstances which were superficially different, but all three had their origins in the convulsions of the second world war and the enemy occupation. In the first case, in 1943–44, the Communists had the only considerable armed force (known as ELAS.) in Greece apart from the Germans, who were largely indifferent to what was going on in the mountainous areas which they did not occupy. Indeed, they encouraged civil war within the Resistance movement, because it helped to minimize guerrilla interference with their own lines of communication and promised trouble for the allies when the occupation came to an end. The immediate cause of the Communist attempt to eliminate all rival Resistance forces was no doubt the belief—erroneous, as it turned out—that the collapse of Italy and the allied landings in southern Europe foreshadowed the early liberation of Greece.

Having realized their mistake, the Communists reverted to a less bellicose policy in early 1944. Major O'Ballance rightly stresses the division of opinion within the leadership of the KKE between advocates of a hard policy of seizing power by violence and a soft policy of creeping into power by infiltration and subversion. The hard policy, of which Aris Veloukhiotis was the protagonist, had failed; the soft policy, advocated chiefly by George Siantos, Secretary-General of the KKE, was then tried in its place. Up to the day of liberation in October 1944, there was good reason to think it might succeed. But the returning Greek government and the British high command proved more stubborn than had been expected, and in consequence the advocates of the hard policy came into their own again.

The outcome was the second round: the rising of December 1944 in Athens, put down with great difficulty by British forces diverted from their main task of fighting the Germans in Italy. Defeated once more, the Communists reverted once more to legal instead of revolutionary activity. But they talked openly of the 'third round' still to come, and Aris Veloukhiotis even took to the hills at once in 1945, vainly repudiating his colleagues' surrender. It was not until 1946 that the KKE, under new leadership, formally re-opened the civil war in the mountains and put the Greek authorities to their severest test during the next three years.

In the third round there continued to be the same divisions within the Communist leadership, but the issues were different. One was a matter of tactics. The successor of Aris, Markos Vaphiadis, believed in a purely guerrilla type of warfare; the successor of Siantos, Nikos Zakhariadis, who had spent the years 1941–45 in a German concentration camp, repeated the errors of the earlier period in seeking to build up a conventional army capable of beating the National Greek Army in open battle. As Major O'Ballance convincingly shows, the training and equipment supplied by the British and American military authorities in succession made this a hopeless endeavour.

There were other divisions too. The most serious was over the political issue of Macedonia, a more or less undefined territory lying partly in Greece, partly in Bulgaria, partly in Yugoslavia. The Greek Communists could never live down their unpatriotic reputation of being willing to cede Greek Macedonia to their northern neighbours. Undoubtedly the KKE was itself torn over this issue, which was one of those that weakened the party and promoted the propensity among its leaders, so fortunate for Greece as a nation, to liquidate each other.

Major O'Ballance rightly emphasizes the effect of internal feuds and errors of judgment in destroying the chances of victory for the KKE. In part these reflected the great schism between Stalin and Tito, which also contributed to their failure; but Major O'Ballance gives persuasive reasons for not regarding Tito's closure of the Greek-Yugoslav frontier to the rebels as decisive in their defeat. He lists many other contributory factors, not least of which, of course, was the determination of the British and American governments, expressed in massive material and moral support, to ensure that Greece should not pass behind the Iron Curtain.

It remains for one who shared in a good deal of the struggle and tribulation which Major O'Ballance so lucidly narrates to add a personal word on what was certainly a necessary, if not a sufficient, condition of the survival of Greece as a free nation. This was the Greeks' will to survive. Alike in their resistance to the German occupation and in their refusal to submit to Communist tyranny, the spirit of the Greek people was beyond praise. There have been few more conclusive illustrations of Napoleon's dictum that in war the proportion of moral to material factors is as three to one.

C. M. WOODHOUSE

Preface

The pattern of Communist insurgent warfare is now clear, having been slowly evolved since the late 1920s. After lying dormant during World War II, it gathered momentum to reach its peak in 1949. Successful examples are the Communist insurgent wars in China and Indo-China.

This pattern was not so clear in World War II when the Allies, Britain in particular, were in contact with the Communist guerrillas in Occupied Greece. The British officers, parachuted into that country to stir the guerrillas into active sabotage came up against a new and totally unfamiliar form of warfare. Today, the progressions of the Communist Insurgent blue-print stand out indelibly, but they have only belatedly been appreciated and fully understood.

After forming a national Party, the Communists establish an intelligence net-work and infiltrate 'cells' into all strata of society. The unvarying Communist objective is to gain control of the country as soon as possible. No holds are barred. A prematurely unsuccessful coup may drive the Communists underground, or else into the less accessible parts of the country, where they become hunted and harried guerrillas.

From this time onwards, the blue-print is studied. After the 'survival', or guerrilla, stage has been weathered, all plans and initiative go to establishing and building up a large conventional army capable of defeating that of the Government in battle. The Communists have never deluded themselves that the 'guerrilla' phase is anything but a passing one, to be got over as soon as possible. They realize that the only way the Government forces can be defeated is to beat them decisively on the battlefield. The intermediate steps, such as Protracted and Mobile Warfare, are but periods of preparation.

The Communists in China prepared the blue-print for Insurgent War, and others have striven to follow it faithfully. Sometimes, being too impatient, they have moved on to one progression before they are really ready, with disastrous results, only to be forced to revert a step to re-coup.

This was how it was in Greece, and one can trace the efforts of the Greek Communist Party to follow the accepted Communist pattern of insurrection, which they were certain must end in success.

The insurgent war in Greece was concurrent with the closing stages of the one in China, and the victories of Mao Tse-tung were so resounding that the result of the war in Greece was overshadowed and largely overlooked. This was a great pity, as in Greece the Communists were defeated, and a study of the war reveals many of their weaknesses.

The Communist defeat in Greece is usually ascribed to Tito closing his frontier, and many pundits are convinced, even to this day, that had this not been done, the insurgent war would still be in progress. This is not so, and the reasons can be discerned in this account of the struggle. They are briefly summarized and analysed in the last chapter.

Unfortunately, in this account several different sets of initials have to be frequently quoted. This is unavoidable, as there are no apt, short, descriptive phrases to replace them. They are listed in an Appendix.

EDGAR O'BALLANCE

CHAPTER ONE

Background to Strife

The Greek Civil War lasted from 1944 until 1949, but it was merely the continuation of the struggle for power that had been started by the Communists in the resistance movement during the Axis occupation of Greece in World War II, and its roots and causes went back farther still.

In this war of insurrection the Communists were defeated, a fact that is all too often overlooked, as it coincided with, and was overshadowed by, parallel but more momentous events that were taking place in China, where Mao Tse-tung's victories were ascribed to the magic supremacy of the techniques of Communist insurgent warfare. The completeness and immensity of the victories of the Red Army of China—when belatedly they were fully comprehended—caused a depression to settle on Western statesmen, generals and military theorists, as conventional warfare seemed to be impotent against it. Hardly any attention was paid to the defeat of insurgents in Greece, which was a great pity as a study of them would have revealed several premises that are only now, sixteen years afterwards, becoming more widely known and accepted.

In many ways Greece provided an ideal setting for Communist insurgent warfare, the people having warlike traditions and a record of resistance to the Turkish régime that was imposed upon them for nearly five hundred years. The very nature of the country and its economy lent themselves to resistance tactics, whether they were conducted against the Axis Occupation Forces, those of the Greek Royal Government, or against other non-Communist insurgent bands.

Background to Strife

It will be necessary to examine briefly some aspects of Greece as she was in 1939 (when this account can conveniently begin) together with a résumé of recent history, Greek territorial expansion and political stresses to provide the background against which events can be unfolded.

From a geographical point of view Greece is notable for the length of her coastline, due to numerous inlets and deep gulfs, in comparison to her size, which is about 55,000 square miles. Over the centuries this has inevitably resulted in a marked maritime element in the character of the country.

Basically a Balkan country, Greece consists of the southern part of the Balkan Peninsula, a narrow finger of land reaching eastwards over the top of the Aegean Sea to Turkey, and a large number (about 250) of islands scattered around her coasts, the largest of which is Crete. Her mainland neighbours were, to the north-west the (then) independent Kingdom of Albania, and to the north, Yugoslavia and Bulgaria, while Turkey just touched her to the east.

About sixty per cent of the 'mainland' is covered with craggy mountains and barren rocky patches, with the chief mountainous backbone running southwards down the centre of 'Continental' Greece. There are in fact no fewer than twenty-five mountain ranges in the country. The mainland is frequently referred to as 'continental' Greece to distinguish it from the Peloponnese, the large expanse on the extreme southern tip of the peninsula which is literally made into an 'island' by the Corinth Canal. Another fifteen per cent of the mainland is covered with forests.

The economic basis of the country rested on agriculture, but a few simple calculations show that only about a quarter of the land was available for that purpose. Moreover, the soil was generally poor and the methods used old-fashioned and uneconomical. Although about fifty-five per cent of the working population was employed on the land they were unable to produce enough to feed the country unaided. A number of agricultural reforms were carried out in the early 1920s, when the large landed estates were broken up, but these barely affected the problem. In the mountainous interior pastoral pursuits were followed.

Even though the country was not self-sufficient in agriculture, much of the grain was sold abroad, and luxury products, such as tobacco, grapes, olives, dried fruits and wines, were cultivated for export.

The dearth of fuel and raw materials, apart from cotton, retarded industrial development. The country was known to have mineral wealth, including iron ore, zinc, copper, lead, silver and manganese, but these deposits were neither fully exploited nor had they been completely surveyed and assessed. Greek industry was small and technically backward.

Poor agricultural yields and lack of a strong industrial potential caused Greece, a seafaring nation to some extent, to become a trading country, and in the course of trading she had built up a flourishing merchant marine which in 1939 was the third largest in the Mediterranean.

The population of Greece had expanded from about 1 million in 1829 when it first became a modern state in reality, to about 7.3 million one hundred years later. This increase was only in part accounted for by natural causes and was chiefly due to the absorption of populations as more territory was acquired during a period of Greek expansion. There were also influxes as, for instance, after the disastrous war against Turkey in 1922, when about 1.5 million Greeks living in Bulgaria and Anatolia were exchanged for Moslems who resided in Greece at the time. After this mass population movement, only tiny foreign minorities remained, and the 1928 census quotes these as being about 86,000 Turks, 18,000 Albanians and 17,000 Bulgarians. These figures would not have altered greatly by 1939.

Practically all the people (ninety-three per cent) had Greek as their native language, but there were small pockets of Turkish-speaking population in Western Thrace and some Slav ones in Macedonia. There was generally an inborn and inbred traditional dislike of the Slav by the Greek, fostered by centuries of strife and rivalry between the two.

About half the population was grouped on the plains of the Greek mainland and the coastal strips of the northern Peloponnese, and about a million people lived on the many islands. The remainder were scattered over the rest of the countryside, which in parts was sparsely populated, especially in the mountainous regions. Athens, the largest city and the capital, had a population of about 400,000, and adjacent to it the main port, Piraeus, contained some 300,000 people. Elsewhere in the country were only about twenty cities with more than 20,000 inhabitants.

The peasants who lived in the interior, forming about forty per cent of the population, were a hardy race who led a tough life, having to eke out a scanty living from pastoral pursuits or agriculture.

Living generally in widely separated villages, they had by force of nature and circumstances developed traits of sturdy independence and self-reliance, but at the same time a rather narrow and parochial outlook. For generations past they had formed the backbone of resistance movements and they had a traditional suspicion of, and opposition to, authority. The Turks, when they had tried to rule the land, had left them alone as much as possible to their own devices.

Apart from the small Moslem element and an equally small Jewish one, all were members of the Greek Orthodox Church, which played an influential part in all their lives. Abroad, its clergy were criticized for being poorly educated by comparison with their Western counterparts, but even so it was they, practically alone, who kept Greek culture and traditions alive during the period when Greece was part of the Ottoman Empire—and especially was this so before the spirit of nationalism began to flourish in the nineteenth century. It is also true that the Greek Orthodox Church was a large land-owner and was hardly progressive in many ways.

In 1939, some forty per cent of the people were illiterate.

Lack of land communications, coupled with the mountainous nature of much of the country, lent itself to insurgent fighting and successful resistance movements. There were under 10,000 miles of motorable roads in 1939, as compared with Britain, a country of roughly the same size, and which then had over 180,000 miles. These chiefly ran along the coasts or linked the main towns of the interior; few went directly over the mountain ranges. Those that did were frequently snowbound for weeks in the winter, when at times only pack-mules could get through with extreme difficulty. Many cart tracks existed that were useable for a greater part of the year, but these were mostly impassable in the depths of the winter and also in the spring when the snows were melting. The primitive road network in the interior underlined the importance of the few towns that commanded the mountain passes.

There were only about 2,000 miles of railway, mainly single track (as compared with Britain's 32,000 miles of double track). There were two railway net-works, one spreading north from Athens to link the main cities of 'continental' Greece, and then creeping into Thrace, while the other tentacled south from the capital to the towns of the Peloponnese.

Local trading was carried on around the coasts in small boats, and the Corinth Canal, which was about four miles long, cut through between the mainland and the Peloponnese, facilitated the passage of coastal shipping. Reliance on this form of transport, together with a lack of capital, tended to retard the improvement of interior land communications.

After eventually falling under the domination of the Roman Empire, when that Empire split in half, Greece came under the Eastern, or Byzantine, part, which for centuries lingered on in a decline, surrounded by rapacious enemies, pagan, Moslem and Christian.

In the fifteenth century successive portions of Greece were seized by the growing Moslem Ottoman Empire. The conventional date for the commencement of Turkish domination over Greece is 1453, when Sultan Mohammed II captured Constantinople. Some parts of Greece were not taken over by the Turks until later, such as Rhodes in 1523, Cyprus in 1571, Crete in 1669 and Tenos in 1715. A few parts, such as areas of the Ionian Islands, almost entirely escaped Turkish occupation.

At first Turkish domination was not quite the tragedy that may be supposed, as, owing to the bitterness of the schisms of the Christian Church, Greece had already been at the receiving end of numerous attempts by Western Christians, or 'Franks' as they were then more generally known, which under the guise of winning them over to allegiance to Rome, were really rapacious raids and foraging expeditions whose aim was loot and plunder. The doctrinal schism of Christianity between Greek Orthodox and Roman Catholic Churches reached such a bitter, savage pitch that the possibility of an alternative subjugation by a western country, rather than by the Turks, was dreaded.

The new Turkish overlords were strong enough to discourage Frankish raids and depredations on Greece, and under their protection the Greeks were able to live in reasonable security for those times and to indulge in trade, the warlike Turks not caring much for that sort of thing, but preferring to stick to military, governmental and administrative posts.

The Greek people as a whole, protected by the Turks and prospering in trade, seemed fairly content with their lot for quite a long time. They also enjoyed freedom of religion and their taxes were moderate. They did, however, have to contribute young male children to the Janissaries, which at one period amounted to as many as one-in-five.

The Janissaries were the household troops of the Turkish Sultans, and consisted originally of Christian youths who were taken completely away from their families at an early age, forcibly converted to the Moslem faith and trained to be soldiers. Thus they had no ties with, or sympathy towards, any of the many Moslem factions or cliques within the Ottoman Empire and so could be more wholly relied upon by the ruler. The Janissaries were feared and respected on the battlefield for nearly four centuries, and they played a great part in winning territory for the Sultans. At first their code and ideals were extremely strict, the corps being equated with a western knightly order at its best, but later it degenerated and developed into a sort of Praetorian Guard. It was destroyed by force in 1824 by the new Turkish army.

Being on the fringe of the Christian and Moslem borderland, the Greeks suffered occasionally for that reason, and at times they were co-opted into fighting for and helping both sides. In 1571, for example, a sea battle took place between Don John, of Austria, and the Turks, known as the Battle of Lepanto, and Greeks were forced to serve in both fleets. The Greeks on the mainland were encouraged to rise in support of Don John, and a small section of the population did so, but the Turks put down this revolt harshly. However, there were few after-effects and the Greeks did not seem to bear the Turks any particular ill-will for their severity. It is true that the odd small revolt and spasm of dissidence occurred in the sixteenth and seventeenth centuries, but generally they drew little deep support from the Greek populace, nor was there much enthusiasm for them. In fact Greeks increasingly entered and became influential in the Turkish civil service, and so were drawn closer to the alien régime.

In 1687, a Venetian general, Morosini, invaded the Peloponnese, and he managed to persuade some of the Greeks there to revolt against the Turks. This came to little and soon fizzled out. Morosini's invasion is now best remembered for the damage his artillery[1] did to the Parthenon at Athens. Later, the Venetian Republic held the Peloponnese for a short period.

On the whole the Turks left the Greeks alone as much as they could, giving them a measure of autonomy. They did not, for example, bother over-much about the interior of the mainland, especially in the mountainous regions, or Crete or some of the other islands. This policy resulted in the rise of lawlessness with bands of brigands, known as Klefts,[2] or Klephti, roaming areas where Turkish authority was indifferent or uninterested.

---

[1] A cannon ball struck a Turkish powder magazine in the Parthenon, and the resultant explosion partially destroyed it.
[2] From the Greek word 'klephtes', meaning thief.

These Klefts were originally Greeks who had been forced to take refuge in the mountains after the initial conquest and seizure of their lands by the Turks. They lived a wild life, existing by robbing Turks and rich Greeks indiscriminately, but their activities caught Greek imagination. Many ballads were composed about them and many tales told of their exploits.

To keep some sort of order in the interior the Turks enlisted local Greeks into an armed gendarmerie, known as the Armatoloi, to put down the Klefts. In many cases the Armatoloi were little better than the brigands themselves, and in the course of the long tussle between the two, insurgent methods and guerrilla tactics became second nature to both.

In the latter part of the eighteenth century certain European powers, particularly Russia, began to show an interest in Greece and an increased hostility to the Ottoman Empire, which was now visibly beginning to decay. They hoped to speed the decay and in the process either grab bits of it for themselves or establish their paramount influence in selected parts. This was generally the era of political awakening of the masses, an era of change and revolt, profoundly influenced, first by the American and later by the French Revolutions. These momentous events had a stirring and stimulating effect on political and nationalist emotions in parts of Europe that were still suffocating under old-established tyrannies.

So it was with Greece, and this became apparent in 1770, when Catherine the Great of Russia, engaged in one of her periodic disputes with Turkey, sought to raise rebellion in Greece in order to divert and distract the Ottoman régime. For the first time Russian overtures struck a responsive chord which resulted in a revolt in the Peloponnese when Russian warships appeared offshore. This can be said virtually to mark the beginning of Greek nationalism and of her modern history as a nation. The Turks put down this revolt with Albanian Moslem troops, but the spark had been ignited and it began to glow. Rumblings of discontent now sounded within the country, where in several places groups of Klefts were in open rebellion.

The Russians claimed the right to interfere and support Greece against her rulers on the strength of the common bond of the Christian religion, matched against the Moslem faith of the Turk, and the ties created by the marriage of the daughter of the last Byzantine Emperor to Grand Duke Ivan III, of Muscovy, in the fifteenth century. In 1547, Ivan IV assumed the title of Czar

(Caesar) and took the Byzantine double-headed eagle as his crest.

By the turn of the nineteenth century other European powers became more interested in Greece; notably Britain, which had problems of security of routes to India, and also France, Britain's rival. In 1814, the Ionian Islands, which lay just offshore from Greece in the Ionian Sea, were occupied by Britain, the Turks being unable to prevent this move, and these islands became a refuge for Greek revolutionaries, refugees and agitators from the mainland.

Early in 1821, there was an unsuccessful attempt to throw off the Turkish yoke. This was followed, on April 6th,[1] the same year, by the Archbishop of Patras unfurling the national flag and so starting the Greek War of Independence. Interested European nations encouraged the Greeks, who took to insurgent warfare. The Klefts in the mountains became the backbone of the struggle, which continued indecisively.

The war attracted foreign sympathy, but the Greek leaders quarrelled amongst themselves and so marred a unified effort. In 1824, the Turkish Sultan called in an Egyptian army, which invaded the Peloponnese and had some success against the Greek insurgents there. Britain, France and Russia were openly in favour of the Greek cause and agreed that Greece should become a separate nation divorced from the Ottoman Empire. When Turkey refused to accept this decision, action was taken and in October 1827 the combined fleets of Britain, France and Russia, under a British admiral, defeated that of Turkey off Navarino.

Pressure was exerted and during the following months Turkish forces were withdrawn from what is now the southern part of present-day Greece. The last action took place in September 1829, which virtually marked the successful end of the Greek War of Independence. The London Conference of Allied Powers issued its decision to support the establishment of a sovereign Greek state in February 1832. Turkey had been bludgeoned into accepting Greece as an independent nation and another piece of territory had been eased from the cracking Ottoman Empire. After this the Klefts, who had played such a big part in the war, became progressively less active until they finally disappeared, but their traditions, ballads and folklore lived on in the mountains.

When independence had been gained, Greece consisted only of the Peloponnese, the southern part of 'continental' Greece and some islands, but during the next hundred years there was a steady terri-

[1] Now celebrated as Greek Independence Day.

torial expansion, which was encouraged by certain European powers so that it would further weaken the Ottoman Empire. This expansion began when Britain ceded the Ionian Islands to Greece in 1864. In this quest for more territory there were setbacks. In 1879, for example, eager Greek troops prematurely moved into Thessaly and Epirus (both now forming part of northern Greece) after the Battle of Plevna, when Turkey was defeated by Russia. British pressure caused them to withdraw again, but not for long, as both these provinces were eventually made over to Greece in 1881, when the Greek frontier was advanced northwards by the Conference of Constantinople. In 1897, Greece entered into a short war against Turkey over the island of Crete, but she was defeated, with the result that Crete did not then become part of Greek territory as she had hoped.

Prior to the Balkan Wars, which began in 1912, Greece had grown to encompass an area of about 25,000 square miles. In that year she joined together with Serbia, Bulgaria and Montenegro to form the so-called Balkan Pact of Christian nations, to attack the Moslem Turk. Turkey admitted defeat in May 1913, and as part of her share of the spoils of war, Greece obtained Macedonia, part of Thrace, and Crete. A few months afterwards, in a fight with Bulgaria over part of Macedonia, Greece held on to all the territory she had obtained, which then amounted to about 55,000 square miles.

Shortly after emerging as an independent nation, Greece adopted a monarchy, the first king being Otho of Bavaria, who arrived in the country in 1833. He tended towards autocratic rule and introduced a preponderance of Germans into his Government, as well as trying to implant German culture on the country. None of these measures was popular and a rebellion, directed primarily against them, occurred in 1843. The following year, King Otho agreed to become a more constitutional monarch, but he still did not gain popularity and another rebellion, in 1862, caused his abdication.

He was succeeded the following year by another monarch, King George I, of the Glucksburg dynasty, who remained on the throne until he was assassinated in 1913. His reign coincided with a period of Greek expansion.

George I was succeeded by his son, Constantine, who had strong pro-German sympathies. His wife was the Kaiser's sister. His influence prevented Greece from participating in World War I until 1917, which led to his being replaced by his son, Alexander. On this dethronement there was a brief political upheaval and Eleutherios

Venizelos,[1] a Liberal politician, became the Prime Minister and brought his country into the war against the Central Powers. The Greek army took part in the autumn Allied offensive of 1918 in Macedonia which brought about the Bulgarian capitulation.

In 1920, King Alexander died as the result of a monkey bite and in the general election of that year Venizelos was defeated. A plebiscite was held and Constantine was recalled.

In March 1921, Greece launched a general offensive into Asia Minor, which failed, but it was renewed in June. By September, the Greeks were being pushed back by the Turks, and in August the following year (1922) the Turks, under Kemal Ataturk, drove the Greeks from Asia Minor. The area of Greek territory was accordingly reduced to about 50,257 square miles. After this defeat, sections of the Greek army gathered under General Plastiras, who headed an anti-royalist revolution which secured King Constantine's abdication.

Constantine, who had also tried to be autocratic, was succeeded by his son, George II, who did not reign long, being packed off into exile in December 1923. A Republic was declared in March 1924, but by this time Greece was in a troubled state internally and political animosity sharpened between the main parties.

In January 1926, General Pangalos, the Prime Minister, assumed dictatorial powers, and in April became the President. Later that year (August) he was deposed by a *coup d'état*, led by General Kondylis, who was actively supported by another officer, Colonel Zervas, who controlled a semi-autonomous armed force, known as the Republican Guard.[2] There was fighting in September 1926, when the Republican Guard was forcibly dissolved.

In 1928, Venizelos returned to power as Prime Minister, but a financial crisis in 1932 brought him down, when the Popular Party leader, Tsaldaris, managed to form a coalition government. The Popular Party had royalist inclinations. In 1933, an unsuccessful *coup d'état* was led by General Plastiras, who was forced to flee to France, being sentenced to death *in absentia*.

In 1935, an abortive *coup d'état* to put Venizelos, now a confirmed republican, back into power failed. As this revolt died away, George II was recalled and the Republic gently faded out. The period of the Republic had been one of instability, confusion and political

---

[1] Eleutherios Venizelos, a Cretan, had in fact revolted in 1916 and founded a short-lived Provisional Revolutionary Government.

[2] Sometimes referred to as the Republican Battalions.

strife in which democratic government had been discredited.

In January 1936, a general election resulted in a deadlock between the Liberals, who had republican aims, and the Popular Front.[1] Inter-party bitterness was such that no working coalition was possible. For a while the balance of power in the National Assembly was held by the Communist Party, which had fifteen seats. A series of deaths in the Popular Party brought General Metaxas, a former Chief of Staff of the Army, to the fore to become Prime Minister.

Metaxas became convinced that, under the cloak of a general strike to be called in August (1936), the Communists planned to seize power; so to forestall them he persuaded King George II to dissolve the National Assembly. The King, who dreaded the possibility of a civil war instigated by the Communists breaking out in Greece, such as was currently happening in Spain, signed the necessary order. This left Metaxas with dictatorial powers, and he governed with a firm hand using all methods available to him, including censorship, secret police and imprisonment without trial. His administration was efficient by Greek standards, and this strong central control prevented Greece from devolving into civil war or a state of anarchy.

Metaxas was hard on both the Liberals and the Communists, imprisoning many and banishing others. Officers in the armed forces with republican sympathies were removed, some being dismissed and others placed on half-pay. The peasants in the mountains were largely indifferent to the change in régime as they were little touched by it materially, and their only complaint was that, in the interests of good husbandry, Metaxas restricted the number of goats each was allowed to keep.

The Greek Communist Party had been formed in November 1918, and was at first known as the Socialist Labour Party of Greece. In 1924, it adopted the name of Kommounistikon Komma Ellados, the KKE. It had made a slow start, being initiated by a small group of Greek intellectuals and some students, who were inspired by the success of the Bolshevik Revolution in Russia. Party members were recruited from amongst tobacco, other industrial and railway workers, then from amongst refugees from Anatolia who lived in overcrowded, miserable conditions, and then the inhabitants of the larger cities. Following the Marxist-Leninist line, the Party looked for support from the workers rather than the agricultural peasants,

[1] The election results were: Liberals, 143 seats; Popular Front, 142 seats; Communists, 15 seats.

but although some headway was made in Athens and other provincial cities and towns, the Communists made practically no impact on the countryside.

The KKE became a member of the Comintern in 1920, and followed the official policy as dictated from Moscow. It managed to infiltrate into trade unions, snapping up key positions until about half of them were Communist-controlled or dominated. The KKE labour expert, known as Kostas Theos, rigged it so that many of his Communist colleagues were elected to the General Labour Confederation, which was a sort of combined trade union conference.

The leader of the KKE was Nicholas Zakhariadis, who after studying in Moscow had returned to Greece in 1924. Most of the governing Central Committee of the KKE had been in Russia at some time or another, and Zakhariadis had been nominated by the Comintern for the controlling position as Secretary in 1931. He became the Secretary-General of the KKE in 1935, when that post was created.

The KKE was a small unpopular party with an unpopular programme. It never managed to obtain as many as ten per cent of the votes in any election, and only gained seats in the National Assembly when the system was changed to one of proportional representation. The KKE's slavish adherence to the Comintern line of thought, its support of the Balkan Communist Federation and its advocacy of autonomy for Macedonia and Thrace were contrary to the majority Greek opinion and inclination. The Greek people as a whole favoured democracy, tended to be suspicious of their northern Balkan neighbours and were nationalistically jealous of every inch of Greek soil.

The KKE had its brief hour of glory and importance in 1936 when its fifteen seats, gained by proportional representation, held the balance between the Popular Party and the Liberals; but when Metaxas assumed full powers, he drove this organization underground, imprisoning as many members as he could lay his hands on. However, true to Communist form the KKE lay low, worked hard underground and schemed for the future.

And so we find we have an almost perfect setting and background for Communist subversive infiltration and insurgent warfare. The country was largely wild and barren, with only sparse communications, inhabited by a people who were poor and, in parts of the interior, existing only a little above starvation level. With the general poverty went attendant ills, such as disease, poor housing, lawlessness, superstition and illiteracy, and some sections of the population were rent with age-old feuds and vendettas.

The townspeople were remote from the peasants in thought and ideas, and the inhabitants of Athens were even more contrastingly sophisticated and cut off from real contact with the people of the countryside. The politicians of Athens, scheming and plotting in cafés, were largely self-centred and lived in a world of their own far removed from the hopes, fears, needs and feelings of the majority of the Greek people.

There were also strong political tensions, the main opposing elements being the Popular Party, with royalist inclinations, led by Metaxas, and the Liberals, with republican views. But there were others too, the most important of which was the tiny, but extremely virile, underground Communist Party, the KKE.

The army was perhaps the most stable factor in the nation, but even its officer cadre was inwardly rent by political affiliations. Several generals had already stepped into the political arena with varying fortune, and they had many ambitious imitators, or would-be imitators, amongst officers of equal or lesser rank. There were also a large number of officers who considered themselves aggrieved, either by one government or another. There was no doubt that the alternation of Republic and Monarchy had left a cleft in the officer cadre of the Greek armed forces, as well as in the nation as a whole.

Metaxas frankly governed by decree as a dictator, from strength rather than from popular mandate and support, and he could only be unseated by a *coup d'état* or a successful civil war. The Communists were not the only ones to seriously consider these alternatives.

CHAPTER TWO

World War II

In the unsettled period of the late 1930s the foreign policy of Metaxas seemed to favour the Germans, and it was remembered that he had been against Greece coming into World War I on the Allied side, but despite this the friendly relations established by Venizelos[1] with Britain and France remained to the extent that no rift occurred to mar the smooth surface. Metaxas tried to be friendly with everyone. From a strategic point of view Britain required a friendly Greece on her east Mediterranean flank. If Greece were to fall under the sway of either of the Axis dictators, the British sea route to the Middle East and India by way of the Suez Canal could be made untenable in war.

The Balkan countries, in which expression Turkey can be loosely included, were uneasy and suspicious neighbours, with ambivalent feelings and little warmth for each other. This was the heritage of centuries of strife and antagonism, fanned by memories of more recent wars and disputes. Most were dissatisfied with the existing state of affairs, and each felt that it had been badly done by at one time or another for the benefit of one or more of the other Balkan countries.

Bulgaria was particularly resentful, and in 1933 Turkey and Greece made an agreement lest she attack them. The Balkan Pact of the following year (1934), signed by Greece, Turkey, Yugoslavia and Rumania, was a mutual defensive arrangement by which those countries agreed to keep within their existing boundaries. Generally since coming to power Metaxas had done what he could to strengthen

[1] Eleutherios Venizelos died in Paris in March 1936

the Balkan Pact, but met with no success. All he managed was a separate non-aggression agreement with Bulgaria in 1938.

Dissatisfied with her frontiers Bulgaria had not joined the Balkan Pact, and neither had another tiny Balkan country, Albania, ruled in almost feudal style by King Zog. Small and backward, with a population of only just over one million, Albania seemed ripe for picking to include in the growing Italian Empire. King Zog, the son of a clan chieftain who had distinguished himself in the Yugoslav incursions just after World War I, had become Prime Minister in 1922, and King in 1928. The Albanian army, consisting of merely a handful of infantry units, with only small arms and a few elderly cannon, was more of an armed gendarmerie than a defence force.

Looking upon Albania as a potential bridgehead into the Balkans, Mussolini launched his army against the country on April 7th, 1939, the Italian soldiers landing at dawn at the ports of Durazzo, Valona, Santi Quaranta and San Giovanni di Medua, the only ones of any size and capacity. The Albanian army was incapable of resisting them. Italian troops entered Tirana the next day, and King Zog and his Government crossed into Greece where he was sympathetically received.[1] Within a few days the Italians made good their possession of the whole country.

Mussolini made a declaration to the effect that he 'had no designs on Greece', but the fact remained that he had forced himself right on to the doorstep of that country and was glancing slyly towards Athens and the Dardanelles. Fully realizing the strategic significance of Greece, and how militarily weak she appeared to be, Britain and France joined together to give a 'guarantee of her integrity'. This was unsolicited, and there are some doubts as to whether this was actually what was wanted by Metaxas at the time, as it might be more liable to provoke than deter. The Munich Pact of 1938 had not produced a good impression abroad of British determination and ability to protect or guarantee the security of any other nation. However, it was neither repudiated nor refused by Metaxas.

One good thing Metaxas had done for Greece was to improve the armed forces. There was no doubt that some improvement was needed. The Greek army, defeated by the Turks in 1921 and 1922, had been demoralized and the alternating Republic and Monarchy had exacerbated dissensions within it. Metaxas had removed over 2,000 officers with known or suspected Republican or Communist sympathies or connections.

---

[1] King Zog remained in exile for the rest of his life, dying in Paris in April 1961.

The Greek army consisted of conscripts, the men serving for two years before being posted to the reserve. In 1939, the standing strength was about 5,000 officers and 65,000 men. The officers were professionals. A framework of 15 infantry and 1 cavalry division and other infantry brigades existed, designed to be filled out on mobilization by reservists. When the Italians invaded Albania, General Papagos, the Chief of Staff, discreetly began to mobilize a few formations, doing this as unobtrusively as possible as the Greek Government did not want to give the Italian army an excuse for attacking Greece.

The arms were far from modern, being mainly small arms for the infantry, while the artillery had only small numbers of French and German mountain and field guns, for which there were limited stocks of ammunition. There were less than 140 anti-aircraft guns in Greece, and no modern anti-tank ones at all. The army had little motor transport and relied largely upon ox-drawn vehicles to carry its equipment and supplies. The Greek army had no tanks.

The Greek air force was small, with about 3,000 personnel, and having just over 160 French and Polish aircraft, for which there was a lack of spare parts. The Greek navy consisted of a cruiser, 10 destroyers, 11 torpedo boats, some smaller craft and 6 submarines.

Despite lack of modern arms and equipment, owing to the nature of the terrain and the fact that its training and morale had been improved by the Metaxas reforms, the army had a good defensive capability. The Greek soldier was a sturdy fighter, and on his own ground in the mountains it was hoped that he would be able to hold the Italians if they started to push their way southwards to Athens from Albania.

On September 1st, 1939, Hitler's divisions crossed into Poland, leaving Britain and France no option but to declare war on Nazi Germany. Poland was soon overrun, and then followed the long lull known as the period of the 'Phoney War', in which little military action took place. Italy stayed out of this European conflict for a time, and the Balkan countries hoped to be able to keep clear of it too. An attitude of watchful suspense prevailed in the Balkans throughout the winter of 1939–40, each country being on its most correct behaviour internationally.

In May 1940, Hitler's panzer forces tore their way through Belgium, and by June France had fallen and the British Expeditionary Force had been evacuated from Dunkirk. With things going so well for Nazi Germany, Italy stepped into the war on her side. Now that

Britain stood alone (America had not yet committed herself), her chances of survival, let alone victory, did not seem to be so good.

Beneath the apparent calm surface that formed in Greece as the people tended to draw together under Metaxas in the face of external dangers, political resentments bubbled on underground. One erupted in July 1940, when a rising against the Metaxas régime occurred in Crete, which had a strong republican tradition. Metaxas acted firmly and with speed, and the revolt quickly fizzled out, but the underlying tension remained, and was reflected in other parts of the country.

Mussolini by now was almost ready to seize Greece. He was growing bolder, and he also wished, for prestige reasons, to establish himself in the Balkans before his Axis partner. Mussolini impatiently began to commit acts of provocation, and in August 1940 the Greek cruiser *Helle* was sunk by an Italian submarine whilst at anchor at Tenos, with some loss of life. Still Metaxas held his hand and Greece remained passive.

Hitler also began creeping southwards into the Balkans and in September, when King Carol was forced to abdicate the throne of Rumania, the country became a German military protectorate with German troops stationed at key points within its borders. Seeing this Mussolini thought that he could not afford to dally much longer or else Hitler would be in Greece before him.

Hollow and superficial formalities had already been observed. In September 1939, Italy had made a declaration of friendship with Greece, and in April 1940 Greece had replied by recognizing the Italian Empire, which included Abyssinia. These niceties meant little to Mussolini, who in October handed an ultimatum to Greece accusing her of allowing British warships to use her waters and of fostering espionage and border troubles with Albania, and demanding that Italian troops be allowed to occupy the Greek islands of Crete and Corfu, parts of Epirus and the port of Piraeus. This was rejected by Metaxas, who at once gave the order to mobilize. This firm 'no' in the face of Italian demands made Metaxas immensely popular and the majority of Greek people supported him in his stand.

Early on the morning of October 28th, Italian troops moved over the Albanian border into Greece, where they struck unexpectedly stiff resistance. Mussolini had initiated this move without previously informing Hitler of his intentions, as he had hoped to steal a march and present him with a *fait accompli*.

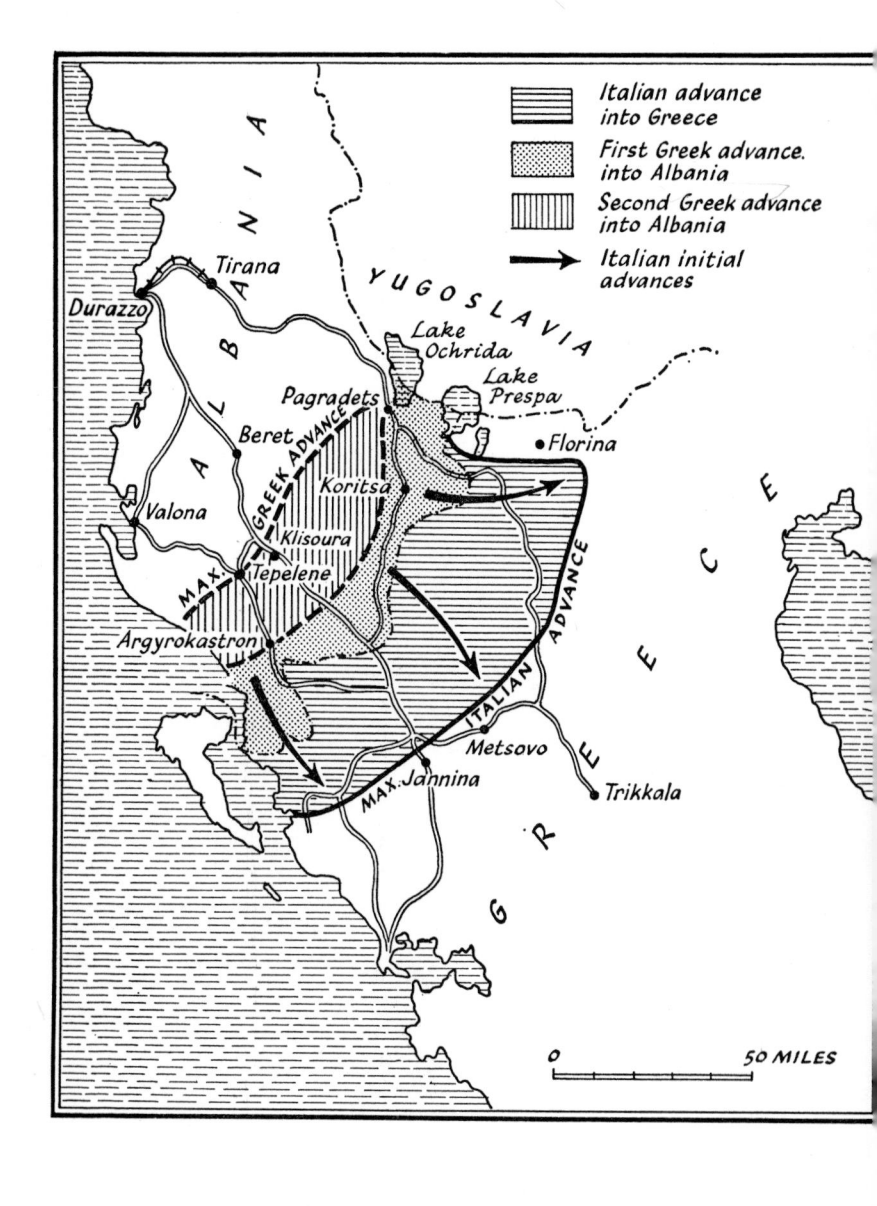

Legend:
- Italian advance into Greece
- First Greek advance into Albania
- Second Greek advance into Albania
- → Italian initial advances

Tirana
Durazzo
YUGOSLAVIA
Lake Ochrida
Lake Prespa
Pagradets
Beret
GREEK ADVANCE
Koritsa
Florina
A L B A N I A
Valona
Klisoura
MAX
Tepelene
ITALIAN ADVANCE
Argyrokastron
G R E E C E
Metsovo
MAX Jannina
Trikkala

0   50 MILES

For the invasion the Italians had assembled about eight divisions in Albania, one of which was armoured, and over 150 aircraft, as it was hoped to achieve a swift victory before the snows came to block the mountain passes as well as to penetrate deep into Greece before the effects of full Greek mobilization could be felt.

However, Greece was not taken completely by surprise as she had already mobilized the equivalent of about three divisions, of which two were lying in wait adjacent to the Albanian frontier. This had been an under-cover mobilization, and these were the troops that moved to block the Italian advance. They came as something of an abrupt shock to the Italians, who had expected little serious opposition. Behind these first Greek divisions in the field, the others were activated and deployed to their battle positions.

The Italian objective was Jannina, and then on to the key mountain pass near Metsovo, through which went the only really good road southwards. Another Italian thrust was intended to seize Florina and then push on to hit the Aegean Sea at Salonika. The Italian armoured division was the spearhead of the advance and as, owing to the lack of armour and anti-tank guns, the Greek infantry had to avoid the open ground, it was able to force its way into Greek territory. As more Greek troops were deployed the advance made heavy going, slowing down until by November 7th it had been forced to a halt. Even though well supported by infantry divisions and aircraft, it was not able to push any farther forward. The thrust to Salonika also failed.

It was the Greek turn next, and as soon as sufficient troops had moved into position on November 14th, they counter-attacked, their first successful action being fought in the Pindus mountains, where they pushed the Italians back. This sharp jolt caught the invaders unawares, and the Greek momentum gathered impetus so much that by the 22nd, not only had all Italians been ejected from Greek soil, but the Greek army had taken Koritsa, the principal Italian base, and Pogradia, two towns well over the Albanian border. The first Greek assault came to a stop on the 23rd, when after a pause it was recontinued. On December 8th, Argyrokastron, an army depot, was reached. This second assault ran down by December 28th, by which time a section of Albanian territory up to thirty miles in depth had been occupied, when the bad weather forced a stalemate to set in.

Although built up to a strength of fifteen divisions, undoubtedly Mussolini's troops were saved from further ignominious withdrawal, partly by the winter snows and partly by the fact that the Greek formations were unable to quickly exploit the favourable situation owing to lack of motor transport and ammunition. As it was, although the Greeks had taken the small Albanian port of Santi Quaranta, in the mountainous centre they were held up in front of the Tepeleni cross-roads. This successful phase of Greek fighting was conducted under the direction of General Papagos.

The Metaxas Government remained reluctant to invite British troops into Greece to help in case this should be regarded as a provocation sufficient to bring direct German intervention. Their successes against the Italians on the Albanian front made them feel that they could manage alone provided the German army did not take an active part against them. Britain was pressing offers of aid, partly because she was anxious lest some of the Greek islands, which had great strategic value, fall into Axis hands, and partly for political reasons. Although loth to avail himself of these offers, Metaxas did allow a small British party to land on Crete the day after the initial Italian attack had been made.

In the air the Greeks were not quite so sure of themselves, as their small air force was taking a pounding from the faster, more modern Italian aircraft, and early in November it was agreed that the RAF should operate over Greece in conjunction with the Greek air force. By the end of 1940, the Greek air force had practically ceased to exist, and in January 1941, the RAF took on its role. That same month four squadrons (of Blenheims and Gladiators) went to Greece but were not allowed to establish themselves north of Thessaly. The RAF task was to give ground support to the Greek infantry and despite British advice General Papagos would not agree to it carrying out bombing of airfield installations and other military targets inside Albania. Battling with the Italian air force cost the RAF over thirty aircraft within a month.

Metaxas died on January 29th, 1941. Just before his death, on the 13th, an offer of British troops had again been refused, but now the Greek Government, headed by Koryzis, reconsidered. It was true that the Greek army was holding the Italians at bay in Albania, but the Italian strength there was increasing. They had already assembled a force of twenty divisions, with supporting troops, and more reinforcements were arriving daily. What was more important was that their arms and equipment were vastly superior to those of the Greeks. Also, the Germans were feeling their way southwards into the Balkans. Certainly the Greeks had done very well so far, but now doubts crept in as to how long they could keep it up.

The Greek answer to these problems was indicative of the spirit of the people at this moment. It was to launch a winter offensive, which they hoped would batter the Italians and deter the Germans. If it was successful it would obviate the need for foreign assistance, and if not, then British ground forces might have to be accepted as well as the RAF.

When the Italians invaded Greece, Metaxas arrested all the known Communists and those with suspected Communist sympathies he could get hold of. Few prominent members of the KKE remained at large and such as escaped the net went farther underground, and worked to start up a 'cell' organization in the provincial towns. Republican officers who had been removed from the army by Metaxas clamoured to be allowed to rejoin to fight for their country against the Italians, but although there was an acute shortage of trained and experienced officers who were increasingly more urgently needed as the army swelled on mobilization, none were re-employed.

By February 1941, the Greek forces on the Albanian front had been increased to the equivalent of fourteen divisions, which were opposing about twenty-one Italian ones, and on the 13th General Papagos commenced an offensive which had the object first of all of taking Tepeleni, which barred his way in the centre, and then going on to seize the port of Valona. He had already made a similar but unsuccessful attempt in mid-January. The weather was exceptionally bad, and although the Greeks fought hard for a few days and actually gained a few square miles of territory, generally they had little success, and the operation had to be discontinued. The RAF had given close ground support to the Greek formations in this attack, but at the Greek request it was still not allowed to bomb targets inside Albania. It was painfully obvious that the Greek army required modern weapons, such as anti-tank guns, heavier field guns and armoured fighting vehicles, before it could hope to break through against the superior Italian armament.

Meanwhile, to the north-east there were ominous German troop concentrations in Rumania, aimed at Bulgaria. This overt threat resulted in a pact being signed by the Bulgarian Prime Minister on March 1st, allowing German forces to move across his country towards Greece. Just previously, in February 1941, Turkey had signed a treaty with Bulgaria, declaring herself to be neutral. Danger to Greece now appeared on this flank.

The failure of the February offensive finally decided the Greek Government in favour of accepting the offer of British troops, and the first detachments landed in Greece on March 5th. Others followed.

Determined to beat his fellow dictator to it, Mussolini arrived in Albania at the beginning of March, where he had assembled a total of 28 divisions and nearly 300 aircraft. On the 9th he launched a massive attack along a 20-mile wide front in the central sector, but despite shortages of ammunition, food and clothing and the privations they were suffering, the Greek soldiers dug in their toes and held on doggedly. The men had been in the front-line areas all winter under severe conditions and had just about reached the limit of their endurance. They were ill-clad, ill-fed and ill-equipped, but they all rose to the occasions and time after time blocked the Italian attacks. The RAF again gave close ground support, and for the first time, on the 14th, was allowed to switch to bombing airfields inside Albania as well. The fighting went on for ten days, after which it died down. Mussolini's offensive had failed. His well-equipped divisions were held by more primitively armed Greek ones.

It had been a costly failure in men as well as prestige, and it was reported that the casualties amounted to as many as forty per cent of the whole Italian force, which was estimated to be about 120,000 strong. The Greeks in their turn also suffered heavy casualties. Mussolini, who was reputed to have personally directed operations, was unfortunate, as he had hoped to snatch a quick victory over the Greeks before the Germans stepped in.

By the end of March, about 31,000 British, Commonwealth and Polish troops had arrived in Greece, and during the ensuing three weeks this number was increased to a total of about 57,000. Eventually it rose to 74,000. The decision to intervene and use British[1] troops in Greece was a political one. There was no military justification for it. The British military situation in the Middle East and the North African Desert was in itself tenuous and uncertain. Only slowly and painfully were troops being gathered together in Egypt to face the Italian armies in Africa. Many doubted the wisdom of sending part of this hard-scraped-together force to Greece on the grounds that it would be too small to make an effective contribution should the Germans attack in strength down through the Balkans, which seemed an extremely likely course, and that it would only correspondingly weaken the British forces facing the Italians in the

[1] The expression 'British' is used through the remainder of this chapter for brevity, but it, of course, includes not only Commonwealth troops but Polish and other Allied ones as well.

Desert. The British force sent to Greece amounted to three divisions
and two brigades, with some additional supporting and logistic
units.[1]

Although better equipped than the Greek divisions, especially in
respect of motor vehicles, the British troops were more tied to the
far from adequate road system, already overcrowded with hordes of
Greek army ox-carts, and were plagued with the problems of ferrying
supplies forward, right from the start. The British advance base was
at Larissa, about 190 miles north of Athens, and reached only by a
single road and a single railway line.

The direct threat was now from the Germans to the north, who
could enter Greek territory at several points along the wide length of
the northern boundary. The plan was that the British force should
hold the Aliakmon Line, which was from the mouth of the river of
that name, along the heights to the south of the river, by Mount
Olympus and the Pieria Mountain Range, through Veroia and
Edessa and on to the Yugoslav frontier—a fairly natural defensive
line that could be held if sufficient troops were available.

With the British force were three weak Greek divisions. Another
three were forward near the Yugoslav and Bulgarian frontiers,
covering Salonika. The British wanted these brought back to strengthen the Aliakmon Line, but General Papagos would not agree.
When the Germans eventually did strike these 'forward' Greek
divisions, they were brushed aside and dispersed in four days. The
narrow finger of Greek territory that was formed by Thrace was
held by only thirteen Greek battalions.

The weak point of the Aliakmon Line was its left (western) end
where it could be out-flanked by troops advancing southwards
through the Monastir Gap. This danger was obvious and the British
urged General Papagos to withdraw his divisions, which were tied
down in a stalemate in Albania, in order to block this route, to
strengthen the Aliakmon Line, to provide a reserve, and to form
'lie-back' defensive positions to bar the enemy from advancing down
country towards Athens should he break through at any point.
General Papagos was reluctant to consider this, and in fact hesitated
until it was too late.

The German 12th Army, consisting of four armoured and eleven

[1] The British force sent to Greece consisted basically of—
  1st Armoured Brigade (British)
  6th and 7th Australian Divisions
  New Zealand Division
  Polish Independent Brigade

other divisions, was detailed to take Yugoslavia and Greece. On April 6th, Germany declared war on these two countries and unleashed three armoured and two other divisions in a three-pronged attack into Greece from Bulgaria. One prong bit through Yugoslavia, a centre twin-prong cut through the Struma and Vardar Valleys, while the third one jabbed at Thrace, aiming at the coastal town of Kavalla. Belgrade had been entered the same day (6th), and a few days later the Yugoslav armies surrendered.

Supported by Luftwaffe dive-bombers, the German armoured columns spread out south and westwards, moving quickly into northern Greece and southern Yugoslavia. One column reached and took Monastir, in Yugoslavia, a town just to the north of the Greek border, which commanded the Monastir Gap. This was a good jumping-off place for it to get behind the Greek divisions tied down in Albania.

Another German column came down the Struma Valley to burst through the Rupel Pass into Greece, while just to the west of it another German armoured one turned slightly westwards along the Strumitsa Valley before going south to cross the Greek frontier near the rail town of Doiran. Brushing aside the Greek units that tried to bar their progress, both columns raced towards Salonika, which they entered on the 9th.

Farther east, another German column had been successful in breaking into Thrace to take Kavalla. Hostilities ceased in that sector on the 10th.

The British forces now took up a shortened line running westwards from Mount Olympus, which the Germans reached and attacked with their mechanized troops and dive-bombers on the 12th. These assaults were held for a while, and then a withdrawal was ordered. Briefly, to avoid being outflanked and encircled, the British forces withdrew southwards in successive stages, holding positions in line with Larissa, which the Germans hit on the 22nd, and then in turn at Volos, Lamia and Thermopylae.

While this British withdrawal was in progress, a German force moved westwards across the Pindus Mountains to meet up with the armoured column moving south from Monastir, which had reached Jannina on the 10th, thus effectively blocking any possibility of contact between the Yugoslav forces and those of Greece. On April 17th, Yugoslavia capitulated. This was a severe blow to General Papagos who had counted on active Yugoslav-Greek military co-operation in the field against the German attacks. The Greek

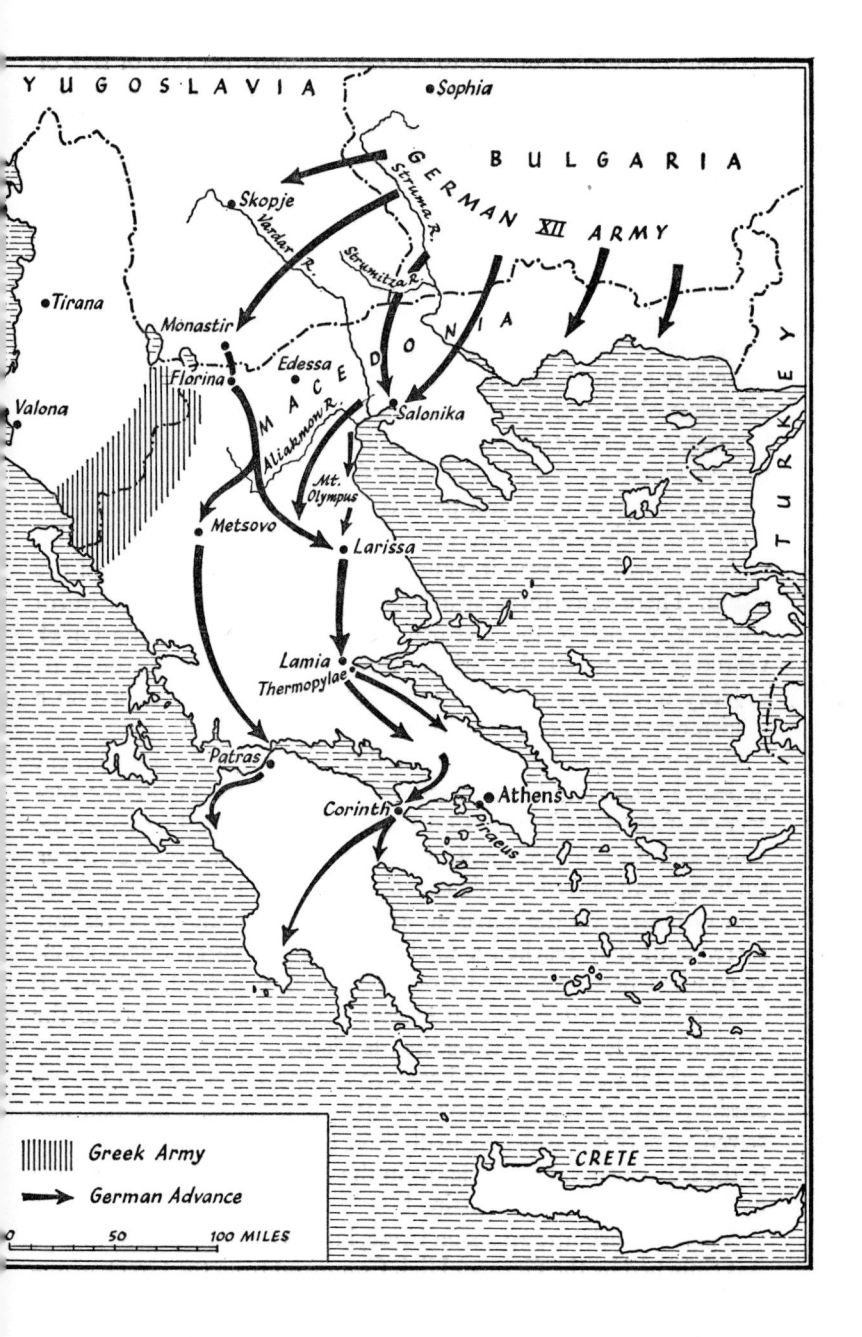

YUGOSLAVIA • Sophia

BULGARIA

• Tirana

Skopje

GERMAN XII ARMY

• Valona

Monastir

Florina • Edessa

M A C E D O N I A

Salonika

TURKEY

Metsovo

Mt. Olympus

Larissa

Lamia
Thermopylae

Patras

Corinth • Athens

Piraeus

||||||| Greek Army

——► German Advance

0   50   100 MILES

CRETE

43

divisions in Albania, unable to withdraw rapidly because of lack of transport and cut off from Greece, were forced to surrender on April 22nd. About 300,000 men were taken prisoner and disarmed, which was about half the mobilized strength of the Greek armed forces.

The day previously, the 21st, the decision was made to evacuate British troops from Greece. The British withdrawal had frustrated German attempts to encircle them, and the Royal Navy was able to take off successfully some 50,600 men from the Greek mainland, before the Germans entered Athens on the 27th.

Anxiety about the adverse strategic effect should the Axis Powers gain control of all the Greek islands led to the decision to hold the larger one of Crete and to make a stand there. Crete, with a population of about 400,000, was about 160 miles in length and about 40 miles across at its widest part. It had a long backbone mountain range for much of its length, with peaks of up to 7,000 feet in height. Only one road traversed it, running along the northern edge of the island. There were three airfields, but no harbour facilities worth speaking of. Before the German advance into Greece, the Greek Government shared the British view that the Italians would be unlikely to attempt to take Crete, but it was decided to station a British brigade there to deter them all the same.

Crete remained the only possibility if the Greek Government hoped to retain any Greek territory at all, and just before the surrender of the Greek armies on the mainland to the Germans, the King and the Government, together with about 10,000 Greek soldiers, were moved to this island. Also, more British troops were sent to bolster up the garrison, and to reinforce the 6,000 already there, until they reached a total of about 32,000, of whom about 21,000 had been evacuated from the Greek mainland. All British guns and motor transport in Greece proper had been lost to the Germans or destroyed before the men left.

Meanwhile, the Germans began to occupy Greek islands in succession, and on May 6th took Mytilene and Chios. They had just seized Samothrace which virtually gave them control of the entrance to the Dardanelles. Other islands in the Aegean Sea fell to them one by one, until only Crete remained.

A gigantic airborne attack on Crete, known as Operation Mercury, was launched by the German High Command from the Greek mainland and the Dodecanese Islands. The Germans used a force of about 22,000 men and a total of 716 aircraft for this purpose. Known as the German 11th Air Corps, it consisted of an airborne division of paratroops, an assault air group of paratroops and glider-borne troops, and a mountain division.

About 6 a.m. on May 20th, the air attacks on Crete began. Two hours later paratroops started to drop and German gliders came in to crash-land, many coming right in amongst the positions of the defending troops. The battle was joined, and its quality has been well and often described since. Here it is sufficient to say briefly that gradually the Germans pressed the British troops backwards towards the airfield at the western end of the island, which was one of the main defensive bastions. All German attempts to land from the sea were repulsed.

The fighting raged for twelve days, but the odds were against the defenders, who were at a disadvantage in the air as the RAF had to operate from Egyptian bases about 300 to 400 miles away, while German aircraft, using Greek territory, had much shorter distances of only just over 100 miles to cover.

On the 21st, the airfield at the western end of the island was lost, and on the 27th the decision to evacuate was made. Embarkation began the next day. Again the Royal Navy came to the rescue, taking off about 18,000 British troops, of whom 1,800 were wounded, and carrying them back to Egypt. By June 1st the evacuation had been completed, leaving all Greek territory in Axis hands.

The ferocity of the fighting during this hectic fortnight can be judged by some of the casualty figures. The Germans suffered about 6,000 casualties, of whom about 4,000 were killed or missing. They also lost about 220 aircraft destroyed and many more damaged. British losses were 1,800 killed and about 12,000 taken prisoner, while the RAF lost about 46 aircraft over Crete in this period. The total British casualties in the fighting in Greece exceeded 30,000.

The Greek King George II and the Government had been taken from Crete to Egypt. Koryzis, the Prime Minister, who had succeeded Metaxas, had committed suicide, and on April 18th the King appointed Tsouderos, a Cretan, in his place.

It has been said that this stiff resistance by the Greeks, latterly aided by a small British force, delayed the German attack on the Soviet Union. The German operations against Crete, for example, were scheduled to take only four days—instead, they took twelve. Certainly Hitler originally planned to launch his offensive on Russia on May 15th, 1941, but had to delay it until June 22nd. Some insist that this unexpectedly fierce opposition to the Axis invasion of

Greece may have saved the British forces then assembling in the Middle East, as had Greece given way suddenly and Hitler's drive into the southern part of the Soviet Union been made earlier and had been more successful (as it might in such circumstances) the two Axis prongs, one from the southern part of the Soviet Union and the other from North Africa, might have crushed them in a pincer before they were strong enough to resist. This was not improbable—but as always the balance of war hangs upon many such probabilities.

CHAPTER THREE

The Axis Occupation

The Axis Occupation swiftly encompassed all Greece and her islands and the general policy adopted was one of fostering traditional and existing antagonisms and Balkan dislikes. The Germans occupied only certain parts, mainly Athens, Piraeus, Salonika and some islands. The Bulgarians were permitted to move southwards and take over Eastern Macedonia and Thrace, and the remainder of the country was left to the Italians. A Greek puppet government was formed, and the Axis powers found enough collaborators with pro-German sympathies to support their administration. General Tsolakoglou became the first puppet Prime Minister. Tsolakoglou had been a corps commander in the Albanian fighting, and it was he who signed the Greek Armistice with the German and Italian commanders.

After a short sojourn in Cairo, the Greek King went to London where he set up a Government-in-Exile. Greek troops who escaped to Egypt were given British arms and equipment, and placed at the disposal of the British Commander-in-Chief, Middle East. A number of Greek warships that escaped Axis clutches were placed under the orders of the Royal Navy. Also, a handful of Greek pilots and air force personnel were formed into an aircraft squadron.

The Greek reaction to the Axis Occupation was at first apathetic. A small trickle of adventurous spirits escaped across the Aegean Sea in caiques[1] to join the Free Greek Forces that were forming in the Middle East. There seemed to be little else for them to do. The scattered, minor, unco-ordinated acts of sabotage brought swift and

[1] Caiques are Greek sea-going boats.

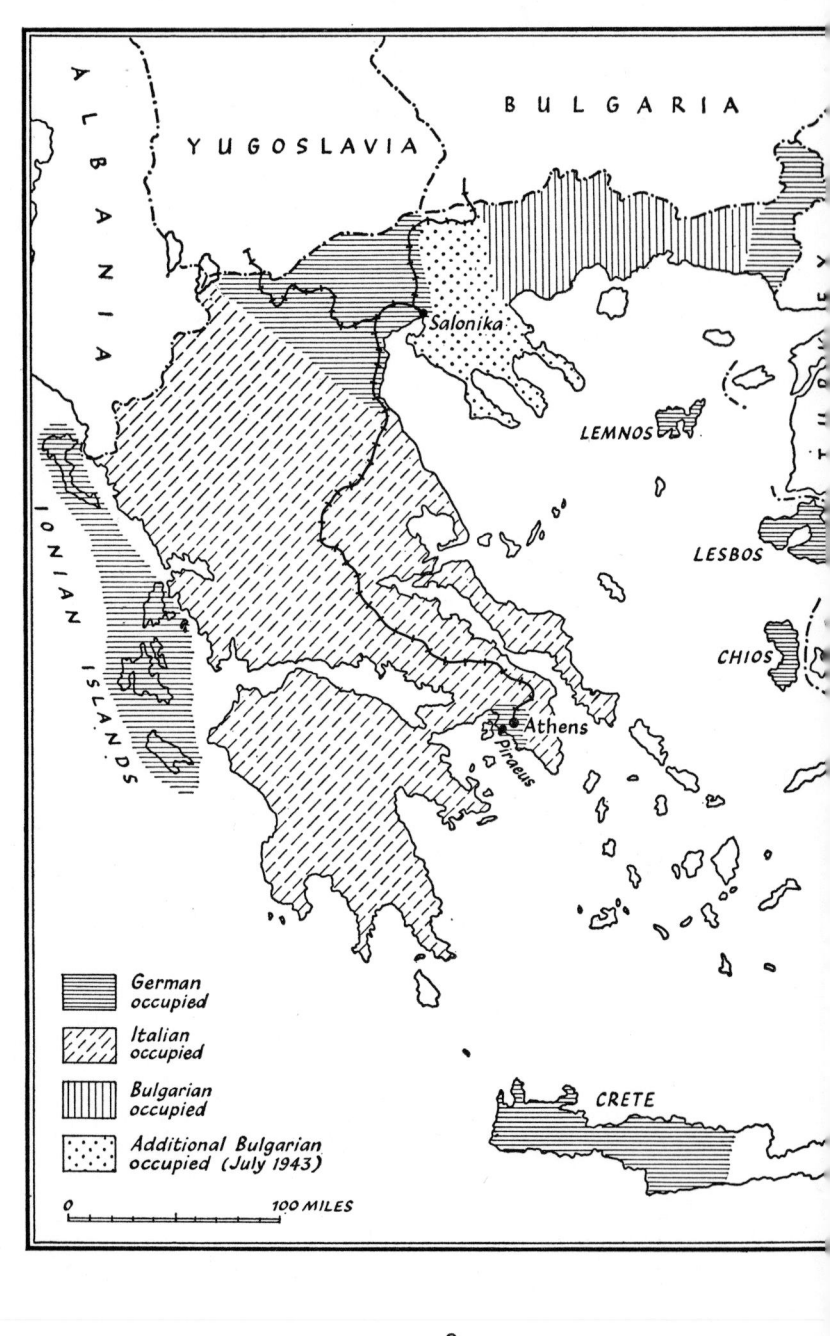

ALBANIA

YUGOSLAVIA

BULGARIA

TURKEY

Salonika

LEMNOS

IONIAN ISLANDS

LESBOS

CHIOS

Athens
Piraeus

German
occupied

Italian
occupied

Bulgarian
occupied

Additional Bulgarian
occupied (July 1943)

0   100 MILES

CRETE

vicious retribution, and no competent and compelling subversive organization or leaders beckoned. As the months slipped by, so did minds and tongues loosen, causing a resurgence of cautious whispering. It was quickly noted that the Occupation Authorities had no violent distaste for mild republican politics, provided they were not subversive, and in fact encouraged them as an antidote to the Royalist Government-in-Exile. During the Metaxas régime republicanism had been proscribed, but now it was able to operate more openly again.

While there was a mild reaction to republican political activities, the Axis Occupation Authorities came down heavily on the Communists. Zakhariadis, the Secretary-General of the KKE, was taken off to Dachau concentration camp, and other leading Communists who fell into Axis hands were similarly deported or imprisoned. Several Communists remained at large and they were reinforced by those recently released by the Occupation Authorities under the impression they were merely Socialists or Republicans. Long suppression had made the KKE accustomed to working underground, and so this Communist organization had a long start over others that came later.

Siantos was appointed the acting Secretary-General of the KKE in the absence of Zakhariadis, and under his guidance its virile and able cadre moved quickly. Siantos reformed the Central Committee of the KKE from the survivors in Athens, and then, partly under the guise of patriotism and partly through vaguely propagating a loose socialistic line tinged with Republicanism, it wormed its way into and began to activate various movements.

There existed in Greece a docile Workers' Labour Federation of Trade Unions. Hoping to make Greek labour malleable to their wishes the Occupation Authorities kept this alive, but put their own nominees in key positions. The KKE deputed Theos, one of the Central Committee, to initiate a rival underground labour movement. Theos persuaded two prominent left-wing labour leaders, Kalomoiris and Stratis, to join forces with him to form a strong militant organization amongst the trade unions, having the object of resistance to the Occupation Forces. This became the EEAM.

At this stage hardly any member of the secret and unpopular KKE would ever admit he was a Communist, but invariably professed mild socialism when pressed.

The next step, which was the formation of the Greek Liberation Front, known as the EAM, followed quickly, in September 1941.

This was perhaps the most significant and far-reaching event in the early days of Occupied Greece. The EAM was displayed as being a coalition of six socialist parties and organizations, which merged together to oppose the Axis Occupation Authorities. Other Greek parties and politicians were invited to join it, and as the dominant Communist element was not readily discernible a number were inveigled by patriotism into doing so, but on the whole most of the politicians and senior military officers in Athens were not impressed and had little to do with this infant organization.

The EAM was controlled by a Central Committee, which remained underground in Athens throughout the Occupation. The EAM was in fact directed by the KKE Central Committee, some of whose members were also on the EAM Central Committee. Many believed later on, especially abroad, that the Communists were a minority that eventually succeeded in taking over the EAM, but this was not so. The EAM was Communist conceived, delivered and motivated.

For the first few months EAM concentrated upon recruiting and preparing for expansion. It quickly developed an efficient propaganda department and within weeks pamphlets and circulars were being distributed in Athens, Piraeus and Salonika, putting forward its aims and views. The EAM Central Committee kept a tight guiding rein on all activities and discipline was strict.

With the coming of spring (1942), seething discontent began to break through the surface in Athens, where there had already been mild public demonstrations in the previous November, and over 3,000 students celebrated Greek Independence Day (March 25th) in defiance of a ban. In April, there was a strike of civil servants, and in June there were spasmodic outbursts of sabotage in the city which were echoed by similar incidents against the Occupation Forces in other parts of Greece.

In August, the Axis Occupation Authorities made their first attempts to transport forced labour to Germany. In open protest, the EEAM, the Communist-controlled Labour Movement, which had become powerful in Athens, Piraeus, Salonika, Volos and Patras, organized strikes and passive resistance. The previous month there had been a massed workers' demonstration in Athens of over 8,000, organized by the EEAM, which gives some indication of its efficiency.

About this time a number of other underground organizations—or perhaps cliques would be a better description—germinated in

Athens. They were mainly independent of each other, and of a variety of persuasions and of differing aims, some thinking it was high time they made their presence felt by overt subversive action. One was the PEAN (Patriotic Group of Fighting Youth) which, catching the mood of the moment and encouraged by the success of the EEAM-sponsored strikes, in September, blew up the Greek Fascist Party (the EEE) building in Athens. The EEE operated mainly in Salonika and parts of Thessaly, but had its headquarters in Athens.

Retribution was swift and deadly. There were several arrests, some executions and PEAN was quickly dissolved. These harsh measures put a damper on indiscriminate, light-hearted sabotage activities in the Capital, but the under-current of talk, scheming and plotting continued.

Meanwhile, the more determined and far-sighted EAM, directed by the KKE, made ready for the next stage in its bid to become paramount, when on April 10th, 1942 it announced its decision to put a guerrilla army in the field, to be known as the National Popular Liberation Army. This became known as the ELAS, and it became the armed force of EAM, and like other Communist armies, such as those of Soviet Russia and Red China, it was almost indivisible from the political organization. The EAM and ELAS were so tied up together and interwoven at all levels that at times it is hardly possible to talk about one or the other separately or to discuss them individually. At times it is necessary to refer to them simply as EAM/ELAS.

This Communist guerrilla army, ELAS, was established outside Athens in three main areas where spadework had been carried out during the winter of 1941-42. These were in the mountainous regions of Roumeli, Thessaly and Macedonia. In the initial stages the small guerrilla bands were raised or taken over by personalities, who were invariably Communists, or secret Communists. One of these was known as Aris Veloukhiotis,[1] who already had a flourishing band in January 1942, in the Mount Olympus district. There were perhaps a dozen or so similar Communist-led guerrilla groups in existence before the formal announcement of the formation of

---

[1] His real name is believed to be Athanasios Klaris. I shall refer to him simply as Aris in future. The majority of the Greek Communists followed the practice of adopting *noms de guerre*, and I have had difficulty in discovering the true names of some. In a few cases I am at a loss to know whether the name is a *nom de guerre* or not. Fortunately it matters hardly at all what they chose to call themselves, so there is no need for further comment upon the identity of the Greek personalities mentioned.

ELAS. In the spring more appeared until by August there must have been twice as many.

The EAM/ELAS energetically and ruthlessly set about firmly establishing itself in the mountains and extending its influence. It did this by persuading or bullying people into joining it. The first tasks were to form more bands and then to arm them. Young men were attracted to ELAS, not because of its political colour, but because it was the only offensive guerrilla force in the field. In fact, the extreme youth of some members of ELAS was a notable feature of this insurgent movement throughout its existence.

Initially the arms obtained were those of the disbanded Greek army of 1941, which had in many cases hidden them in dumps and caches rather than hand them over to the Occupation Forces. These were smelt out by EAM/ELAS and distributed to the ELAS bands as they were formed.

The system of command was typically Communist in style, and all units, as soon as they emerged as a formed body, had a 'Three-Man Committee' imposed on them. This consisted of the designated military commander, an administrative officer and a member of EAM. All had an equal say in discussions, but the EAM representative, a sort of military commissar, had the power to override the military commander's decision, which in any case was not valid until countersigned or otherwise approved by him.

The military member was responsible for operations, plans and security, while the administrative member had the job of obtaining supplies, arms and ammunition, and of requisitioning food and accommodation. The third man, the EAM representative, was the one who mattered. It was he who held the political power. Sometimes, as a screen or a disguise, he posed as a military expert, while at others he kept in the shadows as much as possible. There was hardly any open Communistic propaganda, such as compulsory daily lectures, since the EAM was posing as a mild socialistic coalition.

This principle of control by a 'Three-Man Committee' was continued at all levels in EAM/ELAS, and there was a major committee for each of the three regions of Roumeli, Thessaly and Macedonia, which was responsible to the EAM Central Committee in Athens.

The discipline and administration bore a distinct Soviet stamp, but not an indelible one, as few of the Greek Communists had any formal knowledge of Soviet military routine or logistics. The Greek Communists had a distinct distrust of Greek officers, both regular and reservist, Royalist and Republican. They employed very few in the initial stages. The Communists were far more concerned with political reliability than military capability.

As the Soviet Union was in the war on the Allied side, the congenial and conveniently declared objective of the EAM/ELAS was to oppose actively the Axis Occupation Powers by all means possible, including insurgent warfare. It is of interest to note that whilst being slavishly loyal to Soviet ideals to the extent of trying to import Red Army customs, drill and military practices into ELAS, the Greek KKE had no contact at all with Moscow, its former tenuous and unreliable links being abruptly severed by the Axis Occupation of the Balkans.

About the same time another guerrilla army appeared in the mountains of Epirus, in north-west Greece, which became known as EDES (National Republican Greek League), after the underground political organization that begot it. It had fixed republican aims. The nominal head was General Plastiras, but as he was interned in France, his Party was controlled by a committee in Athens, two of the most prominent members of which were General Gonatas and Colonel Zervas.

Colonel Zervas, who had headed the Republican Guard in 1926, was a regular republican officer. He had been released from detention when the Italians attacked Greece, but he had not been allowed to rejoin the Greek army. He was persuaded by British agents to leave Athens, where he had been scheming and dreaming, and to go into the mountains to form a guerrilla army. He went to his native Epirus in June 1942 to put the idea into practice. Recruiting in the region of Valtos, to the north-east of Arta, he had within three months raised a fairly competent band of about 300 guerrillas. Whenever he could, Colonel Zervas employed ex-regular and reservist officers with republican sympathies.

In theory, Colonel Zervas in the mountains was still subject to the instructions of the EDES Central Committee in Athens, but in fact he assumed full and complete charge of his guerrilla army, making his own independent decisions all the time. The Central Committee of EDES, under General Gonatas, became largely ineffective, whilst Colonel Zervas at the head of his guerrillas[1] became the dominant figure in the movement. Thus EDES divided into two parts, the political one in Athens, and the military one in the mountains, and they increasingly drew asunder. EDES in this respect was the

---

[1] At first this guerrilla force led by Colonel Zervas was known as the EAO (National Bands of Greek Guerrillas), but this was dropped and it became simply known as EDES.

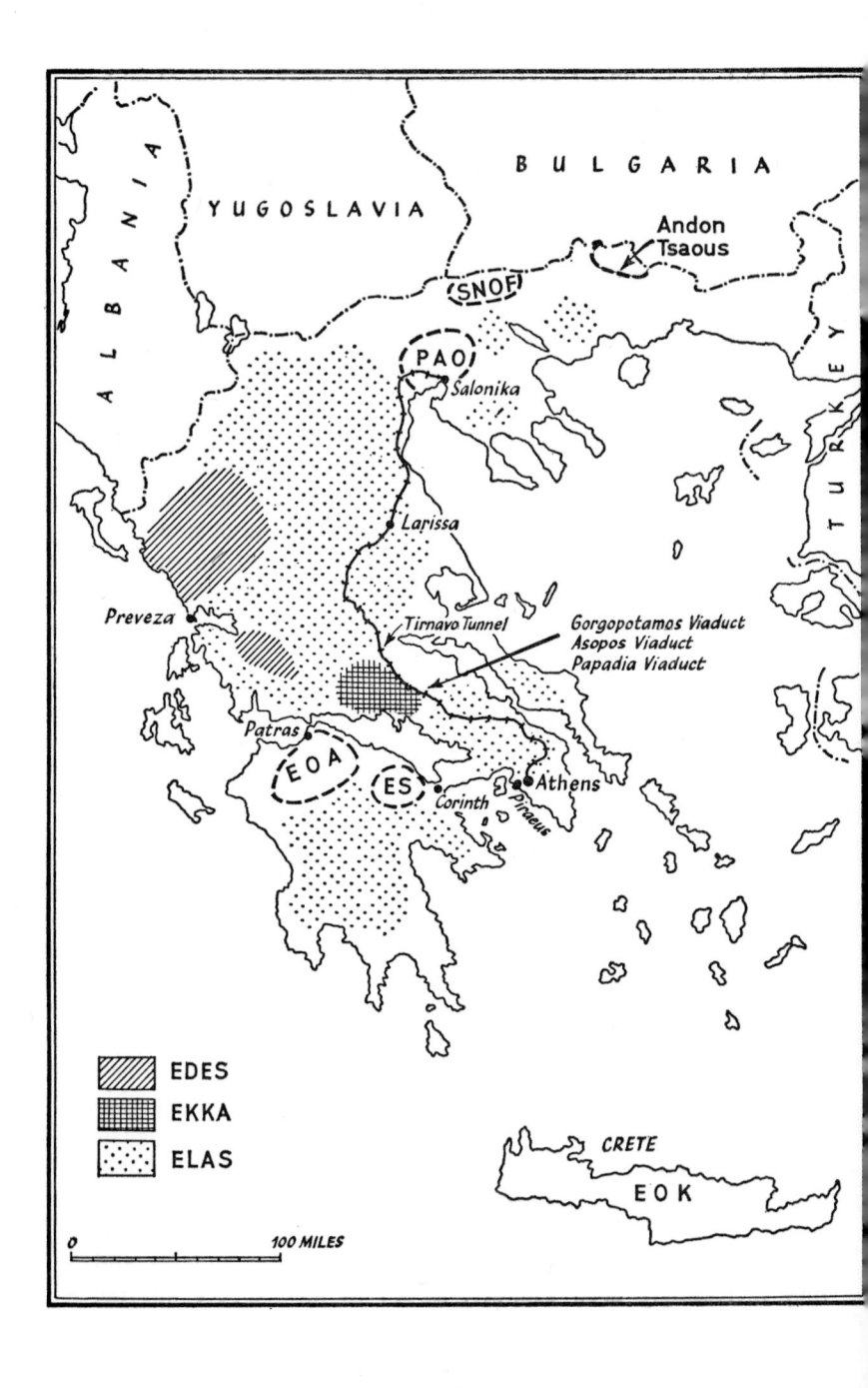

ALBANIA
YUGOSLAVIA
BULGARIA
Andon Tsaous
(SNOF)
PAO
Salonika
Larissa
Preveza
Tirnavo Tunnel
Gorgopotamos Viaduct
Asopos Viaduct
Papadia Viaduct
Patras
EOA
ES
Corinth
Piraeus
Athens
TURKEY

EDES
EKKA
ELAS

CRETE
EOK

0   100 MILES

diametric opposite to its rival, EAM/ELAS, in which the political and the military sections were so completely merged.

It is of interest to note that before he left Athens Zervas had been approached by EAM and offered the job as military commander of ELAS. Zervas had refused, at a time when ELAS was of little account, on the grounds that as a professional soldier he objected to the proposed 'Three-Man Committee' system of command. He later gave other reasons.

Here it should be emphasized that the peasants of the mountains and of the interior of Occupied Greece did not themselves initiate guerrilla activity, as is often supposed; it was forced on them by the political organizations. Generally, the Axis Occupation meant little to them, and after the first few alarms and reprisals they settled down with resignation. Their life was a sparse, hard one anyway and the food shortages of 1941 and 1942 only meant drawing in their belts a shade tighter than normal. The peasants had little to gain from taking to guerrilla warfare and everything to lose, as Axis reprisals would mean imprisonment, deportation as forced labour and the razing of villages, or even worse if Axis personnel were killed or wounded.

No special interest was shown in Occupied Greece by the British military authorities until 1942, which year brought a change of outlook as Britain gathered strength to fight back in the Middle East. As it was on one of the main supply routes from the Balkans to the German Afrika Korps, Greece became important, and when the coming autumn offensive in the Western Desert was being planned, it was decided to encourage, assist and stimulate Greek guerrilla activities to disrupt enemy supplies that were passing through that country to Africa, and to harass the Occupation Forces. But it was suddenly realized that Middle East Command knew little or nothing as to what was going on inside Greece so, beginning in October, a few British officers and men were parachuted into that country, both to carry out sabotage operations and to make contact with the guerrilla bands to assess their potentialities.

A fairly heavy volume of traffic was carried on the single railway line that ran from the north of Greece right down to Piraeus, from where it was transhipped by night across the Mediterranean. It was decided, with the vital Battle of Alamein looming ahead, to cut this line. So far there had been hardly any sabotage on the railway worth speaking of.

One of its most vulnerable stretches was in Roumeli; viaducts carried it over three deep gorges only a few miles apart. From north to south, these were the Gorgopotamos, the Asopos and the Papadia, and all three were guarded by detachments of Italian troops. If any were destroyed it would disrupt the railway until a new one was constructed. The Papadia Viaduct had been destroyed by the RAF in the 1941 withdrawal, but had been repaired. The British decided that the Gorgopotamos Viaduct, across a deep, rocky gorge, about eight miles south of Lamia, offered the best chance of success and would take the longest to repair if destroyed.

The first British group[1] was dropped by parachute in early October 1942, near Stromni, which was in EAM/ELAS-controlled territory, of which the military commander of the Roumeli 'Three-Man Committee' was Aris. Aris, a Communist, although he often denied the fact, was an energetic, shrewd, dedicated but extremely ruthless individual. He certainly had an aptitude for military affairs, but he was a political soldier, and politics always came first with him.

The British officers tried to make contact with Aris to persuade him to help them to destroy the viaduct, but Aris proved to be elusive. This was deliberate as he viewed the arrival of the British party with deep suspicion. He did not want any British interference in his plans, and nor was he over-keen on them finding out too much about the political aims and control of EAM/ELAS. Adhering strictly to the primary principle of Communist guerrilla warfare of self-preservation, the KKE Central Committee had given orders that EAM/ELAS units were not to attack formed bodies of the Occupation Forces, partly because they had not yet reached a sufficient state of training and so would inevitably suffer casualties, and partly because this would invite damaging reprisals.

Apart from this, Aris was not very enthusiastic over the Gorgopotamos Viaduct project as it would bring retribution and unwelcome attention to his territory. He already had between 250 and 300 armed guerrillas in small bands, each of about twenty-five men, scattered throughout the mountains of Roumeli, and he was busy recruiting more. Aris was making the presence of EAM/ELAS paramount in this area and he did not want any competition or diversion until this had been completed.

Aris, personally a brave man, did not shrink from fighting the Occupation Forces, but as a Communist he was only prepared to do so on his own conditions or on his own Central Committee's instructions. However, he realized that contact with the British might prove

[1] Under Colonel (later Brigadier) E. C. Myers.

fruitful in the form of modern arms, ammunition and supplies, of which ELAS was desperately short. Therefore, while remaining elusive he did nothing to antagonize the British party; a month later, for example, when another British sabotage group was dropped by parachute near Karpenisi, also in Aris' territory, he sent it on to join the first group. Aris continued to avoid meeting the British party although his agents remained in shadowy contact making excuses and vague promises.

As there seemed to be little prospect of Aris giving the necessary help to destroy the Gorgopotamos Viaduct, a British officer[1] was sent out to make contact with Colonel Zervas, who was known to be in the Valtos area, over the mountains on the other side of Greece, to the north-east of Arta. Zervas agreed to help in this project, and with about 150 men he marched towards the railway line, but as he approached Aris 'accidentally' bumped into him. Aris realized that if EDES helped to destroy the viaduct it would be rewarded with British arms, ammunition and equipment. He decided to co-operate.

The operation was successfully carried out on November 25th, 1942[2], and not only was the viaduct carrying the railway over the Hellada Gorge destroyed, but an Italian reinforcement train, rushing to the scene after the alarm had been given, was derailed and many casualties caused. The railway was disrupted for six weeks, but there were reprisals, and thirteen hostages from the Lamia concentration camp were taken out and shot.

This was the first big British-instigated act of sabotage inside Occupied Greece, and Aris, a shrewd leader, knew that ELAS must take a leading part in it, when he saw that if he did not participate EDES would do it alone. This act aroused British interest in the guerrilla potentialities in Greece, and more officers were parachuted into the country. These officers eventually merged into what became known as the British Military Mission, which had its headquarters in the mountains to the east of Arta, being thus roughly mid-way between the territory controlled by EDES to the west, and that controlled by EAM/ELAS to the east and north. This headquarters had to move occasionally but generally it hovered around this district for several months.

The task of the British Military Mission was to persuade all

---

[1] Major (later Colonel) C. M. Woodhouse.
[2] According to General Saraphis in his book *Greek Resistance Army*, the actual numbers that took part in the destruction of the Gorgopotamos Viaduct were—115 ELAS, 45 EDES and the British sabotage group.

guerrilla bodies to work under the orders of GHQ Middle East Command and to co-ordinate their activities. It was authorized to control and allocate arms and supplies which were limited due to the lack of Allied aircraft available to drop them.

One of the other guerrilla bands that appeared in the mountains was the AAA (Liberation Struggle Command), which established itself in Thessaly. This was led politically by Papandreou, a Republican politician, while the military commander of the AAA guerrilla forces was Colonel Saraphis, a regular officer with pronounced Republican views.

As a young officer in World War I, Saraphis had been imprisoned for advocating that Greece should enter the war on the side of the Allies, after which he fought in the Greek campaigns in Asia Minor. Subsequently, under the periods of the Monarchy he was exiled or imprisoned, while under the Republic he held important army posts. He had been exiled after an abortive rising in 1935, but had been allowed to return to Greece under the 1940 amnesty, when like so many other officers with Republican sympathies he had not been allowed to serve in the armed forces. In late 1942, after hanging about Athens for some time, he had gone off to the northern Pindus Range to join the AAA.

In areas where the EAM/ELAS was dominant men were 'conscripted' rather than 'recruited', which did much to account for a rapid increase in strength. However, while its political efficiency was apparent, the military side did not function so well.

The British Military Mission did not have a great deal of success in persuading EAM/ELAS to co-operate. Arms and supplies had been delivered, but little was done in return. Whenever ELAS was asked to sabotage anything the whole matter was referred back to the Central Committee of EAM/ELAS in Athens, and a negative attitude adopted.

On the other hand, while EDES and some other guerrilla bands were more responsive to British suggestions, they invariably had less scope. By January 1943, Colonel Zervas had about 500 armed men and twice as many unarmed, but trained, guerrillas. British arms were provided and by the end of the following month he had over 1,500 armed fighting men, so he was able to extend farther afield and establish bands in northern Epirus.

After failing to lure Colonel Zervas, EAM/ELAS looked elsewhere and noted that Colonel Saraphis, who had a sound military reputation, was making an efficient job of the small AAA bands in the northern Pindus Range. In March 1943, proclaiming loudly that all who did not join ELAS were traitors, it attacked the AAA, alleging that Saraphis had been in contact with the Italians. The AAA bands were scattered. Some of Saraphis' men went over to ELAS units, others were captured and shot, while yet others escaped. Saraphis himself was taken prisoner by treachery and sent south to the headquarters of Aris, in Roumeli.

After being kept prisoner for some days in humiliating circumstances and daily expecting to be taken out and shot, Saraphis was released to announce that he had decided to accept an offer made by ELAS to become its military commander. This unexpected move enabled EAM/ELAS to form a strong GHQ in the field to direct operations, which was completed in May 1943. It was on the now familiar 'Three-Man Committee' pattern, and consisted of Saraphis as the military commander, Aris as the administrative officer, and Tzimas as the EAM political representative.

ELAS soon began to number its members in thousands, but only a proportion were armed. In the north, it was successful in Macedonia because the people were more afraid of Slav domination than Communism. In Thessaly and Roumeli it also prospered, until it actively controlled over half the mountainous regions of continental Greece. Only in Epirus, the Peloponnese and Crete did it find difficulty in taking root.

Meanwhile, the idea of guerrilla warfare caught the popular imagination and spread. EAM/ELAS did not have a monopoly in this sphere. EDES, after strengthening its base in Epirus, went on to establish strong pockets in parts of Roumeli, Thessaly and Macedonia, as well as in the Peloponnese, becoming the most powerful and dangerous rival to ELAS.

From the spring of 1943 till the end of the year, other political groups stirred themselves at intervals and began to dabble in guerrilla warfare. One of these was the PAO (Panhellenic Liberation Organization), centred on Salonika, which had been in existence since 1941. It put a small guerrilla force in the field just to the north of that city.

Another was EKKA (National Socialist Liberation Group) which raised guerrilla bands in the area of Roumeli. The political leader was Kartalis, a Republican, and the military commander was General Psaros. EKKA had armed bands in the Parnassus Mountains.

Another armed group was commanded by an individual known as Athis Roumeliotis, who at first had led a unit of ELAS until he quarrelled with Aris, after which he established himself independently in the Pindus Mountains, becoming a sort of feudal chieftain.

In the Peloponnese two militant organizations were formed, consisting mainly of unemployed officers. These were the EOA (National Organization of Officers) and the ES (Greek Army). The EOA was a national movement that recognized the Government-in-Exile, and in the latter part of 1943, when EDES began expanding in the Peloponnese, fighting occurred between the two.

In Crete appeared the EOK (National Organization of Crete) led by Colonel Mandakas, a Republican, which dominated the island throughout practically the whole Occupation. This was one place where EAM/ELAS repeatedly failed to get a permanent footing.

This was the pattern that spread over Greece away from the cities and the towns where Axis Occupation troops actually sat. It was the fashion to be a guerrilla fighter in the mountains, to carry arms and to dashingly wear crossed bandoliers of ammunition. All young men wanted to do this, and there was little to stop them except the shortage of arms and bandoliers, for, away from the main communications, the Axis Occupation Powers cared little about what went on provided there was no sabotage or disruption. They knew these bands were being established, but they also knew how much they hated each other, so they merely did what they could to aggravate internal dissension.

In an attempt to further churn up local hatreds, the Italians organized the Vlachs into units of 'Legionnaires' to hunt guerrillas. The Vlachs lived in south-west Macedonia, being Slavs of Rumanian stock, and so were the natural enemies of the Greeks.

In June 1943, the effects of the guiding hand of the conventionally trained Colonel Saraphis could be seen as the framework of ELAS was forged. So far ELAS had consisted of mushroom-like growths, grouped in three main regions, that flourished where circumstances were favourable and foundered when they were not. Frequently they were dependent for existence upon the energy, ability and personality of the local leader or founder. The political cement was strong, but the military mortar was weak.

Saraphis formed a 'GHQ Committee', which was a sort of general staff to control and administer the ELAS Territorial Commands, which had increased to six. Four of these now came directly under the GHQ Committee. These were the Macedonia Command which had about 4,500 guerrillas, the Thessaly Command with about 4,000, the Roumeli Command with about 3,000, and the smaller Epirus Command which had only about 500 guerrillas.

The two other Territorial Commands still came directly under the EAM/ELAS Central Committee, in Athens, and were the Peloponnese Command with about 1,500 men, and the Attica Command which had less than 800. Not all the guerrillas in the Commands were armed, but a fair proportion, which varied from about half to two-thirds, were.

The basic field unit was the 'band', which was more like a company than a platoon. This still varied in size, from perhaps 30 men to as many as 100, or more, and there was already a tendency to group the 'bands' into battalions. The Three-Man Committee system of command survived at all levels. Discipline was maintained by the familiar Communist methods of reprimand and confession of faults and omissions at unit parades. Known collaborators, traitors and anti-Communist dissidents were given a summary public hearing, which inevitably preceded a swift execution.

A certain amount of thinly veiled Communist propaganda was put over to all the guerrillas at the daily parades, but this was done discreetly, and the techniques and pressures varied from band to band. It existed, but was never overdone to the majority for the obvious reasons that EAM did not want it to be too widely known that ELAS was primarily a Communist army. Private indoctrination was given to selected personnel who invariably held, or were earmarked for, key positions.

The uniform was that of the Greek Army whenever such items could be obtained, and failing this, any other military uniforms, Allied or Axis, were used with all the insignia taken off. A forage-type cap was worn with the Greek National emblem and the initials 'ELAS' on the front.

About this time Colonel Saraphis regularized the 'ELAS Reserve'. He realized that it was little use to have large numbers of unarmed men, as they would be a burden to feed and hardly any value in combat, so he formed the bulk of this unarmed surplus into the ELAS Reserve, which was organized into Home Guard-type units. The men stayed and worked in their own villages, received some military training and were always available as reinforcements at short notice. Each village in EAM/ELAS territory had at least a platoon of ELAS Reservists. The men seldom had uniform or arms.

During the summer of 1943, EPON (United Panhellenic Youth

Organization) blossomed out. This was an EAM-inspired and controlled youth movement for boys and girls. They were given some elementary military training and formed into small groups that were attached to ELAS Territorial Commands, where they carried out the 'house maid' tasks, such as staffing the cookhouses, mess halls, the offices, distributing rations and stores, and acting as messengers and guides.

Another EAM-controlled organization that can be mentioned was ELAN (National Popular Liberation Navy). This was the naval counterpart of ELAS, and operated small boats around the coast and across to the islands. However, in May 1943, when ELAS withdrew into the Pindus Mountains to avoid Axis punitive operations, and thus evacuated long stretches of coastline from which ELAN had operated, ELAN was not able to continue and for a short while ceased to exist. In July 1943, when ELAS again spread out and controlled sections of coastline, ELAN was re-established.

The British Military Mission was instructed to begin widespread sabotage in Occupied Greece in the first week of June 1943, but it did not have a great deal of success in rousing guerrilla activity against the Axis Occupying Powers. There was an attitude of cautious passivity on the part of the guerrillas towards them, which contrasted with their bitter feelings towards each other. With the Sicilian landings imminent the plan was again to cut the railway, the main north-south artery, and to undertake country-wide sabotage with the object of deluding the Axis Powers into thinking that Allied landings in Greece were about to take place.

This time the Asopos Viaduct on the railway was selected to be destroyed, and both EAM/ELAS and EDES were asked to assist in this project. EAM/ELAS at first agreed to help, but then retracted, pointing out that it had just previously (on May 28th) blocked the Tirnavo Tunnel, a few miles north of Lamia, successfully trapping a troop train and killing over 300 German soldiers. This had been done on EAM/ELAS initiative and not at the request of the British Military Mission, but the underlying reason was partly to obtain arms, partly to counter the allegations that ELAS took no action against the Occupying Forces but only fought rival bands, and partly to inspire the confidence of the British Military Mission so that more arms could be demanded.

Again, perhaps the fear of reprisals deterred ELAS, because after the Tirnavo Tunnel incident the Germans said they would shoot fifty Greeks for every German soldier killed. Harsh German reprisals already carried out hinted that this might not be just an idle threat. EAM/ELAS did not want to needlessly attract any more unwelcome attention, and having done one prestige sabotage act, it wanted to be left alone to eliminate or absorb some of its adjacent rivals quickly.

Colonel Zervas, of EDES, said he was not in a position to help as the Asopos Viaduct was right in the centre of a strong EAM/ELAS region, and it would be suicide for him to try and get there.

In the end the Asopos Viaduct was destroyed on the night of June 24th–25th by a small British sabotage party, and the railway was disrupted for four months. The Tirnavo Tunnel incident had only put it out of action for a few days. There were, it is true, other incidents of sabotage in various parts of the country, such as blowing road bridges, cutting telephone wires and ambushing small parties of Occupation troops, which were continued until July 11th (Sicily was invaded on the 12th), but they were largely the work of personnel of the British Military Mission, although they were helped by guerrillas in many cases. However, such destruction as was carried out alarmed the Axis Powers, causing them to think that an Allied landing was about to take place in Greece. Certain reinforcements meant for Italy were diverted to Greece, and two German divisions were moved into that country from Yugoslavia.

The invasion of Sicily marked the end of a phase of resistance in Occupied Greece. During it, guerrilla forces had been established in the mountains. They had been slow to develop, but the British had been slow to step in and aid them. Under British pressures, promises and threats some sabotage against the Axis Occupation Authorities had been carried out, but not nearly as much as GHQ, Middle East Command wanted, anticipated or hoped for.

The secret Greek Communist Party, the KKE, had been at work making its every move with calculated shrewdness and far-sighted political acumen. Its insurgent army, ELAS, was being moulded, preserved and prepared for a sinister purpose – the ultimate seizure of power.

CHAPTER FOUR

Civil War Begins

The unmistakable approach of liberation affected all the guerrilla forces, and each did its utmost to expand its size and influence so as to be able to obtain maximum recognition from the Allies when they arrived. EAM/ELAS now began to make more strenuous bids for supreme power, and lashed out viciously at lesser rivals. In May, it had struck at the remnants of the AAA, and in the subsequent fighting dissolved them completely. Next, it prepared to march and crush EDES.

In an effort to get them to work together–or at least to leave each other alone–the British Military Mission persuaded the three with the largest guerrilla forces, the EAM/ELAS, EDES and EKKA, to set up a Joint GHQ, together with the British Military Mission, which would take orders from SOE (Cairo).[1] This became known as the 'National Bands Agreement', and the Joint GHQ was eventually set up near Pertouli, in the Pindus mountains, to the west of Trikkala. It was officially recognized as part of the British Middle East Command.

At the time of the signing of the National Bands Agreement (July 1943), ELAS had about 16,000 guerrillas in the field,[2] EDES about 3,000, and EKKA about 400. These were the numbers claimed by the guerrilla organizations themselves for which the British Military Mission was expected to pay them at the rate of one gold sovereign per man per month.

[1] Special Operations Executive.
[2] Saraphis says there were 12,500, but he does not include those in Athens, the Peloponnese and some of the islands.

EAM/ELAS made overtures to General Psaros, of EKKA, to merge with it. Helped by the British Military Mission, EKKA was expanding fast, and soon had about 1,000 armed men, and ELAS wanted both Psaros, for his military ability, and his men, for their arms. Kartalis, the leader of EKKA, had left Athens to join it in the mountains, but both he and Psaros were non-committal.

EDES, strong in Epirus and also pretty firmly based in Evrytania in Central Greece, which lay alongside the EAM/ELAS-held territory in Roumeli, struggled to expand to the north and to the east at the expense of ELAS whenever it could. The Arakhtos River formed a natural boundary between them, but both foraged over it into the others' territory. EDES had also managed to establish armed groups in other parts of the country, notably Thessaly.

Joint GHQ demanded that a joint delegation be sent to Cairo to discuss the situation, and a landing strip was secretly prepared near Neraida, about twenty miles south-west of Karditsa. On August 9th,[1] a British aircraft took off six of the leaders. All the delegates were insistent that the King should not return when Greece was liberated until after a plebiscite had been held, and the Communists, ostensibly representing ELAS, demanded that ELAS be recognized as part of the Greek National Army, that officers be exchanged between it and the Free Greek Forces in the Middle East, and that it be given three places in the Cabinet of the Government-in-Exile. These demands caused much argument, but little clear cut emerged, and the delegation was flown back to Greece. Aboard the returning aircraft was Colonel Bakirdzis, a Republican who had escaped from Occupied Greece in 1942, and who on arrival joined EKKA.

Meanwhile, Saraphis had made progress with organizing ELAS, and in September 1943 the Territorial Commands were turned into 'divisions'. As 'bands' had been grouped into battalions, and battalions into regiments, a system of numbering units and formations was adopted. This was a trifle haphazard. The divisions were:

1st (Thessaly) Division—about 8,000 men.
3rd (Peloponnese) Division—about 2,500 men.
8th (Epirus) Division—about 2,000 men.
9th (Western Macedonian) Division—about 4,500 men.
13th (Roumeli) Division—about 3,000 men.

[1] The delegates were:
    For EAM/ELAS—Siantos, Tzimas, Roussos and Despotopoulos (all Communists).
    For EDES—Pyromaglou (the second-in-command).
    For EKKA—Kartalis.

The divisions were still territorially based and recruited, and as can be judged from their estimated strengths, contained varying numbers of battalions and regiments. The battalion was settling down to an average strength of about 500 men. The 1st (Thessaly) Division had long had a cavalry detachment for use on the edge of the Thessaly Plain, and other divisions followed suit if they were able.

Each division had an EPON unit of young people, a training school for junior leaders, as well as engineer, communications, supply and medical companies. Attention was given to the training of specialists. Communication between, and within, the divisions was mainly by telephone, but a few wireless sets had been received from British sources.

On the whole there was a keen spirit of willingness and cheerfulness in ELAS, despite minority reservations, but Saraphis himself admitted that it was backward in training and lacked competent officers. In August, an officer-training school was set up at GHQ to instruct selected personnel, giving a three-month course. By the end of the year nearly 400 young officers had passed through it, which tended to ease the situation.

The previous penalties of public reprimand and confession were changed for the more conventional military ones of detention and confinement to camp. A procedure for courts martial was laid down for soldiers who transgressed the ELAS military code. Neither officers nor the men received any pay, the gold sovereigns given to ELAS by the Allied (as it had become)[1] Military Mission going to the EAM/ELAS funds. Officers were clearly designated, and the ordinary ranks of the Greek army came to be used.

ELAS had several hundred German, Italian and Bulgarian prisoners-of-war, who were used as forced labour to improve roads, carry supplies and construct buildings.

Despite the tendency to formalism, political control had remained rigid, and in October Siantos left Athens and came to EAM/ELAS GHQ replacing Tzimas as the EAM member. Tzimas went off to contact Tito in Yugoslavia. A slight relaxation of the firm political grip occurred when it was decreed that each member of the Three-Man Committees would be equal in status, and that the military commander would in future have the casting vote if there was any difference of opinion. The military commander no longer required the counter-signature of the EAM member on all the orders he issued.

[1] Two American officers had joined it so its designation was changed.

In September 1943 Italy capitulated, and while the majority of the Italian Occupation troops in Greece were hastily removed by the Germans who took over their responsibilities, about 12,000 armed Italian soldiers contacted the Allied Military Mission, asking to be allowed to keep their arms and fight against the Germans. One complete formation with this intention was the Pinerlo Division, at the time occupying Thessaly. It was about 7,000 strong. It was arranged that this division should keep its arms, leave its present location, disperse into small units in the mountains, co-operate with the guerrillas (who were EAM/ELAS) and prepare to take part in harassing operations against the Germans. One of the first tasks given to the Italian division was to attack the German-held airfield at Larissa, which it assaulted on October 1st. The operation dragged on for ten days, and was not successful.

The appearance of an organized, disciplined, armed formation of 7,000 men in the mountains of Occupied Greece, under the control of the Allied Military Mission, dismayed EAM/ELAS, and it persuaded the Allied Military Mission to disperse it more widely in smaller detachments. On the morning of the 15th (October) the 1st (Thessaly) Division surrounded the Italian detachments and disarmed them, seizing the division's twenty-odd mountain guns and all its other equipment. This duplicity gave EAM/ELAS at one stroke a large quantity of arms, which it used to form a new division known as the 16th (Thessaly) Division. It also removed from its midst the only armed force that could block its plans. The Italians were put into crude concentration camps in the mountains and used as forced labour.

The ELAS Reserve—the village Home Guards—had been increased in strength, and was used as a reservoir of semi-trained manpower that could quickly be called upon for rapid expansion of the regular ELAS insurgent army. ELAS formed yet another division in October, the 10th (Macedonian) Division, and another brigade in Attica.

On October 12th, ELAS units moved into action against EDES in the Thessaly mountains, and everywhere a welter of fighting broke out between the two guerrilla armies. The Civil War can be said to have begun on this date.

As soon as the Italian arms and equipment were seized, the new 16th (Thessaly) Division was rushed over the Pindus Mountains to hit at EDES in Epirus. It is alleged that Aris made an unofficial truce with the Germans to enable him to push his men and reinforcements across country so quickly and so openly. The Italian mountain guns were dispatched to Epirus and brought into action against EDES. It seemed as though the German Occupation troops were keeping out of the way deliberately to allow the rival guerrilla armies to batter each other to pieces.

The fierce all-out assaults on EDES by ELAS, in both Thessaly and Epirus, were kept up for about a week, but although Colonel Zervas was forced to withdraw in places, most of the attacks were held. EDES now had about 3,500 guerrillas, largely armed with British weapons, in the Epirus and Thessaly mountains, and at least another 5,000 unarmed followers loosely organized as Home Guards. Zervas had built his force on the Greek regular army pattern, basing it on small sections, each of about ten men. It was comparatively well trained and reasonably well led.

On the other hand, ELAS, despite its strong political discipline and numerical advantage in arms and men, was unable to make more than local gains. Its military quality was still low. Saraphis, Aris and Siantos, the GHQ Three-Man Committee, had hoped to obliterate, or at least severely cripple, EDES before the winter snows set in, but they had not realized how raw and untrained ELAS was. Saraphis probably guessed, but hoped that overwhelming numbers and arms would carry the day. They did not.

ELAS made other offensives elsewhere, and in the Peloponnese, units of the 3rd (Peloponnese) Division attacked not only EDES but also ES and EOA, with some success. In Macedonia, ELAS struck out at the Salonika-based PAO, dispersing it, and the tiny army of the colourful brigand, Athis Roumeliotis, had to draw in its horns quickly. The net result of this EAM/ELAS October offensive, which lasted just over a week in all, was that whilst some of the lesser guerrilla bands were badly mauled, EDES remained strongly ensconced in the mountains in Epirus, Roumeli and Central Greece.

This failure was a disappointment to EAM/ELAS, and another one followed. EAM/ELAS had been of the opinion that the Germans were completely indifferent to what was going on in the mountains away from the beaten track, but this was not so. Having lulled the guerrillas into a false sense of security, German forces struck hard when they had just paused for breath, attacking them from both the western and the eastern sides of the Pindus Mountains. German units cut right into the mountainous areas and got in amongst the guerrilla units. The very best of the ELAS fighters could not stand up even to second-rate German troops, and were compelled to disengage rapidly and withdraw in order to survive. The Germans inflicted many casualties and carried out harsh reprisals, destroying villages and shooting hostages and captured guerrillas. EDES units also suffered from these German sweeps into the mountains, but not to the same extent.

The German offensive was a prolonged one, lasting about three months, until the winter had firmly set in, and during this period ELAS had all its work cut out to keep clear and remain intact as a fighting force, and so had little time or energy to spare to assault EDES. To teach the Macedonian guerrillas a sharp lesson, the Germans also mounted vicious and successful operations against them, especially in the area around Salonika.

The Germans had done what the Allied Military Mission had been unable to do, and that was to stop the fighting between ELAS and EDES, at least temporarily. Owing to these German offensives against the guerrillas, which were continued on until the end of December, Joint GHQ had been forced to move into the Karpenisi area.

Concerned about the shortage of manpower for occupation duties, the Germans allowed the Bulgarians to take over a further slice of Macedonia. Another device they employed was the Security Battalions. These were officially sponsored by Rallis, the then puppet Prime Minister, who thought they were a good idea. So did many other Greeks who had become disgusted and appalled at the activities of certain guerrilla groups and the degree of lawlessness to which parts of the country had sunk. These battalions, composed of Greeks, under Greek officers, were lightly armed and formed primarily to combat the guerrillas. All the personnel in them were strongly anti-Communist.

Their operations were at first confined to the Peloponnese and Attica, where they had some success against ELAS units. Later, they were increased in number and they extended their activities to Central Greece. ELAS guerrillas feared them, and accordingly loudly denounced them as collaborators, but they were popular with many sections of the population as they brought stability and order which had been so sadly lacking since the Occupation began. Before the Security Battalions started to operate, the Axis Occupation Forces had been largely indifferent to the sufferings of the ordinary people, who had consequently been frequently exploited, first by one guerrilla organization and then by another, and in the conflict between rival guerrilla armies had often suffered doubly.

October 1943 had been a bad month for ELAS, bringing disappointments and defeats. Its offensive against EDES had revealed many weaknesses. The men were only partially trained, leadership in the field was bad, the men had been unable to use their newly acquired Italian arms, and their ideas of making the best use of and co-ordinating fire power were elementary and vague; there had been a lack of determination and aggression in battle and communications had failed hopelessly. All these and many more flaws brought to EAM/ELAS GHQ the realization that ELAS was far from being an efficient and reliable instrument.

Military commanders who had shown themselves to be incompetent were relieved, and not a few were punished. A number of commanders and men were discharged from the ELAS in deep disgrace. The crude supply system had broken down almost as soon as units moved from their home base. This was patched up and an EPON platoon of young volunteers was attached to each regiment and battalion to carry out supply and logistical duties.

Recruiting was intensified to make good the losses incurred in October, and all surplus EPON personnel were conscripted into ELAS proper, which meant that it now contained a proportion of youthful members of both sexes. In theory, the girls took their place beside the men, but in practice they were kept together in separate squads and employed on logistic tasks. A few demonstration sections of women guerrilla fighters, armed and accoutred, were kept to show off to visitors, but if they were not engaged in administrative work, they almost invariably went into the political or educational branches. Very few actually took part in the fighting.

ELAS had relied almost wholly upon telephones for communications, and once the Germans realized this they got in amongst the guerrilla units and cut the telephone wire system to pieces, which effectively caused confusion and bewilderment. To prevent such a disaster from happening again, special efforts were made to obtain radio sets for transmitting and receiving, and personnel were trained to operate them.[1]

It was decided to use the remainder of the winter to recruit, train and prepare for the spring. The units were instructed to concentrate upon weapon training, guerrilla tactics and ambush techniques. Hardly any ammunition was available or allocated for training purposes. The strategy to be adopted, as laid down by Colonel Saraphis,

[1] Saraphis claims that ELAS captured a total of fourteen wireless sets from the Occupation Forces.

was one of 'active defence', which he defined as consisting of quick raids and frequent ambushes.

Some units were rooted out from the villages where they had been living in comparative comfort and placed in better tactical positions, from where they could control road communications, move out to raid at short notice and be better able to reinforce counter-attacks. Units were to be 'blooded' gently.

As these directions came out from GHQ, EAM/ELAS, all sounded very grand and efficient, but they were only very slowly put into effect, and the reason for the sluggish action was lack of competent officers. ELAS consistently refused to take ex-regular or reservist officers (there were a few exceptions), even though they were republicans, and its own officer-training school had not been functioning long enough to make much difference. Lack of good unit and staff officers was a big drawback to ELAS all the time.

Supplies began to be a problem, especially in view of the increasing size of ELAS, as food and fodder were scarce in the mountains anyway, and the imposition of a large insurgent army made things more difficult. The cavalry regiment of the 1st (Thessaly) Division had about 1,600 horses, and the other divisions had developed similar, but smaller, detachments. The onset of winter brought a huge fodder shortage, so it was decided to disband most of the cavalry units for the season and send the horses down to the peasants on the plains until the spring.

ELAS now held about 15,000 prisoners-of-war, living in elementary camps in the Pindus Mountains, where they had inadequate shelter and often not enough clothing. The majority were Italians, but there were numbers of Germans and Bulgarians. Not quite knowing what to do with them, and failing to blackmail the Allied Military Mission into taking responsibility for them, ELAS 'lent' them out to work for peasants, who in return housed and fed them.

EDES was also busy recruiting, but was restricted to the regions of Arta, Jannina and Valtos, and thus did not have the same scope as ELAS, which now had about four-fifths of the mainland to recruit from. EDES strength began to decline from its probable maximum of between 11,000 and 12,000 men.

The winter of 1943–44 was a hard one for the people of Occupied Greece. The Germans blatantly lived off the land, stripping the country of anything and everything that was required back in Germany, such as machinery, horses and farm animals, thus aggravating the already dire food shortage. Many died of starvation. The Greeks in Macedonia and Thrace perhaps suffered far more than their countrymen elsewhere in Occupied Greece, as the Bulgarian administration rode heavily upon them. Many atrocities were committed and reprisals taken for acts of subversion were frequent. In the latter eighteen months of the Occupation, over 50,000 Greeks from Macedonia and Thrace were deported to Bulgaria as forced labour.

Recovering a little from the October setbacks, ELAS resumed attacks on EDES in January 1944, and the fighting continued into February, in Epirus, Roumeli, Thessaly and the Peloponnese. The weather restricted activities but there was plenty of skirmishing. The Allied Military Mission did its best to arrange a truce, but its efforts to bring about a cease-fire between the two ran into difficulties over zones of influence and boundaries. This time ELAS was more successful and the dwindling forces of EDES looked like being eventually overwhelmed.

The Allied Military Mission did at last succeed in bringing about an armistice between EAM/ELAS and EDES. Known as the Plaka Agreement, it was signed on February 29th, 1944, when representatives of both sides, and the Allied Military Mission, came together near the Plaka Bridge, in disputed territory in Epirus. Plaka was on the River Arakhtos, which flowed southwards into the Gulf of Ambracia. It was the most convenient and practical dividing line between the respective territories controlled by the rival guerrilla armies.

Both agreed to stop fighting each other and to co-operate with the Allied Military Mission against the Occupying Powers in return for arms and supplies. EAM/ELAS agreed to leave EDES alone in its now fairly small area in Epirus. This was a victory for EAM/ELAS, as EDES, virtually locked up, had an extremely meagre recruiting potential, which meant that it would have difficulty in maintaining its present strength, let alone expanding. EAM/ELAS had good reason to be pleased with itself as it managed to entice about 1,000 armed men from Colonel Zervas at the time of the Plaka Agreement. Both guerrilla armies had a deserter problem.

The state of the various guerrilla groups in March 1944 was that EDES, with less than 6,000 men, was confined to part of Epirus. Elsewhere EDES bands had all succumbed. General Psaros, of EKKA, with about 2,000 armed men, remained at large in southern Roumeli. The Salonika area had been cleared of PAO elements by

ELAS, but Andon Tsaous, who had an anti-Bulgarian band, was still firmly established to the east of the River Strymon.

In the Peloponnese, the ES and EOA, both anti-Communist in outlook and mainly composed of ex-regular and reservist officers, were having a rough time at the hands of ELAS, which had eliminated all the EDES fighters from the region. The EDES guerrillas either joined the Security Battalions or entered the ranks of ELAS, depending upon inclination and circumstances. Apart from the places just mentioned, EAM/ELAS, with a strength of about 30,000 armed men, was predominant in the mountains of Greece.

Having failed to eliminate EDES by force of arms, EAM/ELAS had to think again. There seemed to be two distinct lines of thought within the KKE, one advocated by Aris, which was that the way to achieve power was by violence, while the other, put forward by Siantos, was that a better way to achieve this objective was by infiltration and political penetration. The former having failed, it was decided to try the latter. The KKE then made a plan to sponsor an alternative government in the mountains, which was to be a practical rival to the Government-in-Exile.

This was announced on March 26th, 1944, and was known as PEEA (Political Committee of National Liberation). Colonel Bakirdzis was persuaded to desert EKKA to become its first temporary president, and other prominent politicians, some of whom were non-Communists, were attracted or deceived into joining it. PEEA was recognized by the Soviet Union, which so far had supported the Greek Government-in-Exile.

Next, on April 17th, EAM/ELAS attacked the remnants of EKKA, in southern Roumeli, scattering them and killing General Psaros. Some EKKA fighters were killed, a few changed sides and joined ELAS, but most escaped to Patras where they were incorporated into the Security Battalions.

With the establishment of PEEA, EAM and ELAS tended to disentangle themselves a little as the political energy of KKE was concentrated on it. One member was designated Secretary for War, who nominally took over the political control of ELAS. Saraphis was promoted major-general (by PEEA) and became the military head of ELAS, with Aris as his administrative assistant, or capetan.[1] This trend was followed and gradually the Three-Man Committees were

---

[1] Capetan is from the Greek word 'kapetanios', a chieftain. This was a title many early Greek guerrilla leaders took, but as time went on, within ELAS, it came to have more of a political meaning.

reduced to 'Two-Man Committees', as the EAM representative was withdrawn from them for other work. A political department was set up, which spread its tentacles outwards and downwards into all formations and units. On the Two-Man Committees the first member was the military commander and the second was the capetan, who, although still carrying out administrative duties, took over most of the political responsibility. The capetan has been called a military commissar or a political officer, and this is largely correct, although he also had military work to do.

General Saraphis made further alterations and innovations that formalized ELAS. Ranks were clearly defined and the saluting of officers was made compulsory; decorations were instituted and promotion regulations were brought out.

He formed at his GHQ a heavy weapons battalion, consisting of detachments of artillery, mortars and machine-guns, which was both available for local protection and for use wherever required. The divisions, as far as they were able, copied this innovation. So far ELAS had consisted almost exclusively of guerrilla infantry, but now it began to be the fashion to develop specialist sub-units, and Austrian, Czech and other escapees were used as instructors, as well as some German and Italian prisoners. The training school at GHQ for ELAS reserve officers, which had been established a few months previously, was enlarged. The ELAS Reserve itself was increased in size and some arms were allocated to it. Local leaders were given training. It is difficult to assess its actual strength at any given time or its capability, but most villages in EAM/ELAS territory had a small detachment. The figure of 30,000 has been mentioned, and may be used as a rough guide. No uniforms were available for the ELAS Reserve.

In the regular ELAS, changes were made within the divisions as units were more evenly grouped into regiments. Recruiting in Macedonia had been going well, enabling ELAS to form yet another division (the 11th Macedonian Division), making three in all in that part of Greece. However, the 16th (Thessaly) Division was reduced to a regiment and incorporated in the 13th (Roumeli) Division, and so the total number of ELAS divisions remained at seven, with a brigade in Attica. These were still largely static, having only a limited capacity to operate outside their own districts.

ELAN in the meanwhile was flourishing and its expansion and operations had been facilitated by the withdrawal of Italian warships from Greek waters on the Italian surrender. PEEA established a naval section under the Secretary for War. From July 1944, ELAN came under GHQ, ELAS, but the respective squadrons came directly under the command of the relevant ELAS division from whose territorial region they operated.

The ELAN squadrons were commanded by a Two-Man Committee, and they were of some nuisance value against German shipping. In July 1944, the Germans mounted operations against their shore bases, and ELAN was forced to abandon several and to scuttle a number of its ships. ELAN strength rose to over 1,200 men, and it had at its height over 100 small armed boats of different sorts and sizes, dispersed in seven squadrons, and three or four independent flotillas of up to half a dozen craft each.

With PEEA, the rival insurgent government in the mountains, an accomplished fact, it next demanded consultations with the Government-in-Exile. A meeting was arranged which took place in the Lebanon, under the chairmanship of Papandreou. This became known as the Lebanon Conference. Papandreou agreed to form a government and allot five seats to PEEA members.

EDES and EKKA[1] both agreed to put their armed guerrilla forces into a national army that would be directly under British GHQ, Middle East Command, but ELAS, whose spokesman was General Saraphis, would not endorse this.

During the summer of 1944, the Allied Military Mission kept EDES supplied with arms and ammunition, so that practically all Colonel Zervas' men, less than 5,000 in number by now, had some sort of weapon, but he was instructed not to take any action against the German Occupying Forces so as not to provoke any damaging reprisals.

On the other hand, ELAS was given very little material aid, few arms and practically no ammunition. The shortage of ammunition and the need to conserve it were the only things that caused ELAS to hold its fire and curtail its activities. However, it did manage to infiltrate and set up a thriving battalion near Preveza, on the west coast, near the Gulf of Ambracia, right behind the EDES-controlled region.

The question is often asked why, once the true nature of EAM/ELAS was known, did it continue to receive any material aid from the Allied Military Mission. The answer was simple. EAM/ELAS occupied the territory through which went the main

[1] Actually EKKA did not have any armed forces at this time, at least not acting independently as such.

Axis lines of communication, while the territory controlled by EDES was comparatively unimportant strategically to the Allied war effort. In adjacent Yugoslavia, the Communist partisans under Tito were carrying out effective guerrilla warfare and sabotage against the Axis Occupying Forces. The Allied Military Mission, whose object was to further the prosecution of the war against Germany by every means in its power, knew that, should it choose to do likewise, EAM/ELAS had both the means and ability, and the Mission always hoped, regardless of the ultimate political ambitions at stake, that EAM/ELAS could be persuaded to emulate the Yugoslav Communist partisans.

Throughout the summer, EAM/ELAS guerrillas put pressure on ES and EOA, the two small groups functioning in the Peloponnese. Gradually they were overcome, and by August both had ceased to exist. Many of their members made their way to Epirus to join EDES. However, in their turn the ELAS fighters took some punishment from the Security Battalions that were operating fairly effectively. The strength of the Security Battalions totalled about 15,000, and they were made up in units of about 500 men each. There were about eighteen battalions in the Peloponnese, six in and around Athens and six in central Greece.

Having both a deserter and a recruiting problem, coupled with fear and hatred of ELAS, Colonel Zervas accepted practically all refugees from EAM/ELAS actions, regardless of who they were. This broad policy tended to water down the efficiency and fighting ability of his units, as many were of small value as guerrilla fighters. Some refugees were a distinct handicap, and others made exaggerated claims as to their military status and ability.

Colonel Zervas took action against the Chams, a Moslem minority in Greece, who had been stirred up and armed to harass Greek guerrillas in Epirus. They did not prove to be very aggressive or enthusiastic fighters, but they had an irritating nuisance value. Zervas drove them from his part of Epirus and they took refuge just over the border in Albania. This cleared his decks for action to some extent.

So turbulent was the ebb and flow of Greek politics that, while some guerrilla groups had been submerged and had passed from the scene, others rose to take their place. One group that can be briefly mentioned was SNOF, a Communist-controlled body of Macedonian Slavs, under Gotchev, which at first professed affiliation with EAM/ELAS. Gotchev would not unquestioningly follow

EAM/ELAS instructions and lines of thought so there was constant friction and hardly any co-operation between the two. On one or two occasions there were abrupt ruptures that almost led to hostilities. After this SNOF turned to Tito, of Yugoslavia, and declared that its intention was to work for an autonomous Macedonia within a Communist Southern Slav Federation. SNOF had produced its first armed bands in November 1943, since when it had quickly increased in strength until it had nearly 2,000 armed men. Not very much was heard of its activities until it definitely split with EAM/ELAS. ELAS took action against SNOF whenever it could, but generally it was more than fully occupied against the Bulgarian Occupation Forces in Macedonia.

Since 1941 there had been no contact at all between the Soviet Union and either the Central Committee of the KKE or EAM/ELAS in the mountains. It is believed that the Greek Communists had attempted to keep up some sort of liaison with Moscow, but that this had been discouraged and then quashed by Stalin. It will be remembered that in May 1943 he dissolved the Comintern, which had formerly been the medium for giving out instructions to foreign Communist parties, both legal and illicit. Throughout the Occupation the Greek Communists had been forced to plough a lonely furrow without guidance or support from the fountainhead. Suddenly, from out of the blue, on July 28th, 1943, eight Soviet officers arrived at EAM/ELAS GHQ, and two others were dropped by parachute to ELAS forces in Macedonia.

The complete severance of all contact between the Greek Communists and Moscow is all the more surprising owing to the unusual position of Bulgaria. In March 1941 Bulgaria had signed the Tripartite Pact, thus becoming virtually a satellite of the Axis Powers, and she provided them with troops, installations and other assistance. However, Bulgaria still remained on full diplomatic terms with the Soviet Union at the same time.[1] Inside Bulgaria there were spasmodic attempts to stir up guerrilla warfare against the pro-Axis régime, but none ever came to very much, despite clandestine aid and support given by the Soviet Union. Many of these tiny, weak bodies were Communist-inspired, and there was an active, underground Communist movement in existence which could easily have

---

[1] The Soviet Union declared war on Bulgaria on September 5th, 1944, and the next day Bulgaria replied by declaring war on the Soviet Union. Soviet troops invaded the country and by the 9th, Bulgaria was in Soviet hands with a pro-Soviet puppet government installed.

made contact over the border with the Greek Communists had it wanted to do so, and vice versa. Perhaps traditional Balkan dislikes and suspicions were stronger than the ties of international Communism.

From January 1944, following the liaison visit by Tzimas to Tito in Yugoslavia, EAM/ELAS had been in radio communication with Tito's headquarters. EAM/ELAS had continually asked that the Red Army supply it with arms and ammunition, but there had never been any reply to these requests. EAM/ELAS also asked that Soviet officers be sent to see it at work in the mountains of Greece. There had been no reply to that proposal either. A change of policy occurred in mid-1944, when the Red Army was advancing towards the Balkans, and it was decided to look in and check up on the Greek Communist guerrillas to see what they were doing and what their potential was. The activities of the Yugoslav partisans had no doubt stimulated this interest.

This Soviet Military Mission, which had come from Tito's headquarters in Yugoslavia, was not very impressed by what it saw of ELAS, and the result was that no military aid was forthcoming from the Soviet Union. Perhaps it was unfair to compare ELAS to the Yugoslav guerrillas; but in any event, for the time being at least, the ever-practical Stalin lost interest in it.[1]

By early September, the German Occupation Forces had obviously begun to concentrate preparatory to withdrawal, and the Red Army was getting nearer the Balkans. With the liberation of Greece so near at hand, Britain still hoped that political squabbles could be postponed until it had been achieved, so another attempt was made. A conference, known as the Caserta Conference, was called to discuss preparations for the Greek liberation. On September 26th, General Saraphis of ELAS and Colonel Zervas of EDES were flown to Caserta in Italy to take part in it. A British general, General Scobie, was nominated to be in command of all Allied forces designated to land in Greece, and both Saraphis and Zervas agreed to place their troops under him. Other spheres of influence and interest were laid down, and Colonel Zervas was confirmed in the territory he actually held in Epirus.

The liberation of Greece by the Allies was carried out in a hurried slap-dash manner. Greece had somehow been overlooked when it

---

[1] Much later I was told by a Soviet officer, who claimed to have read a copy of the original report sent back by the Soviet Military Mission on ELAS, that ELAS was 'just a rabble of armed men, not worth supporting'.

came to making a plan for liberating Axis Occupied countries. The Soviet Union's region of liberation included the Balkan countries but, owing to Churchill's intervention at the Moscow Conference of October 1944, not Greece. Neither had there been advance plans to liberate the country from the Mediterranean. Perhaps the importance of the task had been minimized because only a small number of German troops remained there and no particular difficulty had been envisaged in ejecting them in due course. The Bulgarians had been discounted. When it became obvious that the Germans were about to pull out, a scratch Allied force, mainly of British troops, was mustered to move into Greece on their heels.

By the end of the month (September), apprehensions about probable Bulgarian defection and the advance of Soviet troops into Yugoslavia brought the German evacuation of Greece into full swing, and the Greek guerrilla bands, jostling violently together, began quickly jumping into the places left vacant. The larger ELAS came out of this scramble better than the other, weaker, ones. The Allied Military Mission attempted to enforce the Allied plan prepared for this emergency, known as Operation 'Rat Week', but this was only partially applied by the guerrillas and with scant enthusiasm. They were all too much concerned with jockeying for position. It is true that ELAS did harass the withdrawing troops, but the main motive was to seize arms and material. The plain fact was that Greece was liberated because the German troops left the country, and not because they were driven from it. At times the Greek guerrillas, and the tiny Allied forces acting with them, had difficulty in keeping contact with the German rearguards. In Macedonia and Thrace the position remained the same, as the Bulgarian Occupying troops had changed their colours and were acting as agents of the Red Army.

British troops landed in the Peloponnese on the night of October 3rd–4th, Athens was entered on the 13th, and on the 18th General Scobie set up his GHQ in the capital, where he was joined by the Papandreou Government.

We now come to consider the controversial question of the true value of the Greek guerrillas to the Allied war effort. They are all too often compared closely with Tito's partisans; and as they had few spectacular successes – apart from one or two incidents, such as destroying the Gorgopotamos Viaduct (which was British instigated and partly British effected anyway) and the Tirnavo Tunnel – they do not come out too well by this comparison. This is a rather unfair comparison that does not take into account many of the circum-stances, and the varying background of the two countries and their individual guerrilla potential. To assess their real value Greek guerrillas should be viewed alone in their own setting.

It should be emphasized that the fact that Greek guerrillas existed at all made them of some value to the Allies—it is merely a question of how much.

The first fact that has bearing on their value is that the bulk of the guerrillas were fairly late in the field, and the activities had certainly not reached their peak efficiency in 1942 and early 1943, when the Allies could have used them to the best advantage.

Next, the Greek guerrillas received only limited arms and stores from the Allies with which to carry out subversive activities and sabotage.[1] This was partly because in the first instance hardly any Allied aircraft were available to drop these supplies in Occupied Greece, and partly because later they were deliberately restricted, as they were being used primarily against each other and not against the Occupying Forces. It is perhaps now easy to speculate that had arms been given on a more generous scale the Greek guerrillas could have been of greater value to the Allies, but there is no real reason to think that this might have been the case.

Another factor to consider was that Axis reprisals were harsh and exemplary, and this discouraged subversive activity. When praising the achievements of Tito's partisans, one is apt to forget that the cost was about one million civilian dead. In Greece, whenever successful subversive operations were carried out heavy penalties were inflicted, hostages were shot, peasants who lived nearby were frequently imprisoned or worse, and their houses or villages demolished. For example, in March, April and May 1944, the Germans admitted shooting 4,100 hostages in Greece. With barely sufficient troops for occupational purposes they chose this cruel method of repressing subversion. One of the most publicized reprisals occurred on December 13th, 1943, at Kalavryta in the Peloponnese, when about 1,000 people were machine-gunned or burnt to death. Another occurred on July 29th, 1944, at Kleisoura, when after a German patrol had been ambushed, about 250 women and children (the men of the village had fled to the mountains) were shut in a building

[1] Saraphis claims that ELAS was given by the British (later Allied) Military Mission during the whole period of the Occupation '10 mortars, 30 machine-guns, 100 sub-machine-guns, 300 automatic rifles, 3,000 rifles and very little ammunition' (*Greek Resistance Army*).

that was set on fire. Many were burnt to death. When ELAS blocked the Tirnavo Tunnel, the Axis Authorities took 118 Greeks from the internment camp at Larissa and shot them at the scene of the incident. There were many other lesser incidents.

Over 2,000 villages[1] were razed or partly destroyed by the Occupation Powers, so it can be seen that there was heavy retribution for acts of sabotage. At the end of the Occupation it was estimated that about 1·5 million people were either homeless as a result of their houses being deliberately destroyed by way of reprisals, or were living in abject conditions for the same reason.

On the other hand, it was soon seen that, provided nothing was done against the Occupation Authorities, the guerrillas were usually left alone to their own devices as long as they kept out of the way in the mountains. This was a big temptation to 'live and let live' that only superhuman determination could overcome. The peasants, themselves not over-blessed with this world's goods, had everything to lose and little to gain, except the vague satisfaction of knowing that by hindering the Axis war effort they were being patriotic and were indirectly helping the Allies.

Another factor was that amongst Greek guerrilla groups there was a multitude of conflicting motives and ideals, and each was primarily concerned with expanding and extending its own influence. The many leaders individually saw themselves as at least taking part in the post-war government of Greece. The main energy of the guerrillas was expended in fighting each other, which the Occupation Authorities did what they could to encourage.

The quality of the guerrillas themselves was not always of the highest. There is no doubt that all the guerrilla bands had their hard core of fearless, dedicated fighters, but they also had a large proportion of 'hangers-on', attracted by the romantic notion of posing as a sort of patriotic brigand roaming the mountains, and those who were reluctantly caught up in the movement by an accident of circumstances, such as being conscripted. The military value of such individuals was low, and consequently restricted the hitting and defensive ability of the guerrilla bands. This bred a certain amount of caution in the leaders, who had no desire to see their own particular unit dispersed to the wind, and so hesitated to commit it to action if this could be avoided lest it be defeated and destroyed.

It can be said that the first object of the Greek guerrilla bands was

---

[1] There are higher figures quoted by other authorities but these invariably include villages partly damaged by inter-guerrilla reprisals.

that of self-preservation, the second that of expansion, and the third that of elimination of rivals, while that of hindering the Axis war effort came a poor fourth.

The strongest in numbers and best organized politically was ELAS, directed by a shrewd Central Committee hidden away in Athens, whose policy was put into effect by such merciless characters as Aris. This Committee, of EAM/ELAS, was manipulated by the KKE, the Greek Communist Party, and whatever may be said about the methods and directives of the KKE, it was largely responsible for shaking the Greek people out of the lethargy they had sunk into immediately after the Occupation settled on Greece. The underlying aim of EAM/ELAS, which was to achieve total power in Greece, never changed throughout, and everything and everybody was bent to this purpose. Tolerance is no part of the Communist creed.

The political and propaganda aspects of EAM/ELAS were good, not to say excellent, but its military value was less so. This, despite attempts to conceal it, was a constant weakness. EAM at first tried to entice Colonel Zervas, a recognized military expert and capable organizer, as it wanted him to put ELAS into an aggressive fighting condition. Zervas did not accept this offer, and it is only of academic interest to speculate what might have happened had he done so.

When Zervas could not be tempted to join, EAM/ELAS looked for and succeeded in getting the 'second best' Saraphis. Although Saraphis did tighten the loose framework of ELAS, lay down some elementary tactical drills, run training courses and reorganize the divisions, there was comparatively small increase in military efficiency or fighting ability. The political aspect had been accentuated until it almost blotted out the military. The standard of the unit leaders was often indifferent, their political views and opinions gaining them their jobs. Morale was not always what it was cracked up to be, and despite severe penalties, there were many desertions.

ELAS units reeled back and scattered when hit by the German Occupation Forces in October–December 1944, and had the Germans continued with their campaign against the guerrillas it is doubtful whether ELAS could have survived long as a cohesive body in the field. There must have been something in a Soviet officer's remark to me quoted earlier, that EAM/ELAS was 'merely a rabble of armed men not worth supporting', for, although it always had overwhelming superiority in men and arms of never less than four-to-one, it was unable to wipe out its main rival, EDES.

The only other guerrilla army worth commenting briefly upon in summarizing is EDES, the Republican one, under the leadership of Colonel Zervas, who had become practically divorced from his controlling political Central Committee in Athens, as he believed that the struggle should be directed from the mountains rather than from the capital. He also believed that it was not possible for a committee, wherever it was located, to command an army in the field. In EDES, military ability counted for more than political reliability, and the army was reasonably well organized in small groups on more or less conventional lines in Epirus.

EDES later became established in other parts of Greece, and its maximum strength at one period exceeded 10,000 men. Colonel Zervas had been persuaded to make his organization 'non-political', which he did to some degree. This left him wide open to infiltration by EAM agents, who at times caused havoc within his ranks and ensured that his deserter problem never grew less. Had he been more strict from the political angle he would have been able to prevent much of this. EDES was not only continually harassed in the field by ELAS, but its morale was constantly undermined by EAM activities.

In the latter fighting with ELAS, EDES did not come out so well, but the main body, reduced in strength, remained intact in Epirus. Towards the end its fighting ability was sadly impaired owing to influxes of refugees from other groups, including ELAS deserters. As EDES shrunk in size and the territory it controlled decreased, so was its recruiting potential severely reduced. It became a vicious circle that Colonel Zervas could not break through. During 1944, the Allied Military Mission almost openly favoured EDES, as it realized that EDES was the only obstacle, although a small and decreasing one, to the seizure of the whole countryside by EAM/ELAS. The supply of extra arms and cash greatly assisted in keeping EDES alive.

Before summing up what the Greek guerrillas accomplished, it may be as well to remark briefly upon the attitude of the Allies—or rather of Britain in particular, as she was the chief one involved—towards Occupied Greece. At varying times, owing to the diverse needs of the Allies and the ever-changing war situation, greater or lesser attention was given. In 1941, Greece hardly ever came into British plans at all. Apart from seeking intelligence of enemy shipping and troop movements, which was gained in a disjointed manner, little else was attempted. This continued into 1942.

It was only immediately before the Battle of Alamein and subsequently that Greece loomed up in importance, because it was on an Axis supply route. The British Military Mission was established in the mountains, charged with the task of supplying arms to all guerrillas who would co-operate with it to hamper the Axis forces as much as possible.

The importance of Greece increased in the first part of 1943, when plans were being made for landings in Sicily and Italy, as the Allies wanted a flurry of sabotage, both to draw off and keep occupied as many Axis divisions as possible, and to deceive the Germans into believing that an Allied landing in Greece was imminent.

Once the Sicily landings had taken place and the fighting in Italy developed, Allied interest in Greece waned. The Allied Military Mission remained, but it seemed as though it had just been overlooked, as everyone was so busy elsewhere. When it became obvious that the Greek King had no support from any of the main guerrilla groups operating inside Occupied Greece, the Government-in-Exile became an embarrassment.

During 1944, when Allied attention was focused on the Second Front, Greece definitely became a backwater. The country was no longer—if it ever had been—an important cog in the Allied war machine. This spasmodic interest, sandwiched between periods of indifference and neglect, could hardly be calculated to bring out and encourage the best form of co-operation with the guerrillas inside Occupied Greece.

What then did the guerrillas do to help the Allied war effort?

In the first place, their mere existence tied down about thirteen German, Italian and Bulgarian divisions, about 300,000 troops in all, in occupation duties for many months. When Italy capitulated, the Germans still had to maintain about six divisions in Greece and the islands, and the Bulgarians three, adding up to about 180,000 men in all. True, these were not all first-class formations, but if they had not been required in Greece they would have been available for use elsewhere.

The first appearance of the British Military Mission in Occupied Greece had stimulated a wave of sabotage activity in November 1942, at a time when the British 8th Army was fighting Rommel's Afrika Korps. The destruction of the Gorgopotamos Viaduct, which hampered Axis supplies coming down through the Balkans for six weeks, could not have been accomplished without Greek guerrilla assistance.

In the summer of 1943 before the Sicily landings, despite the realization that severe reprisals would inevitably follow, another wave of minor sabotage of airfields and communications took place, causing the Germans to bring in three more divisions under the impression the Allies were about to land in Greece. Much of this activity, such as the destruction of the Asopos Viaduct, was carried out by British saboteurs, but they could not have operated without the knowledge, help and consent of the guerrilla organizations.

After the Italian capitulation sabotage tended to die down as the various guerrilla armies concentrated solely upon fighting each other and upon their own survival.

As regards facts and figures, which are difficult to prove or disprove, EAM/ELAS, for example, claims[1] that during the Resistance under the Occupation it was responsible for, since the establishment of the ELAS GHQ, killing 19,355 Germans, Italians and Bulgarians, wounding 8,294 and taking 5,181 prisoner. This excluded the Italian Pinerlo Division and other Italian troops that changed sides on the capitulation of their country. ELAS also claims to have destroyed 30 bridges, 85 locomotives, 957 railway wagons and 1,007 motor vehicles. ELAS losses are estimated to be approximately 4,500 dead and 6,000 wounded.

ELAS is silent on how many arms it seized from the Occupation Forces. Although the figures may be slightly exaggerated in some respects, it was roughly indicative of the ELAS achievements, and the other guerrilla groups probably caused similar casualties and did similar damage in proportion to their size and means, depending upon what scope was available to them.

One other thing that should not be overlooked is that the various clandestine groups, especially the Salonika-based PAO, gave valuable intelligence to the Allies, not only about enemy formations and troop movements within Occupied Greece, but also of Axis shipping.

Finally, if it can be said that the Greek guerrillas were only of limited value to the Allied war effort, which was probably correct to a degree, then it should be added that the Allies in return showed only periodic, selfish and materialistic interest in a country that was cruelly hamstrung under Axis Occupation.

In retrospect, one fact seems to stand out; which is that had EAM/ELAS fallen in wholeheartedly with British requests for guerrilla warfare and sabotage action, Britain would most probably have backed it to the hilt and given large quantities of arms and

[1] Sarafis, *Greek Resistance Army.*

supplies, as she had done to Tito's Communist guerrillas in Yugoslavia. Had this occurred, the Communists would have been in a much better position to step into power in Greece when the country was liberated, as did Tito in Yugoslavia. One can hardly assume that EAM/ELAS was deterred completely from carrying out more intense sabotage by Axis reprisals, as dedicated Communists are invariably utterly callous as to the fate of others, so one must assume that to their own detriment they misread the portents of the future.

The first round of the battle between the Greek Communists and the rest of the Greeks had underlined the fact that in guerrilla warfare political and military aims are practically inseparable, and to succeed all guerrilla leaders must be both good politicians and military experts. Many KKE and EAM/ELAS leaders did not combine these two essential qualities, and by appreciating this premise, one can see how the Communists in Occupied Greece only stumbled along in the first round instead of sweeping the board to present the Allies with a *fait accompli* when they landed.

CHAPTER FIVE

The Second Round

A little should be said about the actual Liberation of Greece to give a fuller background to the 'Second Round' of the Civil War between the Greek Communists and the remainder, which began on December 1st, 1944.

The Allied Liberation plan, known as 'Operation Manna', was hurriedly prepared immediately after the Caserta Conference, as it was thought that the German Occupying Forces were on the point of leaving. The designated Liberation Force was small in size and had little heavy armament, being more in the nature of a 'take-over' force than one intended to drive out the occupying troops with the bayonet. The troops available consisted of two British brigades (2nd Parachute and the 23rd Armoured, both acting as infantry) and a few hundred British and some American commandos, to which were to be added the Free Greek Land Forces. The latter in practice now only amounted to the Greek Mountain Brigade (known as the Rimini Brigade as it had just fought well at the Battle of Rimini) and a small commando group known as the Sacred Band, which was in the Aegean Islands. The Free Greek Air Force, consisting of three squadrons, was also to be made available, as were a few Greek warships.

Allied commando units had landed on the Peloponnese in the first days of October 1944, and they moved along the Gulf of Corinth towards Piraeus, expecting the Germans to evacuate almost at once. The plan was that the Parachute Brigade, with appropriate Allied air cover, would take Athens and then clear the road to Piraeus, so that other Liberating troops could be brought in by sea. However, the Germans, who had about 10,000 troops in the area of Athens, seemed to be in no great hurry to pull out, and so operations tended to hang fire.

For a few days there was a tense pause. In Attica, the nominated commander, General Spiliotopoulis, would not allow the ELAS guerrillas, who were technically under his orders in accordance with the Caserta Agreement, to harass the Germans in Athens as he feared they would then do extensive damage by way of reprisals. This example was generally followed elsewhere in the country and the guerrilla units stood off, refraining from provoking German troops.

On the 12th, it was learnt that the Germans were at last moving out from Athens, and the following day British paratroops landed by parachute, secured the Megara airfield just outside the city, and moved into the capital on the heels of the departing occupation troops. The next day, the remainder of the Parachute Brigade arrived at the airfield, from where they spread out into Athens and along the road to Piraeus. In defiance of orders, a small group of ELAS guerrillas seized and held on to the electric power station and the Marathon Dam on the outskirts of Athens, just before the German units departed.

Meanwhile, 'Operation Rat Week' – the objects of which were to harass the German withdrawal through Greece, prevent any heavy military equipment being taken out of the country and ensure that enemy formations would not be fit to go off and fight elsewhere immediately without being re-equipped – did not go so well. Only a few Allied commandos were avilable to augment and support the Allied Military Mission personnel and encourage the guerrillas. ELAS afterwards claimed to have killed over 5,000 Axis soldiers in this operation and to have taken many more prisoner, which was probably largely correct, but it was arms and ammunition they were after. There is no doubt that ELAS was successful in seizing large quantities of arms and ammunition in this withdrawal. Also, the Germans deliberately left quantities of arms, ammunition and explosives behind in dumps in the hope that they would be 'found' and used by guerrillas to promote dissension amongst themselves, and possibly be used against both Allied and Greek authorities.

By November 1st the Germans had withdrawn north of Salonika and Florina, and ten days later had left the Greek mainland completely. German troops remained on some of the Aegean Islands, but they gradually concentrated on Crete, where they continued to hold out. The Bulgarian Occupation Forces, now under Red Army control, stayed where they were for the time being.

General Scobie's instructions were to establish his GHQ in Athens, to maintain law and order and to help the Papandreou Government set up its administration. He was not to interfere in local politics. By the end of October, his III Corps, as his force was known, consisted of about 26,500 British troops and five squadrons of aircraft. The smallness of the Liberation Force meant that it could physically station soldiers only in Athens, Piraeus and one or two other cities and communication centres to 'show the flag', so the rest of the country stayed under the control of the existing guerrilla armies.

According to the terms of the Caserta Agreement, Colonel Zervas was to have most of Epirus, Andon Tsaous the Drama area, and the Chams the Philiates district in Epirus. Elsewhere, both on the mainland and in the Peloponnese, ELAS was in actual occupation, and this fact had been recognized. Salonika and northern Greece were put under the command of General Bakirdzis and Central Greece under General Saraphis. Aris had been nominated by ELAS for the Peloponnese command, but he was not acceptable to the Allies, so another ELAS senior officer had to be named.

Liberated Greece was in a sad state, as the Germans and Bulgarians had systematically and ruthlessly stripped the farms, the smallholdings and the countryside of cattle, livestock and poultry. Starvation faced the population and, in addition, several thousands of Axis POWs were retained in Greece to work on reconstruction and they had to be fed as well. Accordingly, the country was treated more as an UNRRA problem than a possible base for further aggression against Germany, and plans were put into operation to rush in supplies of food, clothing and medicines. An Anglo-American organization, known as Military Liaison, paved the way for the receipt and distribution of the UNRRA supplies.

Before withdrawing, the Germans, despite being deliberately left alone by the guerrilla armies, had destroyed harbour facilities, bridges, factories, roads, communications and machinery. To both help the distribution of vitally essential items and to help repair communications, a large proportion of the British Force consisted of administration units.

Once installed in Athens the Papandreou Government, which still had six PEEA members in its Cabinet, promised a purge of the police and the government services and the prompt punishment of traitors. Members of the Security Battalions were arrested to await trial, as were many other collaborators and suspects.

On the constitutional side, George II agreed not to return to Greece until a plebiscite had been held showing that a majority of the people wanted him, and it was suggested that in the interim a Regency be set up, but there was some argument about this. Archbishop Damaskinos of Athens was proposed as the Regent, but neither King George II nor Papandreou were in favour of him filling this position at this stage.

Expecting that all ELAS and EDES armed guerrillas would automatically place themselves directly under the command of General Scobie and obey his orders, in conformity with the Caserta Agreement, the Papandreou Government began to talk about disarming them and making preparations for reconstituted National armed forces, police and gendarmerie.

The Red Army and Soviet influence closed right up all along the northern Greek frontiers. On the Albanian border, ELAS made more or less friendly contact with Hoxha's guerrillas and a unit of Albanian guerrillas was nominally placed under ELAS command, where it remained until it disintegrated and faded away. In return, ELAS handed over to Hoxha some Albanian war criminals he badly wanted.

On the Yugoslav frontier, ELAS men moved forward into the old frontier posts and buildings wherever they could. One small area was held by SNOF, which stood fast and refused to budge. SNOF, under the leadership of Gotchev, had about 600 armed men and would not co-operate with ELAS. When faced point-blank with overwhelming armed might, Gotchev threw in his lot completely with Tito's partisans, but remained where he was. Anxious to avoid an open breach with Tito, ELAS hesitated for a few days, but suddenly lost patience and drove the SNOF fighters over the Yugoslav border.

To the east, Bulgarian troops, now part of a Soviet Union satellite army, remained in Thrace and Macedonia under the pretext that there was no constituted authority to hand over to. The Allies insisted that all Bulgarian Occupation Forces should be withdrawn before an armistice agreement with Bulgaria was concluded, and the Soviet Union, which wanted the Bulgarian troops free to fight against the Germans in Yugoslavia and Hungary, ordered them to evacuate Greek territory. Hesitatingly they did so and the 'northern corps' of waiting ELAS moved in quickly. The 'northern corps', under General Bakirdzis and Markos Vaphiadis, consisted of the four Macedonian divisions, the 6th (a new one), 9th, 10th and 11th.[1]

Andon Tsaous, with perhaps just under 1,000 armed 'Greek National Guerrillas', remained in position in Drama province where, according to the Caserta Agreement, he hoped to remain. The Allied Military Mission had tacitly allowed the Bulgarian Occupation Forces to give him some measure of aid as he was so violently anti-ELAS. It had unsuccessfully tried to persuade ELAS to co-operate with the Bulgarians against the Germans, but ELAS and the Bulgarians—regular forces and Soviet-sponsored guerrillas—were suspicious of each other. The last Bulgarian troops left Greece by October 25th, and the Bulgarian Armistice was signed on the 28th. ELAS was in effective control of the greater part of northern Greece.

In Epirus there was some initial scuffling between EDES and ELAS, without it to any great extent affecting the territory controlled by the rival armies. EDES took over the island of Corfu, ejecting ELAS troops, and there was friction over the island of Levkas, which was occupied by EDES although given to ELAS at the Caserta Conference. EDES would not evacuate the island, nor would the British order them to do so, despite the fact that on British orders ELAS had withdrawn its battalion from the area of Preveza, and this infuriated ELAS.

ELAS strength had increased until at the moment of the Liberation it had risen to about 50,000[2] armed fighters. Two more divisions had been added to its order-of-battle, the 2nd (Attica) and the 6th (Macedonian). On October 23rd ELAS GHQ moved into Lamia and asked to be allowed to assist the Yugoslavs against the Germans, but this was turned down by the British GHQ in Athens. ELAS then asked to be allowed to take part in the Liberation of Crete and Melos when this was to take place, but this also was turned down.

In continental Greece ELAS was successful in taking physical possession of practically the whole of the countryside (except the enclaves mentioned) and occupying all the cities, towns and villages —except for Athens, Piraeus, Salonika, Patras and other places where British troops were stationed. The Communists quickly saw the smallness of the Allied Liberation Force and noted the small fighting content, as well as the fact that it seemed to be more concerned with

[1] A Bulgarian Military Liaison Mission was attached to General Bakirdzis' HQ.
[2] General Saraphis says the strength of ELAS in mid-October was 5,130 officers 1,070 political officers and 48,940 men.

repairing roads and harbour facilities and distributing UNRRA supplies than penetrating into the interior. EAM/ELAS units were able to spread into the countryside. The abrupt dissolution of the Allied Military Mission, which had come to realize what EAM/ELAS was, and what its aims were, facilitated this. EAM was gaining a sympathetic Allied Press, and British GHQ at Athens was rather inclined to treat it with consideration and respect, thinking that it was the only guerrilla army that had achieved anything during the Occupation, and not to take much notice or heed of the warnings and advice of members of the Allied Military Mission.

As it settled on the country, EAM/ELAS seized the people in its grip, enforcing its administration on them wherever it could. A Red Terror developed, as Security Battalion personnel, collaborators and those with a known or suspected anti-Communist bias were arrested. The EAM secret police, the OPLA (Units for the Protection of the People's Struggle), was the instrument that effected these arrests, and it combed the towns and the countryside looking for victims. Many prisoners were shot and thousands of others detained; there were massacres, especially of Security Battalion officers and men, impromptu executions and hundreds of people were never heard of again. Rumours of this Red Terror, although suppressed as far as possible by EAM censorship, filtered through to Athens, making the British GHQ suspicious and uneasy. Money was demanded by ELAS to pay its men, but was not forthcoming. The Papandreou Government wanted to disarm and disband the guerrillas and had no intention of encouraging them to remain in existence by paying them a regular wage.

Ostensibly to keep order in a countryside entirely devoid of official Government security forces, the EAM formed its own gendarmerie, which was known as the EP (National Civil Guard). This organization had actually been in operation for some few weeks before the German withdrawal in areas controlled by the EAM, but now it swelled in strength and acted as the EAM private police force.

Another EAM sponsored organization was the EA (National Co-operative), which had the object of helping and rehabilitating those who had suffered under the Occupation. It was responsible for distributing a proportion of the UNRRA supplies, but was distinctly partisan, the food and money always being given out to EAM members or sympathizers only.

In Athens EAM was by no means paramount, and it had to struggle hard against several factions, the most powerful and lively of which was X. X was a right-wing underground organization with Royalist inclinations, led by Colonel Grivas, that had been in existence in the city during the Occupation, when little had been heard of it or its activities. Upon Liberation it suddenly blossomed out as an aggressive, anti-Communist body, gaining considerable influence and following in the capital, where it endeavoured to block EAM/ELAS ambitions.

EAM/ELAS had wanted detachments of ELAS to be stationed in Athens, but Papandreou would not permit this, making the excuse that all barrack accommodation in the city was either in use, or earmarked for British or Free Greek Forces. ELAS units were instructed to remain outside. ELAS also asked that its newly formed 2nd (Attica) Division, which had grown from the Attica Brigade, be allowed to march past in Athens, and this was forbidden too. On October 25th General Spiliotopoulis was replaced by Brigadier Katsotas, the commander of the Free Greek Forces, as the commander of the Attica region. On the 30th the Papandreou Government decreed the disbandment of EP, the EAM National Guard, which was making wholesale arrests throughout the country; however, it had no means of enforcing this order, so EP continued its work unhampered.

During the month of November 1944 the situation in Athens deteriorated as EAM agents infiltrated the city accompanied by small groups of ELAS, armed but in plain clothes. Their object was to stir up discontent and to establish guerrilla areas so as to be able to dominate other rival groups, such as X. A Black Market appeared, and this was both exploited and manipulated by EAM to embarrass the Government. Also, EAM did what it could by instigating labour friction to hinder and obstruct the distribution of urgently needed UNRRA supplies.

The EAM began to agitate openly as a political party against the Papandreou Government, and on the 4th it organized a large demonstration in Athens to protest against the alleged killing of ELAS soldiers by EDES. On the 10th the Rimini Brigade arrived from Italy, and this anti-Communist formation provoked further demonstrations. The general lines of the EAM complaint were that Papandreou was protecting collaborators, especially those who had served in the Security Battalions, and giving them good jobs, whilst discriminating against and victimizing EAM, ELAS and other left-wing bodies. It was true that elements of the Security Battalions had been used by the Liberating Forces to keep order and that the original harsh intentions towards them had, by necessity, been softened.

Anxious because the greater part of Greece was in the grip of armed guerrillas who seemed reluctant to accept the authority of the Papandreou Government unless on their own special terms, General Scobie pressed for the speedy formation of a national army, police and gendarmerie, and the early disarmament and disbandment of guerrillas. A conference was called, attended by the major political parties, their military advisers, and the British, to discuss how this should be carried into effect. All agreed that a national army was desirable, but they differed as to how it should be composed.

The British proposed that in the first place it should consist of a large 'mixed' division, which would be gradually expanded into a corps of three divisions with supporting troops. The 'mixed' division was to consist of an ELAS brigade, an EDES battalion, the Free Greek Forces and a few conscripts; a total of about 40,000. All the remaining guerrillas were to be disarmed.

ELAS proposed that all units should be disbanded, including the Free Greek Forces, which consisted of the Rimini Brigade and the Sacred Band that had just arrived from the Aegean Islands, but the British would not agree, as these formations were the only ones the Papandreou Government could rely upon in case of insurrection or internal disorders. Next, ELAS proposed that if there was to be a 'mixed' division, the men in it should be completely integrated, and not just the units. While Papandreou would agree to accept a 'mixed' division, he would not have either the men or the units in it integrated. Eventually, after much argument, a 'mixed' division, as initially proposed by the British, was provisionally accepted by all parties attending the conference, including ELAS.

It was agreed that all other guerrillas would be disarmed and disbanded by December 10th. A new 'National Guard', to police the countryside, was to be formed to take over from the EAM-sponsored EP as soon as possible; as from December 1st the EP was to come under the direct orders of General Scobie. All regular officers with the guerrillas were to be reinstated in the regular army, and 'officers' who had been commissioned in the field by the various guerrilla organizations were to have special facilities to help them become regular officers if they wished to do so. General Saraphis was proposed as Chief of General Staff for the new national army, but Papandreou would not have him.

The growing undercurrent of EAM opposition and obstructiveness alarmed both the British and Papandreou, and on November 15th General Scobie was secretly instructed to prepare for possible hostilities against EAM/ELAS, should it attempt a coup. Two brigades of the 4th Indian Division (which consisted of three infantry brigades) were flown from Italy to Greece as reinforcements in case of trouble, one going to Patras and the other to Salonika. These preparations proved to be timely and justified. General Saraphis, the spokesman for ELAS played for time, quibbling over the conditions for disarming his men, until on November 29th he openly and flatly refused to disarm ELAS.

Two days later (December 1st) the EP refused to hand over its police duties to the new National Guard, and this act can be conveniently regarded as marking the commencement of the 'second round' of the Communist Civil War in Greece, although there had been a few armed clashes between ELAS and the Government forces before this date.

The KKE Central Committee decided that the moment to strike for power had come. It saw the military weakness of the British Liberation Force, its indifference to local politics, its apparent determination to bring back King George II, and its inability to impose the authority of the Papandreou Government in Greece outside the large cities. It also saw that the British Government had become aware of Communist intentions and had already begun to reinforce the British III Corps, even though World War II still raged and British troops were urgently needed elsewhere. The KKE felt that it was time to change from the policy it had adopted of infiltration and political intrigue to one of force. It estimated that it, or rather ELAS, had gained a certain amount of sympathy and admiration, added to which for ideological reasons it was thought that the Soviet Union, the other great ally, would be strongly in its favour, so that Britain might be forced to be circumspect if suddenly faced with a successful Communist *coup d'état* in Greece. The longer the KKE hesitated, the stronger the British force might become and the more prepared the Papandreou Government might be to counter such a move. The decision to revolt was that of the KKE Central Committee. It was alleged later by Markos Vaphiadis that Stalin had sent a message to the Central Committee of the KKE which induced the revolt, but that when asked for help Stalin prevaricated. The KKE was now ready for war, and ELAS units moved right up to the outskirts of Athens and Piraeus.

The EP had a convenient practical, as well as ideological, objection to handing over to the newly formed National Guard, as it consisted of raw, ill-disciplined, recalled reservists, sprinkled with officers and men of the former Security Battalions. The Government plan was to quickly raise a National Guard, of about 22,000 men, which was to consist of some thirty-five battalions (each 630 strong) to be manned with recalled reservists of the 1936 conscript class. These began to be recalled in mid-November, and were hardly capable of taking on the difficult job by December 1st.

On that day the six PEEA members resigned from the Papandreou Cabinet, and EAM made preparations for the struggle to seize power in Greece by force of arms. It reconstituted the ELAS Central Committee, which met at Lamia where GHQ ELAS was established, to discuss the plan of campaign. The whole ELAS army was divided into two parts each given separate tasks.

One part, the southern one, came directly under the newly re-formed Central Committee, of which the two most prominent members were Siantos and General Mandakas, and consisted of the 2nd (Attica), the 3rd (Peloponnese) and the 13th (Roumeli) Divisions. It had a fighting strength of about 18,000 armed men.

The other, northern, part came directly under the command of GHQ ELAS, which in effect meant General Saraphis and Aris, and consisted of the 8th (Epirus) and the four Macedonian (the 6th, 9th, 10th and 11th) Divisions. It had a fighting strength of about 23,000 men. Its first task was to prevent EDES marching to reinforce Athens, then to clear the northern parts of Greece of the remaining hostile elements, and finally to close in and destroy EDES. By December 2nd, ELAS formations were on the march, and GHQ ELAS prepared to move from Lamia to Trikkala farther north. The Central Committee of ELAS, which had appointed General Mandakas to be the military commander in the battle for Athens, moved to Thebes, where it intended to establish its operational GHQ.

Once its mind was made up no opportunity was lost, and while ELAS divisions were moving to their battle stations, EAM used all its political and disruptive weapons to the full. A massive EAM demonstration against the Government was called for in Athens, to be followed by a general strike. The general strike aimed, amongst other things, at paralysing the communications of the country and preventing the distribution of UNRRA relief, thus indirectly increasing discontent and misery, for which it hoped to blame the Government and the Liberation Force which were responsible for speedy distribution of food.

The EAM demonstration was called for December 2nd and permission was given to hold it. Papandreou did not seriously think, with British troops in Greece, that EAM would try to take over by force. Permission to demonstrate was later withdrawn by the police but it went on regardless of the ban. Eye-witnesses were astonished at the ability of the organizers to assemble and handle such huge numbers. The demonstrators clashed with the police and shots were fired. Several demonstrators were killed and many arrested. The police also suffered casualties.

The next day of the general strike, the situation became tense as ELAS sub-units, armed and in uniform, openly appeared in the suburbs of Athens. There were clashes between them and the Government security forces.

On the 4th fighting started seriously as the 2nd (Attica) Division moved into the Athens suburbs in strength, while a few miles to the south the 3rd (Peloponnese) Division crossed the Corinth Canal and was establishing itself in the outskirts of Piraeus and around the port area.

When it was realized that armed revolt had broken out, General Scobie ordered all ELAS units to move out from the Athens and Piraeus area, stating that if they did not do so they would be treated as enemy troops after the 6th. He gave instructions for the isolated detachments of British troops to concentrate at Salonika, Athens or Volos. A large part of the British force was dispersed, either helping to repair damaged communications or assisting the distribution of UNRRA supplies. The proportion of combat troops was comparatively small.

Papandreou offered to resign but the British would not allow this. ELAS openly refused to withdraw from Athens and Piraeus and the EAM stated that its aim was to set up a 'Government of National Unity'.

In Athens, on the 4th, British troops on patrol in the city clashed with ELAS, and two ELAS battalions were disarmed after a shooting incident. In Piraeus, ELAS units attacked Navy House, the Anglo-Greek Naval GHQ. but were repulsed by British troops holding it.

On the 5th British troops became increasingly involved in scuffles with ELAS soldiers on the streets of Athens. The 2nd (Attica) Division was joined by the 13th (Roumeli) Division and both worked their way through the suburbs, forcing the evacuation of all police stations in their path. In Piraeus troops of the 3rd (Peloponnese) Division closed in a ring around Navy House and the port. Later in the day a determined attack was made by ELAS and Navy House fell. The road from Athens to Piraeus was now completely in ELAS' hands, and the British and Government forces were unable to use it.

The powder keg that was Salonika, where one British brigade formed the garrison, was not ignited, but ELAS troops under General Bakirdzis and Markos Vaphiadis, moved right into the town and the port area.

For the next week the pattern of the fighting was much the same, with British and Government forces being cooped up in the centre of Athens by the more numerous ELAS attackers. A few sweeps had been made to try and clear additional space, but as fast as British troops moved through the streets, ELAS fighters gave way before them only to re-appear in their former positions when they had passed on. ELAS units made periodic sallies, and they seemed to have plenty of mortars and ample ammunition for them. In addition, they also brought a few guns into action. Sniping was prevalent, and the British task was made more difficult by the fact that a proportion of ELAS fighters did not have uniforms, but all had a weapon of some sort.

The road to Piraeus remained firmly blocked, and in Piraeus itself ELAS were in almost complete possession of the port. RAF aircraft came into the picture and made rocket attacks on ELAS positions, as well as machine-gunning ELAS troops and dropping leaflets. There were four RAF squadrons in Greece and three Greek ones, but Papandreou asked that the Greek Air Force should not be used.

In the north of the country the first phase of General Saraphis' plan had gone well, and by December 6th Andon Tsaous' band, down to about 650 National Greek Guerrillas, was scattered. Andon Tsaous escaped to Athens, where he was eventually accepted by the new regular army as a captain.

ELAS also managed to smother a small group of villages in the Mikhalagas district of West Macedonia that had accepted arms from the Germans during the Occupation to fight ELAS. Since the Liberation they had steadfastly refused to surrender to ELAS. When this small 'blob' of opposition was removed the whole of the northern Greek frontiers were in ELAS' hands, and it only remained for General Saraphis to turn and destroy EDES in Epirus.

The British position was so critical and the request for reinforcements so urgent that Field Marshal Alexander (who became the Supreme Allied Commander, Mediterranean, on the 19th) flew in to see for himself what the situation was. On the 11th he landed at an RAF airfield about six miles from Athens, and his armoured car was shot at during his journey into the city. He found that the British and Greek Government forces were virtually besieged in a small, vulnerable area in the centre of the city; the road to Piraeus was blocked and the British were unable to use the Piraeus port as most of it was in ELAS' hands. He also found that the British forces had only six days' rations and three days' ammunition supply left.

Clearly the British force was much too small to be effective, whatever plan of operations was adopted, and he diverted the 4th Division,[1] which was on its way to Italy, to Greece. A fortunate lull in the fighting in Italy allowed him to do this.

Field Marshal Alexander's plan was first of all to clear the road from Athens to Piraeus and re-occupy the port completely so that supplies could again flow in, after which British troops could eject ELAS fighters from the two cities and surrounding districts. The latter was in itself a formidable task, there being an estimated fifty square miles of built-up area.

On December 12th, ELAS representatives called upon General Scobie and asked for his cease-fire terms. They knew that Field Marshal Alexander was in Athens (actually he left that day), and it was probably done to give him the impression that they were just about ready to give in so that he might not think it so necessary to order up very large reinforcements. General Scobie replied that ELAS must cease-fire and evacuate Attica. There was no answer.

In fact, ELAS was far from done, and on that very day had captured the Athens Town Hall after some stiff fighting, thus further compressing the British-held centre of the city. General Mandakas had good reasons to be pleased with himself, his plans and his men. ELAS guerrillas had entered into an entirely different type of operation, that of fighting in a built-up area. While they took a little while to get accustomed to this new sort of fighting, after a few days they were successfully adapting themselves to it. They could not stand up to British troops in equal numbers, but by sheer preponderance of manpower they were able to flood the space around the small 'islands' held by British and Government forces.

General Mandakas prepared for the next phase, which he planned would gradually strangle the area held by the British and Government troops in the centre of Athens and eliminate the RAF airfield

---

[1] There were now (amongst others) two divisional formations in Greece with similar titles, which may be confusing. One was the 4th Division, a purely British one, and the other was the 4th Indian Division, which contained both Indian and British troops.

at Kiphissia, about ten miles north-east of the capital. More ELAS reinforcements were being drafted in and weapons and ammunition left behind in dumps by the Germans, of which there were ample mortars, were distributed ready for use. ELAS had a total of nearly 100 artillery pieces of different sorts and sizes, two-thirds of which were given to General Mandakas. There was, however, only a limited amount of shells for these guns.

On December 13th, everywhere in Athens ELAS troops were on the offensive, being determined to take as much ground as they could before pausing to wait for further reinforcements to be absorbed. All day there was fierce fighting in the streets as ELAS units assaulted barricades and buildings held by British and Government troops. During the fighting ELAS used tram-cars, filled with explosives, which they propelled against British tanks on the main streets. All attacks were repulsed; and after the fury of this series was spent there was a comparative lull for a few days. Intermittent mortar shelling and spasmodic skirmishing and sniping continued.

In Piraeus, on the 13th, Indian troops recaptured Navy House, but part of the port remained in ELAS' hands, as did the surrounding area. On the 14th, units of the 3rd (Peloponnese) Division attacked British troops at Patras, but they were beaten off, although some outlying British detachments had to be drawn in.

In Salonika, the dockers were again on strike but so far there had been no open fighting between ELAS and the British brigade that was on the outskirts of the city. There had just previously been a strike, lasting from the 8th to the 10th. General Bakirdzis and Markos Vaphiadis were watchful but cautious, waiting for the Athens–Piraeus sector to resolve itself before they moved into action.

During this pause at least three regiments from the Macedonian divisions in the north moved down to Athens in British trucks. On the 16th, British units were evacuated by sea from Volos, sabotaging the vehicles they could not take with them before leaving, but despite this action ELAS managed to put just over 100 of these abandoned vehicles into working order. These repaired British trucks were used in a shuttle service between Salonika and Athens to carry men, ammunition and supplies.

On the 16th, ELAS replied vaguely and inconclusively to General Scobie's cease-fire terms. There was no intention of accepting them and it had been merely a device to deceive and delay. By this time the EAM Radio Station, which called itself 'Free Greece', was in full voice, pouring forth a stream of propaganda, allegations and threats. EAM had made favourable contacts in America, where it was working to gain American sympathy for its cause and to sow antagonism to the British policy of using troops against former Resistance fighters. ELAS now began to seize hostages in large numbers, mainly from middle-class families with right-wing or Royalist attachments. On the other hand, whenever they could, the Greek Government Security Forces arrested left-wing suspects.

Already, on the 13th, General Plastiras had returned to Athens from exile in France at Papandreou's request. It was suggested that he become the Prime Minister and Archbishop Damaskinos the Regent, but the King would not agree to this. After the Greek army defeats at the hands of the Turks in September 1922, General Plastiras had marched on Athens with a few regiments, forcing King Constantine to abdicate. He executed the Greek Commander-in-Chief and several Royalists, and this George II could not forget.

Meanwhile British reinforcements, in the shape of more units of the 4th Division, were being flown in, and they went to secure the precariously-held bastions. With his forces strengthened, Major-General Hawkesworth, who had been sent in to fight the Athens battle under General Scobie's direction, began to prepare for the operation to open the road to Piraeus. This coincided with the resumption of General Mandakas' offensive, in which he planned to take the RAF airfield at Kiphissia and the Averoff Prison.

The Kiphissia airfield, held by about 350 airmen, was unsuccessfully assaulted on the 18th, after which the attacking ELAS troops, estimated to be a small regiment just over 1,000 strong, closed in to surround the airfield, cutting it off completely.

That same evening (the 18th) at dusk, another ELAS regiment made an assault on the Averoff Prison, which was one of the Government-held buildings in the centre of Athens. It contained about 640 prisoners, one of whom was Rallis, the former puppet Prime Minister. Others were collaborators, war criminals and left-wing personalities. The assault failed, but more ELAS units were deployed and preparations made for a second attempt, which was carried out the next day, when the prison was breached by explosives and set on fire. There was fierce fighting for possession of the building, during which many prisoners escaped,[1] and others were burnt.

---

[1] The British and Government Forces managed to detain 235 prisoners. Rallis was one of those who escaped, but he was later recaptured. Rallis was eventually sentenced to life imprisonment, and he died in prison.

British troops grimly held on to part of the prison buildings, and a stalemate temporarily set in on this district.

On the 20th, the Kiphissia airfield was overrun, just before a British relief column, which was moving towards it, arrived; but British troops did manage to rescue about 100 airmen who had been taken prisoner by ELAS. The remainder of the defenders, about 250 men, had already been taken away beyond reach.

Quite a number of British troops had been taken prisoner by ELAS in the fighting so far, and most were marched off to crude POW camps in the mountains in the region of Marathon, about thirty miles or so north of Athens. Most had a rough time, as often they were deprived of their greatcoats and sometimes even their boots (ELAS troops so urgently needed them), and no blankets or proper accommodation were provided. And this happened in December, which can be, and was, extremely cold in Greece. Throughout this 'second round' of the Civil War, ELAS refused point-blank to allow Red Cross representatives to visit their POW camps. In view of the primitive conditions prevailing, perhaps this was understandable.

On the 20th, General Scobie announced that an all-out British attack on ELAS troops was about to commence, and warned all civilians to leave the area or keep out of the way. By this time the remainder of the 4th Division had arrived, and he was at last in a position to be able to seriously undertake clearing operations. Until this moment he had not had sufficient troops, and although he had been able to hold on to the ground his men occupied, the sweeps that had been carried out so far had been largely ineffective, because as soon as British troops advanced the ELAS fighters gave way before them only to close back in again when they moved on.

For four or five days there was heavy fighting in Athens, especially as the British troops pushed outwards, moving into action against ELAS with artillery and mortars and supported by RAF aircraft firing rockets at enemy strong points. At first this centred around the Averoff Prison sector, but gradually the Government-held area was enlarged as ELAS units were forced back street by street. This was not according to the ELAS plan and General Mandakas urged his men to stand fast while he rushed up more reinforcements to help them, but it was more than they could manage to do.

As ELAS units received blow after heavy blow from the British troops, their morale declined and discipline began to fall off. Some fought very well but others were not so stout-hearted when they saw how deadly the opposition was, and the extent of the casualties discouraged and dismayed them. As ELAS units cracked, completely fresh ones had to be quickly pushed into the gaps to try and hold them. There were many brave and determined men in ELAS, and several groups fought to the last, but generally the lack of efficient regimental officers was the big handicap. The slow progress of these clearing operations was due to the closeness of the built-up area, which was to the defenders' advantage.

The Athens to Piraeus road remained blocked, but in Piraeus the position was much the same, with the British and ELAS each in possession of part of the port. Navy House was again unsuccessfully assaulted on the 20th, but here also the ELAS impetus was losing momentum. The staff of the 3rd (Peloponnese) Division had difficulty in co-ordinating and maintaining the offensive. In Salonika, the uneasy peace was precariously kept between ELAS and the British brigade.

Perturbed by events in Greece, on December 24th Mr. Churchill personally visited Athens to see for himself what could be done to improve matters. British relations with America were becoming strained over Greece, and moreover Britain wanted her troops out of Greece for use elsewhere as soon as possible.

Mr. Churchill's visit prompted what became known as the Athens Conference, which was held from the 26th to the 28th. It was presided over by Archbishop Damaskinos, and attended not only by Mr. Churchill, Eden (the British Foreign Secretary), Macmillan (the Resident Minister), Field Marshal Alexander, General Scobie and Mr. Leeper (the British Ambassador), but by Papandreou and other Greek politicians. Representing EAM/ELAS were Siantos, Partsalidis and General Mandakas. This conference failed to bring about a cease-fire, but there was a reluctant agreement to Archbishop Damaskinos being appointed Regent.

Damaskinos, the Archbishop of Athens, had been deposed by Metaxas and restored to his office by the Germans during the Occupation, but he steadfastly refused to swear allegiance to the puppet government. He had been prominent in denouncing the deportation of Greek labour, the arrest of Resistance fighters, the deportation of the Jews and other measures the Axis Occupation authorities imposed. These protests led to Damaskinos being placed under house arrest in 1944, but they had made him extremely popular throughout Greece.

Meanwhile, with more troops and arms available, **General**

Hawkesworth was successfully tumbling ELAS units backwards as he cleared an ever-increasing area around the centre of Athens. Vainly did General Mandakas rush up more men, and also recklessly expend his diverse stocks of artillery and mortar shells. ELAS morale was stretched to breaking point, and on the 28th it began to snap. On that date, despite the shooting of deserters from the scene of the fighting in front of their units, ELAS troops steadily gave way before British guns. On the 29th, the HQ of the 13th (Roumeli) Division was battered and overrun. This was perhaps the last really hard-fought-for position in Athens, after which the backbone of ELAS resistance was never quite the same.

Stiff opposition was met with in Piraeus, where not so many British troops were available, but in this city also there was a marked change in the state of ELAS morale, and a growing reluctance to stand and fight to the last. Progress had been made in clearing the road from Athens to Piraeus.

On December 31st, ELAS representatives were again in touch with General Scobie, asking him what his cease-fire terms were.[1] This time the approach was far more serious.

In the north of Greece, General Saraphis had been more successful. During the first part of December he had concentrated upon eliminating Andon Tsaous and subduing the recalcitrant villagers of Mikhalagas; and when this had been accomplished he was ready to move against EDES, which was in and around Arta, Preveza, Jannina, Metsovo and Corfu Island.

When the ELAS battalion that had been in position near Preveza had been withdrawn under British instructions, EDES had in return been persuaded to give large quantities of ammunition to ELAS to enable ELAS units to take part in 'Operation Rat Week' (harassing the withdrawing Germans), which left Colonel Zervas very short himself when faced with ELAS attacks. Owing to the critical situation in Athens there was precious little chance of his obtaining more from British sources.

General Saraphis used three ELAS divisions, the 1st (Thessaly), the 8th (Epirus) and the 9th (Macedonian), amounting to about 11,500 armed men in all, and he moved them over the Pindus Mountain range. This took several days as the winter snows had set in, and he used Italian POWs to keep the passes open. At the

---

[1] On December 31st, 1944, the British claimed to have captured in the fighting since the 4th: 3,464 rifles, 85 brens and spandaus, 3 75mm guns and over 1 million rounds of ammunition.

commencement of this ELAS offensive, EDES had about 9,000 armed men opposing him, but this number quickly shrank through desertion, the men either escaping south to the Peloponnese where there were anti-ELAS elements, or changing sides to join ELAS.

At length General Saraphis was ready and on December 20th he made two separate thrusts against EDES, one in the north, coming over the Metsovo Pass, aimed at Jannina and on westwards to Corfu Island, and the other, farther south, aimed at Arta and then Preveza. Arta was taken on the 21st, and the EDES defenders fell back on the small port of Preveza.

In the north, Jannina was entered by the ELAS column on the 23rd and EDES units scattered before it, the men either making their way towards the coast to get to Corfu, or southwards to Preveza to join Colonel Zervas who had set up his GHQ there.

Giving EDES no respite, General Saraphis urged his men against them as hard as they could go, and they succeeded in cornering and hemming in the hard core at Preveza, where Colonel Zervas was making a stand. EDES men deserted daily and the army was cracking up. As resistance was obviously hopeless, the remnants were evacuated by the Royal Navy between December 29th and 31st. On the 30th, ELAS units landed and occupied the disputed island of Levkas.

This was the end of EDES as a fighting force, and the survivors, down to less than 2,000, were disarmed and disbanded. EDES' battle casualties in this week's fighting amounted to 680, thus leaving a silent figure of over 6,000 unaccounted for. The majority had undoubtedly changed sides, although many had quietly made their way to their homes where they lay low for the time being.

The rapid break-up of EDES, a once well organized and formidable guerrilla army, can chiefly be accounted for by lack of ammunition, rife desertion, especially in the latter days, the improbability of obtaining more supplies and ammunition from the British, and the remote possibility of obtaining reinforcements or recruits; added to which it was faced with overwhelming military strength and a devastating political arm.

By the turn of the New Year of 1945, the fighting in Athens and Piraeus had taken a turn for the better as the extra weight of British troops and arms had their effect. General Scobie had got the upper hand and he pressed on with clearing the city of ELAS troops as quickly as he could, but house-clearing was a slow, systematic job that had to be done thoroughly. By January 2nd there were signs that the city was returning to normal, and shops began to open. On the 4th, the public services started to function, and by the following day practically the whole of Athens and its suburbs were clear of ELAS fighters.

By the 7th, Piraeus was completely in British hands, and the road through to Athens was finally cleared the next day. British troops were extending their activities outside the built-up sectors into the countryside of Attica, where their mobility and fire power were more than a match for the ELAS units.

Despite the reinforcements that ELAS had brought in, and the fact that they were fairly adequately armed for house-to-house fighting, morale had declined sharply. For a few days longer the stouter elements of ELAS clung on to their posts and positions until blasted out, but for the remainder only threats of harsh punitive action prevented them breaking ranks and making a mass exodus from the city.

On January 1st, ELAS representatives had again called on General Scobie to ask for his terms. EAM/ELAS was getting anxious, as the Central Committee realized that defeat was staring it in the face. It wished to salvage as much from the wreckage as possible and, of course, the sooner the fighting stopped the more they could hide the broken morale from view. The Communists wanted to live to fight again another day, and this they were determined to do at all costs.

On January 1st, the ELAS Central Committee, responsible for the fighting in Athens and appreciating the adverse situation, brought in Aris from GHQ ELAS, where he had been paired with General Saraphis, to see if he could do anything to retrieve its fortunes. Aris managed to prolong the ELAS resistance in Athens for a few days longer, by applying ruthless methods such as summary execution of men who left their positions in the fighting zone without permission.

He could do little more, as the whole ELAS 'corps' of the three reinforced divisions was crumbling and falling apart. The officers and men had had about as much as they could stand: they were guerrilla fighters accustomed to hit and run, and were neither trained nor conditioned for sustained operations against regular troops. The ELAS organization, with its lack of trained staff and regimental officers, was not capable of fighting a set-piece battle. It had done very well but now too much was being demanded of it. On the 8th, General Saraphis, fresh from his triumphs over EDES, was called south to take over command of the Attica fighting, but he was too late. Several ELAS units were disintegrating and desertion was snowballing. ELAS was in no state to fight on against the British troops, and would probably have mutinied if it had been ordered to resume the offensive, despite the strict EAM political control. British units were now fanning out from Athens and approaching Thebes, the ELAS battle GHQ and Lamia, and ELAS formations dispersed before their advance.

On the political side, the Greek Government was strengthened when on January 1st, 1945, Archbishop Damaskinos was appointed Regent, and on the 3rd General Plastiras became the Prime Minister. ELAS representatives could now only negotiate for a cease-fire from a position of weakness, as not only was the tide of battle full against them, but also it was losing popularity amongst the people of Greece because of its ruthless and selfish activities. The reports of the numbers of hostages seized by ELAS, especially as the battle began to go against it, which were estimated to be not less than 15,000, many of whom were ill-treated and exposed to inclement weather conditions, alarmed public opinion. The news trickled through that a few of these hostages were executed daily. This, together with the rumours of treatment meted out to British POWs and the fact that ELAS would not allow Red Cross representatives to visit them, caused General Scobie to say that fresh cease-fire conditions were necessary. ELAS had little option but to listen and to negotiate to get the best bargain they could.

On the 8th it was announced that ELAS agreed to the British cease-fire terms, and that hostilities would cease at midnight on the 15th. Briefly, the conditions were that ELAS troops in Attica should withdraw 100 miles west and north from Athens, ELAS troops should evacuate Salonika, the Peloponnese and certain islands, and that all Service personnel taken prisoner should be exchanged on a one-for-one basis. There was no mention of releasing the thousands of civilian hostages.

The fighting now ran down, and for the next week there was only spasmodic action as most of the ELAS units were withdrawn from the Athens–Piraeus area. The majority of the ELAS rank and file left willingly enough, but there was a dedicated hard core that wanted to fight on. These withdrew reluctantly with the others, although not a few hid their arms and went underground. At midnight on the 15th, ELAS units observed the cease-fire, and the 'Second Round' of the Civil War, which had lasted about six weeks, drew to a close. On the 17th, British troops re-entered Salonika.

The cost of this round in human lives is not known with any accuracy. A British force, amounting to about 75,000 men at its height, had been involved in the fighting and its casualties were given as being 2,100, of whom 237 were killed in action. ELAS casualties must have been much higher. It was reckoned that ELAS had taken and held over 20,000 hostages.

A political defeat followed the military one for EAM as a split occurred within its ranks. Nominally a coalition of six left-wing parties, EAM had always been KKE-manipulated. On January 10th, two prominent Socialist leaders in the EAM coalition, Stratis and Tsirimokos, broke away from it, alleging amongst other things that over 114 Trade Union officials had been shot by EPON, the KKE Secret Police. Stratis formed the SKE (Greek Socialist Party) and Tsirimokos the ELD (Popular Democratic Union). EAM was left with very little cover to its true Communist character.

The Greek Communists had lost the 'Second Round' of the Civil War. Why was this? Let us just briefly consider some of the salient features when the reasons may become more clear.

Within the KKE, the Greek Communist Party, there were two schools of thought: one that advocated revolution by force, and the other that advocated revolution by political infiltration and disruption. As it was anticipated that the Allied Liberation Force would be strong and well armed, and might temporarily establish itself in Greece in strength to fight what remained of the Axis forces in the Balkans, it was reasoned that it would be suicide to match ELAS against it, so it was planned to keep ELAS in the background for later use, and to concentrate upon political infiltration and disruption to pave the way to final seizure of power.

It was only when it was seen how small and restricted the Liberation Force was that the temptation to seize the country by force of arms arose and was seriously considered. This was probably prompted by Stalin. ELAS had about 50,000 armed men—over twice as many as the British had initially brought into Greece upon the Liberation—and although its organization was faulty, its standard of training low and it lacked competent officers, the decision was made to resort to hostilities against the British and Government forces. It initially had the advantage of surprise, as it was not thought by the Papandreou Government that this would happen, and ELAS units were able to isolate detachments of British troops and to move into the greater part of the urban sections of Athens and Piraeus before anyone knew what was going on. The tiny British force was compressed into a precarious position in Athens, and practically driven out of Piraeus. Had ELAS been better trained, better officered and better organized (its arms were sufficient) it might have been able to take over completely in those first few days. Not reaching that pitch, it failed—but only narrowly.

Once Field Marshal Alexander had visited Athens and ordered up reinforcements, the moment and opportunity had gone never to return, and from then onwards it was not possible for ELAS to wipe out the British and Government forces by direct attack. One might argue and speculate that with such numbers, in such a large expanse of houses and streets, ELAS could hold out almost indefinitely by the simple expedient of applying their guerrilla evasion and dispersion tactics, as they tentatively did to some degree fairly successfully in the face of British sweeps in mid-December in Athens. But ELAS commanders had been re-orientated by the KKE, which saw power within its grasp if it was seized quickly, and they were not permitted to do this, but were expected to hit at the British troops in a conventional manner. They did not prove to be so adept at this, and day by day, after the first flush of excitement and success, morale, enthusiasm and aggressiveness declined until they all but faded away.

ELAS was a guerrilla army, bred and blooded in the mountains on the 'hit-and-run' principle. Positional warfare was beyond its ken and means, something to be avoided, and evasive action had always been the order of the day when faced by regular troops. Overnight, the KKE seemed to expect ELAS to turn itself into a conventional army, able to function smoothly as a 'corps' in a completely new and unfamiliar form of warfare. The members of the KKE Central Committee tended to be rather weak on military strategy, tactics and reasoning.

The job was far too big and complicated for ELAS. For a few days it had fought well as British and Government troops and police gave way before it, but when it came up against strongly held positions its weaknesses and handicaps became apparent. The majority of staff and regimental officers in ELAS were not capable of planning and conducting a co-ordinated offensive, or of being able to fight a set-piece battle at all. ELAS had recruited few ex-regular or ex-reservist officers because they were not completely trusted. Had it done so the ending might have been different. Considering their shortcomings the ELAS officers did remarkably well, but after the first few days the fighting got beyond their control, becoming disjointed and piecemeal. Orders were often misunderstood, sometimes deliberately so when they were unpalatable or regarded as being too risky, and counter-orders were frequent.

General Mandakas, who was in charge of the Athens fighting, realized the position, and when he saw that his men had run up against hard resistance as the British and Government troops were penned up in the centre of the city he planned to contain them and cut off their supplies as best he could. They were to be further compressed by 'commando assaults', brought up and quickly rehearsed for the particular purpose, by special units on individual posts and buildings, while he deployed, trained and conditioned the remainder of his 'corps' to make it fit for the eventual, all-out final offensive.

Had the British and Greek Government garrisons not been reinforced when they were, it is more than probable that General Mandakas' plan of operations would ultimately have been successful. It was not his fault that ELAS did not succeed; he did what he could with the tools and material at his disposal. When his men began to fall back, he fell into disfavour with the KKE Central Committee, and first Aris, and then General Saraphis, were brought in, by which time it was far too late to do anything but stop the whole ELAS 'corps' from disintegrating completely.

The KKE Central Committee was realizing that hostilities had been a great mistake. Had it been content to wait a while and pretend to cooperate with the Papandreou Government, it would have been in a much stronger position, both politically and militarily. Its disruptive activities, in the form of labour stoppages, economic manipulation and political obstruction were already strangling and nullifying Government efforts, and would have continued to have crippling effects. Impatience and misjudgement had committed it to open warfare. Now, in temporary defeat, the other contending school of thought in the KKE Central Committee, led by Siantos. which advocated political infiltration and erosion, took over. The immediate task was to salvage what it could and to plan and prepare for the 'next round'.

CHAPTER SIX

Salvaging the Wreckage

The Communists had come out of the Civil War very badly indeed, but their leaders put on a bold, aggressive front to hide the magnitude of the disaster, and under a screen of bluster and vilification, set to work to salvage what they could from the wreckage. As ever with Communists, a lost battle is never the end, and all effort, skill, energy, deceit and cunning were bent to preparing to fight again another day.

Not only had the Greek Communists suffered a military defeat, of which there could be no possible doubt, but they had also taken a beating from an ideological point of view, as in addition to arousing the dislike of the majority they lost the support of sections of the population that might otherwise have been attracted to their cause. Whereas considerate treatment might have gained many converts, the harshness of the Communist yoke over both foe and potential friend alike caused a swing away from Communism by the uncommitted. Many of the peasant class, with no fixed political convictions, who had found themselves in Communist-dominated territory had been sickened and revolted by what they had seen and experienced.

As evidence of atrocities, particularly the seizing, ill-treatment and killing of hostages, came to light a shudder of horror swept through the nation. Even after the cease-fire was operative, EAM/ELAS refused to release hostages, which aroused widespread anger. Many of these inhumanities were confirmed in their stark grimness by Sir Walter Citrine, who headed a British TUC Mission to Greece in January 1945, and who was able to examine evidence and interview many people. In defeat, the Communists felt the full blaze of public hatred turn against them. This temporarily extinguished the fear people had of them.

On February 2nd, representatives of both sides, and the British, met at the village of Varkiza near Athens to discuss the terms to be dictated. The political representatives of EAM were Siantos and Partsalidis, and Tsirimokos represented the ELD. Agreement was finally reached on the 12th, and the main provisions included the complete demobilization and disarming of ELAS, the release of prisoners and hostages, a plebiscite on the future régime of the country and a general election. This became known as the Varkiza Agreement.

Concurrent with the political talks at Varkiza were military ones, with General Saraphis as the ELAS representative, to arrange the details of the actual demobilization, the disarming and other matters. ELAS agreed to surrender 41,000 rifles, over 2,000 machine-guns of various sorts, 160 mortars and 30 artillery pieces. Former regular officers who had been with ELAS were to be reinstated, and ELAS personnel were liable to serve in the new Greek National Army that was to be formed. The Sacred Band was to retain its special status under Allied command for the time being, so that Greece could maintain token forces against Germany in World War II, which was, of course, still in progress.

Although they twisted and squirmed, the Communists could do little but accept and try to negotiate the best bargain they could in the adverse circumstances. In fact, they came out of the deal quite well, their main triumph being that the KKE was allowed to function legally and openly as a political party in Greece. This meant that the two Communist newspapers that had sprung up could remain uncensored, and that other KKE-sponsored organizations, such as EAM and EPON, could operate openly.

Although rather overshadowed by the more momentous Yalta Conference, the Varkiza Agreement seemed to most to conclude satisfactorily the unfortunate Greek Civil War. After this, as far as most of the Allies were concerned, Greece became something of a backwater on the world's political stage. To some extent this was not entirely unfavourable to the scheming Communists.

Superficial agreement may have been one thing, but the Communists, with a calculating eye on the future and fortified with ample experience of surviving underground, had active secret reservations, and so the Varkiza Agreement was only partially implemented. Great play was made of demobilizing and disarming ELAS, but a number of ELAS members, several sub-units and in some cases a few complete battalion-sized units, found the conditions entirely unacceptable and the prospects bleak, so took to the mountains with their arms, determined to continue the insurgent struggle. The intrepid Aris declared he would never surrender, and with about 100 defiant guerrillas took to the mountains. As Government security forces had hardly materialized, he and the others were comparatively safe for the time being.

Other ex-ELAS fighters, either from political conviction or more likely because they anticipated—probably correctly—what their fate would be were they to give themselves up, gravitated northwards and filtered over the border into either Albania or Yugoslavia, two countries now under Communist Governments. Some also went into Bulgaria, but they were a lesser number. During the latter part of January and in February 1945, it is thought that up to 3,000 guerrillas, either singly or in groups, crossed over from Greece, and that in the following two months, as Government security forces became more active, yet another 1,000 or more joined them.

Apart from these restless extremists, the main body of ELAS was peacefully disarmed and disbanded. Many who had been pressed into service gladly and thankfully returned to their towns and villages, where they frequently faced a cold reception, or worse. Regular officers were formally restored to the Army List but were not actively employed.

Flesh quickly dissolved from the skeleton of ELAS, a once large and formidable army, leaving only a steely, disjointed backbone. Functioning as a political party and acting as the mouthpiece of the KKE, EAM[1] loudly disclaimed any connection with, or control over, the dissident insurgents in the interior who refused to surrender. It also disclaimed responsibility for Aris and his attitude, professing to support wholeheartedly the Varkiza conditions, and denied any contact with the ex-ELAS refugees who were flocking into Yugoslavia, Albania and Bulgaria.

Professing to implement the Varkiza Agreement both in spirit and letter, ELAS handed in a larger quantity of arms than had been specified. These included 100 artillery pieces, about twice as many as it was suspected it possessed, but these were probably given up because there was no more ammunition for them. Also, guns might

---

[1] About this time EAM claimed it had about 1.5 million members, who were mainly young people.

have been more difficult to conceal and easier for the Government security forces to trace. It was noticed that all the weapons handed in were old ones, and that hardly any modern automatic small arms in good condition were surrendered. The best were hidden in caches in the mountains, but later a few of them were discovered, their whereabouts being revealed to the Government by the peasants who felt they no longer had anything to fear from the defeated Communists.

The breach of faith was not completely one-sided, and the Greek Government carried out wholesale arrests of ex-ELAS personnel, allegedly for committing common law crimes, mainly murder. The number of arrests rose until prisons and detention camps were crammed full, causing EAM to voice shrill protests, recriminations and allegations of Government bad faith.

Within the Central Committee of the KKE, the defeat in the field had caused bitter soul-searching. There was some reorganization, but Siantos retained the office of Secretary-General. Moreover, there was a difference of opinion amongst prominent Communists on whether the Greek Communist Party should follow a national or an international policy. Siantos was in favour of the KKE pursuing a nationalist line, but being in a chastened, uneasy frame of mind, and conscious of the nearness of the Red Army and of the baleful malevolence of Stalin, hesitated, as did his colleagues.

Soviet policy was to co-ordinate Albania, Yugoslavia and Bulgaria into some sort of satellite Balkan Communist Federation, and it was not averse to a large chunk of northern Greece, that part occupied by the Slavs being included, which worried the Greek Communists, many of whom were nationalists as much as Communists.

In April, a new twist was given to the Communist dilemma when information came through that Zakhariadis, the Secretary-General of the KKE, was alive in a German concentration camp. There had been no news of him since he had been whisked away when the Germans moved into Greece during the war, and it had been tacitly assumed that like so many others he had simply 'disappeared', having been either killed or died in captivity. Zakhariadis was a Moscow-man, who was previously known to favour international Communism, but as conditions in the world—and in Greece especially—had so radically changed since his internment, no one quite knew how he would react to the new situation. Composing themselves as best they could, the Communist leaders waited for Zakhariadis' release. Meanwhile they used ERGAS (Workers' Anti-Fascist

League) as the instrument to further internal economic chaos.

Zakhariadis returned to Greece in June 1945 and resumed his former position as Secretary-General of the KKE. He remained in favour of international, rather than national, Communism, but in foreign affairs advocated that Cyprus should be given to Greece. He did not support the Greek claims to 'Northern Epirus',[1] which wrung such an outcry, even from his own followers, that he had to modify his statements to favour the inclusion of this territory. But he never laboured this point. It seemed that Zakhariadis was to remain as good a Moscow-man as ever, which increased the unpopularity of himself and his Party in Greece as a whole, as well as causing a certain amount of uneasiness within the KKE.

ELAS' rough-neck rival, the X Organization led by Colonel Grivas, took to armed conflict against the scattered bands and individuals of ELAS, both on the mainland and in the Peloponnese, with zest and enthusiasm. Firmly right-wing and Royalist, X, riding on the wave of the reaction of Communist unpopularity, expanded rapidly, enrolling, for example, many former members of EDES. X had sympathizers in the armed services, the Government and the civil service, and SAN (League of Young Officers) fell under its influence.

In the spring of 1945, the activities of X in certain areas were the only antidotes to the die-hard ex-ELAS elements, such as those led by Aris and others like him.[2] In fact, the ex-ELAS guerrillas at large complained bitterly that not only were they having to avoid the attentions of the Greek security forces, which in parts of the country was not such a difficult problem, but they were savagely attacked by X as well, and that far from the Government merely refraining from taking action against X, at times it actively collaborated with it against them. This was largely, but not completely, true.

In June 1945, Aris was killed in a clash with the National Guard near Arta, when he refused to surrender his arms. X had provided the Government forces with the information that had led to his death. Aris' head was taken to Trikkala and briefly publicly exhibited. Thus died violently a colourful, but cruel and remorseless

---

[1] 'Northern Epirus' consisted of about 1,900 square miles of territory in Albania that Greece claimed.

[2] The X Organization probably reached its peak strength in January 1946, when it claimed to have over 200,000 members. A proportion of these were non-active, being merely sympathizers caught up in the public mood of anti-Communism, but an armed minority was alive and busy.

character, who had been one of the few to keep Communist resistance alive in the days of its dark defeat.

With the changing situation, others now began to come forward, so that by early summer signs of a Communist guerrilla revival were apparent. Many ex-ELAS leaders recovered their confidence and their spirits, and spurred on by what would happen to them if they were arrested, took to the hills and began collecting former comrades around them again. This trend seemed to be spontaneous rather than centrally organized or inspired, but it is most probable that the KKE Central Committee exerted an influence over these mushroom-like growths. The end of the war in Europe, the comparative lack of interest in Greece shown by the major Allies, the expected imminent withdrawal of British troops, the weakness of the Greek security forces and the hovering nearness of Soviet Russia, suddenly indicated that all might not yet be lost for the Communist cause in Greece.

The Central Committee of the KKE tended to be cautious and wanted to concentrate primarily on stirring up political and economic unrest in the hope of stalling the plebiscite and the general election in some vague way, but it was not unaware of the value of an underground military organization, particularly if the Soviet Union could be persuaded to supply arms and give moral support.

Gradually, the anti-Communist National Guard improved in efficiency, although it still fell short in some respects. With this instrument with which to implement them, the Government decreed sterner measures against the guerrillas. Numbers of suspects and sympathizers in towns and villages were arrested by the police. This had the rather contrary effect of forming a steady reservoir for guerrilla recruiting, as it simply drove many ex-ELAS fighters underground to become insurgents again.

In the Greek political sphere, the summer period was one of bitter allegation and counter-allegation. In July 1945, the EAM sent a circular to several foreign countries, alleging that 20,000 people had been detained by the Greek Government and over 500 murdered since the Varkiza Agreement. On September 2nd, the Greek Government announced that already the bodies of 8,752 murdered hostages, many mutilated, had been discovered, and that of the ex-ELAS men arrested some 11,000 were common criminals, of whom 8,700 were charged with murder. The EAM alleged that 2,961 resistance fighters had been condemned to death, but the

Government said it had released many of them by the autumn. And so on.

Although fully recognizing what a dangerous man Zakhariadis was, the Government, having agreed to allow the Communist Party to function legally, had little option but to permit him to be politically active. This may have been partly because it was not sure how the Soviet Union might react if he were arrested, and partly because Britain persuaded the Greek Government to act democratically. However, in July it was announced that Zakhariadis was to be prosecuted for 'spreading malicious rumours', and his trial was set for October, but no serious effort was made to take him into custody. Zakhariadis seems to have been able to gradually fade into the background and then disappear underground, like so many other prominent Communist leaders about this time.

In October, at the Seventh Congress of the KKE attended by some 300 delegates, Communist policy and future actions were sorted out. While it was admitted that some mistakes had been made in the past, no heads rolled and the KKE emerged with a united façade, under the leadership of Zakhariadis himself. The general tone adopted was that it might be possible to foment an armed rising and that steps should be taken to bring this about, but in the meantime all subversive and disruptive political and economic steps should be taken through EAM, ERGAS and other Communist organizations. It was decided that there should be no undue provocation of Government security forces by armed bands until after the plebiscite and the general election, by which time it was anticipated that British troops would have left the country. The leaders, if they had not already done so, went underground to avoid arrest.

EAM actively campaigned in the political sphere against a succession of shaky, unstable Greek Governments. In December 1945, it loudly declared 'no confidence' in the Sophoulis Government, then in office, calling for one with EAM representation. The decision to hold the general election before the plebiscite caused the Communists to indulge in shrill vituperation of the Government. A slight jolt was given to their corporate ego when the Soviet Union recognized the Greek Government. A little later, when the USSR, Britain and America recognized the régime of Hoxha in Albania, practically all Greece howled in protest, demanding that 'Northern Epirus' be annexed. The Communists remained silent.

Under the eyes of observers from America, Britain and France, the general election was held on March 31st, 1946, and it resulted in a victory for the Popularists and the right-wing. There had been several unsuccessful intrigues to postpone it, and the Communists abstained altogether, allegedly because their demands for an amnesty for their men, the dissolution of X and purges of collaborators, were not met. More probably the real reason was because under a fair, secret ballot the KKE's numerical weakness would have been exposed, it being variously estimated that it would have only been able to poll between nine per cent and twenty per cent at the most. A government was formed by Tsaldaris.

Communist reaction was to intensify political agitation against the Government and to increase labour unrest through ERGAS. The election result caused an increase in anti-government insurgent activity as those who had remained defiant all the time were now joined by many former members of ELAS who had been 'stood down', but were now volunteering again in their dozens, partly for ideological reasons and partly because their prospects under a right-wing government were bad. Especially around the Mount Olympus area, the Pieria Range, the mountains north of Salonika and those in the Chalcidice peninsula was there a sudden spate of insurgent bands springing up as fugitive ex-ELAS men fused together.

During August there were frequent clashes between the National Guard and the new insurgent bands, especially in Macedonia and also in the Peloponnese. A visiting British parliamentary delegation gave an idea of the state of anarchy that was evolving when it reported that it found that extremists of both the left and the right were using violence and carrying out acts of terrorism, and that a miniature civil war was in progress in parts of the country.

As planned, the plebiscite was held on September 1st, 1946, and it resulted in a majority (68.9 per cent) voting for the return of the King. Undoubtedly, many with republican convictions voted for the return of the monarchy to ensure that there would be no possibility of a left-wing dictatorship coming into power.

Archbishop Damaskinos resigned as Regent, and George II returned to Greece on September 28th, 1946. This gave confidence to Royalists, who were returned or placed in positions of responsibility in the armed and security services and the civil service. General Spiliotopoulis became the Inspector-General of the Armed Forces, General Ventiris became the Chief of the General Staff, and senior officers with Royalist sympathies were given commands and key posts. There was a corresponding hardening against those with left-wing convictions, and the regular officers who had been with ELAS, and had been nominally reinstated, were imprisoned. Generals Saraphis, Bakirdzis and Mandakas and nearly thirty other ex-ELAS senior officers were banished to the Aegean Islands.

The return of the King to Greece and the consolidation of the Royalists and right-wing elements in power made the KKE realize that it had a long, hard grind ahead to survive, let alone gather strength for the 'third round', which was now seriously contemplated and being planned. Prisons bursting with ex-ELAS personnel brought home forcibly to the KKE that it would never achieve its ends, which were to obtain total power in Greece, by peaceful means alone. Nevertheless, it did not intend to neglect the political weapon, but meant to use it as long and as subversively as it could, whilst secretly preparing for armed insurrection.

The KKE took stock of its position and found that, although far from ideal, its prospects were not by any means completely hopeless. Part of the old ELAS structure had survived underground and armed Communist-led bands of insurgents were springing into existence unasked. Favourable initial contacts had been made with Yugoslavia and also with Albania, and both these countries, together with Bulgaria, were harbouring ex-ELAS refugees. It was hopefully felt that the Soviet Union might provide material aid for an insurgent struggle, which, with the field clear of British troops and with such a large reservoir of trained ex-ELAS manpower to call upon, might be waged successfully against the none too able Government security forces.

British pressures on the Greek Government to rule democratically –which meant allowing the Communist Party to operate openly, publish its own newspaper and to distribute Party propaganda– played into the hands of the KKE. Perhaps Britain was influenced by the fact that the Soviet Union, the Communist fountainhead, was still regarded as a close ally, and that it might be considered an unfriendly act to allow the Greek Government to proscribe all left-wing organizations and political parties.

So it can be seen, with hindsight, that although the Greek Government seemed to hold so many aces in its hand, in the shape of its armed security forces, anti-Communists in key positions, the jails crammed with Communists and the bulk of the feeling of the population sharply against Communism, danger lurked just below the surface, unseen and perhaps largely unsuspected.

There were cracks that could not be concealed in the Government façade. There was political disunity, an uneasy alliance between monarchists and republicans, a discontented people, a ravaged country, a broken economy and the army and civil service were infiltrated by Communists and their sympathizers. Because it was unpopular to voice Communist sentiments out aloud in Greece, this attitude merely forced the Communists underground, an accustomed habitat, where they secretly plotted with practised smoothness.

CHAPTER SEVEN

The Democratic Army

Although the Greek Communists regard February 12th, 1946, as the official opening of the 'third round', the birth of the 'Greek Democratic Army', the successor to ELAS, can be more accurately quoted as being December 15th, 1945. It came into being as the result of a Politburo level meeting at Petrich, in Bulgaria, which was attended by members of the Central Committee of the KKE, and representatives of the Yugoslav and Bulgarian General Staffs. At this meeting the decision was made to reorganize an insurgent army to fight against the Greek Government. Yugoslavia promised massive material aid, and it was hoped that the Soviet Union would help materially too. At first this force was known as the 'Republican Army', and it was not until a year later, in December 1946, that the title of 'Democratic Army' was adopted.[1]

Initially, embittered ex-ELAS leaders were the impetus and inspiration of the Democratic Army, rather than the Communist politicians, who at the time were busily intriguing in Athens against the Government. As early as June 1945, ETA, the old quarter-mastering branch of ELAS, was beginning to revive and to function again, collecting arms from dumps hidden in Greece, and taking them, together with other stores, to the camps that housed ex-ELAS refugees just over the northern Greek frontiers. Volos and Naoussa, towns that had a strong left-wing element, initially provided the personnel engaged in this ETA revival, but by the end of the summer the ETA network was reaching out over large sections of the countryside.

---

[1] Sometimes referred to as the Democratic Army of Greece, or DSE (Dimokratikos Stratos Ellados).

Several senior members of the KKE were dubious about the wisdom, or even the necessity, of re-forming an underground insurgent army just yet. It was not until two months later, in February 1946, at a Plenary Session of the KKE, that it was persuaded, not altogether whole-heartedly, that it was feasible to think about preparing for armed insurrection, and to endorse the decision to raise and support an insurgent army.

The Democratic Army got off to a quiet, almost unobtrusive start. The Yugoslav authorities allowed it to use an army camp outside Bulkes,[1] to the north-west of Belgrade, and others nearer the Greek border. The camp at Bulkes already housed several thousand Greek refugees, including many women and children, as well as ex-ELAS members, so the formation of the Democratic Army could be carried into effect without attracting too much attention. In March, Zakhariadis visited the camp and gave an encouraging pep-talk to the nucleus of the new insurgent army.

Stalin, approving the formation of the Democratic Army, asked Yugoslavia and Albania to give clandestine material aid and support. He also vaguely promised to help, but no supplies or arms ever arrived from the Soviet Union. Little came from Albania at this juncture either. As summer succeeded spring, impatient Communist insurgent leaders led their own little groups over the Greek frontier. The northern borders of Greece stretched over 600 miles and were for most of their length unguarded and unguardable.

Able to successfully avoid the new Greek National Guard detachments, owing to better mobility in the mountains, the insurgents became bolder and their penetrations deeper. They began to use 'hit-and-run' tactics against isolated villages with the primary object of seizing food. Acting more or less independently, and going off where and when they pleased, the extent of their depredations was dependent upon the individual daring and ability of the group leaders. Bulkes was used as a kind of home base, rather than a GHQ from which orders were taken.

In August, the Central Committee of the KKE selected Markos Vaphiadis to take control of the Democratic Army and to organize it properly. He arrived at Bulkes in September, and on assuming command became known as 'General Markos'. A strong and able character, he first of all set about establishing his authority over the several insurgent bands at large. He overhauled the intelligence

---

[1] Also spelt 'Boultes'.

system and instituted political and insurgent warfare training for both the leaders and the men.

Then about forty years of age, General Markos had come from Asia Minor as a refugee in 1923. When in his teens he had joined the Greek Communist Party and had been imprisoned for his political activities. During the Occupation of Greece he had been with ELAS in a political capacity, being the EAM representative on the 'committee command' pattern in Macedonia. Eventually, paired with General Bakirdzis, he had risen to be in charge of the Macedonian Corps. So far, Markos had mainly been a political soldier, but like most of the ELAS 'commissars' he took an active part in the fighting and a keen interest in military operations and problems. He had a flair for soldiering, added to which he had picked up a great deal of military knowledge from the regular officers with ELAS, such as General Bakirdzis, and from practical experience on the battlefield.

With Aris dead and the regular officers formerly with ELAS now reinstated in the Greek National Army (GNA), Markos was perhaps the best and most suitable choice as a field commander for the Democratic Army. General Saraphis, who had done so much to make ELAS efficient and had helped to direct its fortunes in battle, played no part in the formation of the Democratic Army. Had he been so inclined and had he been invited to assist, being a reinstated regular officer retained in Athens in absolute idleness, he was in theory available. Saraphis was not a Communist but that had not prevented him serving with ELAS. Owing to his reputation and proved organizing ability it was probably expected that the KKE would have been keen to obtain him again. This was not the case and no overtures were made to Saraphis, which may have indicated a lack of trust in him. Had Aris, who had worked with and respected Saraphis, remained alive, perhaps an invitation might have been forthcoming. Markos had not been so close to Saraphis, and had in fact differed with him on occasions as to how the Macedonian divisions should be used. He himself aspired to the sole military command of the Democratic Army and had no wish to share this role with a non-Communist regular officer. It is only of academic interest to speculate whether the final outcome would have been any different had Saraphis gone over to the Democratic Army.

By the end of 1946, Albania, Yugoslavia and Bulgaria were firmly in the Soviet orbit and mutually antagonistic in principle to the monarchist régime in Greece, so there was no ideological barrier to providing clandestine bases and aid for the Democratic Army.

When the Germans evacuated Albania in 1944, General Hoxha, the leader of the partisans of that country, set up a Communist government, which in November 1945 was recognized by Britain and other major Powers. In January 1946, King Zog was formally deposed and a People's Republic of Albania proclaimed. By its political nature, this government was sympathetic to the Democratic Army and its aims, and accordingly ex-ELAS and other Greek refugees were allowed to shelter within its frontiers. The fact that the KKE and the EAM, unlike other political parties in Greece, were not keen on annexing 'Northern Epirus' may have been an added incentive to help stir up insurrection against a Government that had that intention. Technically, Albania was still in a state of war with Greece.

Despite Stalin's instructions, the actual material aid given to the Democratic Army in the first place was small and mainly restricted to food, but its unlimited freedom to flit unhampered across the Albanian border into Greece and back again to security whenever harried by the Greek National Guard was of inestimable value. This allowed Democratic Army units to raid into Greece for food and whatever else they could pick up. The Democratic Army was allowed to establish a camp at Rubig, and another one later at Nikolitsa, both being adjacent to the frontier area.

In Yugoslavia, Tito was in control and his Government was recognized by Britain in 1945 and by the USA the following year. He also was not averse to aiding Greek refugees and to secretly sustaining the Democratic Army, but he was a trifle cautious. At first Tito was not over-generous, his actual aid being limited to food supplies, the use of some army camps and a few army transport vehicles, but he allowed the Democratic Army units freedom to cross and re-cross his frontier with Greece.

Although a confirmed Communist, Tito was also an intense nationalist, and he thoughtfully contemplated a Communist Slav Macedonia, detached from Greece, that could later be incorporated or federated with Yugoslavia. Perhaps the KKE and the Democratic Army might be persuaded into helping him achieve this.

Mainly because of the shelter given to Greek refugees and because Tito allowed the Democratic Army to raid over the border into Greece instead of interning it, diplomatic relations between the two countries worsened. These irritations brought old enmities to the surface and national emotions came to the boil. When chasing Democratic Army elements, the Greek National Guard was forced to stop short at the Yugoslav frontier. Greece feared Yugoslavian strength and intentions, so dared not do anything that might provoke Tito.[1] Greek National Guard units refrained from returning the fire that was occasionally splattered on to its members from north of the border. In August 1946, the Yugoslav Ambassador was recalled from Athens.[2] Yugoslav troops stood ready along the frontier to deal with any Greek infringement, and Tito's determination in this respect can be illustrated by the fact that in September 1946 Yugoslav anti-aircraft gunners shot down a Greek Spitfire that was just over Yugoslav territory near Evzoni.

Bulgaria was slower to settle beneath the Communist yoke. In September 1946 a referendum was held in which the monarchy was overwhelmingly rejected, and the next month a general election returned a Communist majority. In November, Dimitroff, a Communist, gained full control of the government and, disliking the political pattern in Greece, he gave shelter to Greek refugees and allowed some Democratic Army units to harbour in his country. In accordance with Stalin's instructions, he gave the Democratic Army a little material aid too. Like Tito, Dimitroff was a nationalist-type Communist, and he did not exclude the possibility that Thrace might be Communized and then merged with Bulgaria. Bulgaria had no diplomatic relations with Greece.

Both Yugoslavia and Bulgaria would have liked an outlet into the Aegean Sea, and the city of Salonika stood out as a tempting prize. By the end of 1946, all three countries, Albania, Yugoslavia and Bulgaria, were Communist in principle and practice. They each formed bilateral agreements of friendship, and economic and mutual aid, and thus were an ominous, unfriendly bloc to the north of Greece.

By September 1946, General Markos had established several small Democratic Army bases in the mountains just inside Greece, which he controlled from Bulkes, and each accumulated its own small store of arms, ammunition and food. The reason for this decentralization was partly so that they would be ready dispersed in sound tactical positions and partly because General Markos was not too sure how his 'hosts' would react to diplomatic or other pressure put on them

[1] Yugoslavia had about 300,000 men under arms, and had 4 infantry and 1 armoured division in Serbian Macedonia.

[2] The incident that sparked off the withdrawal of the Yugoslav Ambassador was the Yugoslav allegation that the Greeks had deliberately wrecked a Yugoslav liner off Patras. In fact, this had been done by RAF aircraft on bombing practice, thinking it to be an abandoned enemy vessel.

by the UN or other Great Powers. He knew that Yugoslavia was intriguing for Trieste, and there was no telling to what lengths Tito might go to achieve this end, even to the extent of clamping down on fellow Communists. Markos knew only too well that Communists do not necessarily stick together against a common enemy. Stalin's cold, calculated treachery might well be imitated by Tito. Owing to the vagaries of power politics he could not be sure that his headquarters at Bulkes might not be suddenly shut down and he and his men interned.

The need for some sort of command and staff organization was necessary, and in October 1946 Markos announced the formation of a 'GHQ in the field'. A larger part of this GHQ was actually in Bulkes, but it did allow him to have a smaller operational headquarters which was mobile and could be much nearer to Greece, which was divided into regional commands. Markos intended to be on hand to command personally any operations of any size and consequence.

By autumn, Democratic Army activity, formerly confined mainly to eastern Macedonia, had spread across the whole of northern Greece, as under Markos' urging and exhortations the insurgents recovered much of their confidence and aggressiveness, which had been dampened in defeat. He ordered his Democratic Army units to strike at isolated villages, which were looted and often burned. When National Guard detachments rushed to the scene the insurgents withdrew. It was 'hit-and-run' tactics, the 'hits' being made against undefended villages in a widening area, which gradually spread southwards towards Larissa. One of the largest of these raids was made against the village of Deskati near Mount Khasia, in Thessaly. Within a month, over 120 people had been killed, and the Greek Government was forced to declare martial law throughout the whole of northern Greece.

In October, Markos intensified these 'hit-and-run' raids with the object both of obtaining supplies for the coming winter and of spreading the awe of terrorism. In these raids his men took hostages, shot village gendarmes and executed pro-Government peasants, so that before very long all the villagers in the north went in fear of the Communists. One of the largest raids in this month was made by about 400 men of the Democratic Army on Naoussa, which was taken by an assault aided by a fifth column within the town. The small National Guard detachment was overpowered, several people were executed, stores were seized and when National Guard rein-

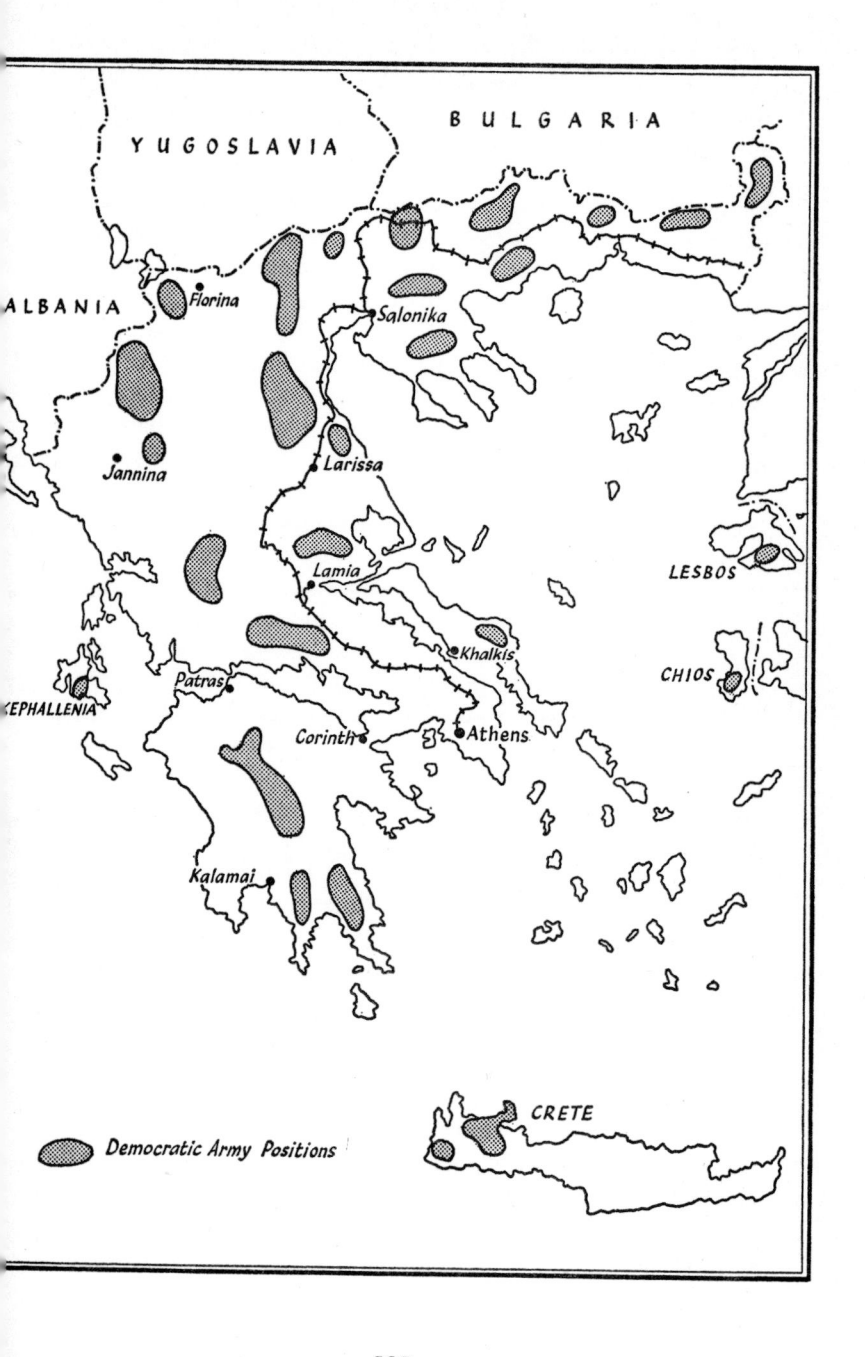

Democratic Army Positions

forcements appeared the Democratic Army insurgents disappeared.

When General Markos assumed command of the Democratic Army he had about 4,000 armed men, which he realized were not sufficient to carry out the plans he had in mind, so he sent out the call for ex-ELAS members to join him. Many did so, the men creeping over the border and making their way to Bulkes or one of the other camps, or to join one of the other of the groups established in the mountains inside Greece. In this manner, the Democratic Army quickly rose to a strength of 5,000, and then to 6,000 by the end of October.

Concurrent with the revival of co-ordinated activity of Democratic Army units was the revival of the Communist underground network in the towns and villages, which provided the essential intelligence service as well as recruits and supplies. The persistent efforts to infiltrate the Greek security and armed forces to suborn them from their allegiance to the Government were not always without success. For example, sixty officers and men of the GNA were convicted by court martial in the Larissa area for helping the Democratic Army and the Communists in October.

In November the tempo quickened as Markos was determined to establish the Communist grip firmly on the inhabitants of northern Greece before the winter set in. His policy was to pick out a village, concentrate three or four of his small units to attack it, kill the gendarmes and selected villagers and then quickly withdraw, taking all stores and food that could be foraged. Skra, a large village near the Yugoslav border, was taken in this manner and held for a few days, only to be abandoned when Government reinforcements, which had been delayed by heavy snowfalls, came rushing on to the scene. Similar assaults were made on villages in the region of Jannina and Grevena, when hostages were seized and summary executions carried out.

By mid-November the situation was such that the Greek Government was forced to admit that it did not have full control of the area north of Mount Olympus.[1] This was understating the fact, as large sections were under Democratic Army domination, to the extent that it was able to issue 'passes' to the inhabitants to travel from their homes. The seeming inability of the National Guard, which invariably arrived on the scene too late, to protect the peasants from Democratic Army terrorist activities, caused fear once again to

---

[1] In November 1946, the Greek Government formally requested a UN investigation into foreign aid given to the Democratic Army.

descend upon the countryside. General Markos had succeeded in the first phase of his plan.

The British, who were advising upon Greek security problems, saw the insurgent activities as an internal police matter, something the National Guard had been raised to cope with, and were reluctant to approve of Greek regular troops being employed in a counter-insurgency role. But the Government security forces, which consisted of the National Guard in the countryside, armed gendarmes in the villages and police in the towns[1] were unable to compete against the carefully planned 'hit-and-run' Democratic Army tactics. As the National Guard was much too small to be everywhere it was needed at once, with tacit Government approval, it unofficially took to arming anti-Communist individuals in villages[2] to protect themselves and their homes from raids. These came to acquire a sort of official status and were known as local defence volunteers or home guards, being auxiliary to the National Guard.

In October, Britain was asked for more arms to give out to civilians. This request was refused, but by this time the adverse situation was so apparent that Britain agreed that the Greek National Army should be brought into action against the Democratic Army, to work in conjunction with the National Guard. At last it was recognized that it was civil war, and not just a case of 'bandits' against the National Guard.

The GNA, then about 100,000 strong and not too well equipped as regards transport and arms, was at last brought into play against the insurgents. It had little more success than the National Guard, but for different reasons. From the start it was tied down in static defence as powerful politicians used their influence to ensure that troops guarded their own local areas, and they were loth to see them moved away. Accordingly, units of the GNA could not be easily and freely switched from one place to another as required. This deprived the GNA of the mobility essential to deal with insurgent warfare. Another retarding factor was that the General Staff, under heavy political influence, was rigid and over-centralized. Divisional commanders could not move any of their units without its permission. This lack of initiative and mobility was a distinct advantage to the Democratic Army.

[1] The Greek security forces, excluding the GNA, were just over 30,000 strong at this time.
[2] The EAM alleged that by October 1946 over 5,000 people in Central Macedonia, 3,500 in Western Macedonia and 300 in Thrace had been given rifles by the National Guard.

Because of the extremely poor economic situation, Greece was having trouble in supporting her own armed forces. Britain had helped fairly generously in the first place,[1] but by 1946 she too was feeling the economic pinch. It had been visualized that Greece would be able to be militarily independent by January 1946, and when it was obvious that this target could not be met Britain agreed to continue to help until March 1947. This gave little promise of providing the numbers of trucks, weapons and other equipment required to enable the GNA to carry out anti-insurgent warfare. The vague Greek military plan was that it was hoped that Democratic Army units would not become too entrenched during the winter in the mountains inside the country, so that it would be possible to sweep them clear in the spring, by which time the GNA might be slightly better trained.

The Greek domestic political scene was not a happy one, and Tsaldaris, the Prime Minister, tried vainly, under British urging, to broaden the basis of his government. In November, he exasperatedly excluded all opposition parties, which caused muttering and discontent. He also closed down one of the two Communist newspapers for printing extracts of General Markos' announcements and proclamations from his 'GHQ in the field'.

The Democratic Army plans for the winter were far more positive. General Markos intended to step up his 'hit-and-kill' tactics on as broad a front as possible, not only on the mainland but also in the Peloponnese. He realized that insurgent activity in the Peloponnese would give an outward impression of national support and spontaneity which might indicate general discontent with the Government, untinged with incitement from either Yugoslavia or other Balkan countries. Democratic Army activity in the Peloponnese would distract attention from the more serious Democratic Army efforts in the north of the country, and would show that it could operate in the south without the aid of a conveniently friendly adjacent country.

General Markos estimated that to stir up full-scale insurrection he would need an army of about 50,000 men, and he began to plan on this premise. Having absorbed the bulk of the potential volunteers and the ex-ELAS men who were willing to return, he now had to resort to conscripting manpower. Pressed recruits were taken in

[1] The GNA was largely clad in British battle-dress, boots, and greatcoats, and wore British webbing-type equipment. Half the soldiers were armed with British rifles, and each unit had a few British bren guns.

village raids, and the men and women induced to serve in the Democratic Army under threats of reprisals against their families should they fail in action or desert. By the end of 1946 Markos had about 7,000 in his army, a tiny proportion of whom were young women. Despite threats, carried out in many instances, Markos began by November to have a deserter problem, one which never left him during the whole war. The Greek Government offered clemency to Democratic Army deserters who gave themselves up—an offer renewed at intervals—and over 600 did so in the last two months of the year.

General Markos had placed high hopes on the Soviet Union providing food and material for his campaign, but despite vague promises Stalin sent nothing at all, except a few Soviet officers to act as observers and report back what was happening. They merely kept an eye on how the KKE was behaving and what the insurgents were doing.

Anxious and disappointed about his supply problems, but not nonplussed, the resourceful Markos made the round of Balkan capitals and by personal negotiation was able to obtain limited military aid from Yugoslavia, and also some from both Albania and Bulgaria. This was enough for him to continue his insurgent struggle. He did not obtain nearly as much as he wanted and his supply problem remained one of his major worries throughout. In fact, until more arms arrived, the Democratic Army temporarily limited recruiting as Markos was no believer in unarmed soldiers.

This foreign help, which came mainly from Yugoslavia, was only extracted at a price, and in return Markos was compelled to make agreements that would have been very detrimental to Greece had the KKE ever come to power, as they involved frontier adjustments in favour of Albania, Yugoslavia and Bulgaria. He also had to support the detachment from Greece of its Slav regions. These arrangements, which had been made by General Markos largely on his own initiative, were only endorsed in a lukewarm fashion by the Central Committee of the KKE. Siantos, a nationalist, was firmly against them, as were other members, but perhaps in true Communist style they never had any intention of finally honouring them. They were regarded as an expedient that could be ignored in due course.

By January 1947 General Markos was able to claim that he held over 100 villages, which was not an idle boast, as this number of villages at least were his for the simple reason that Government

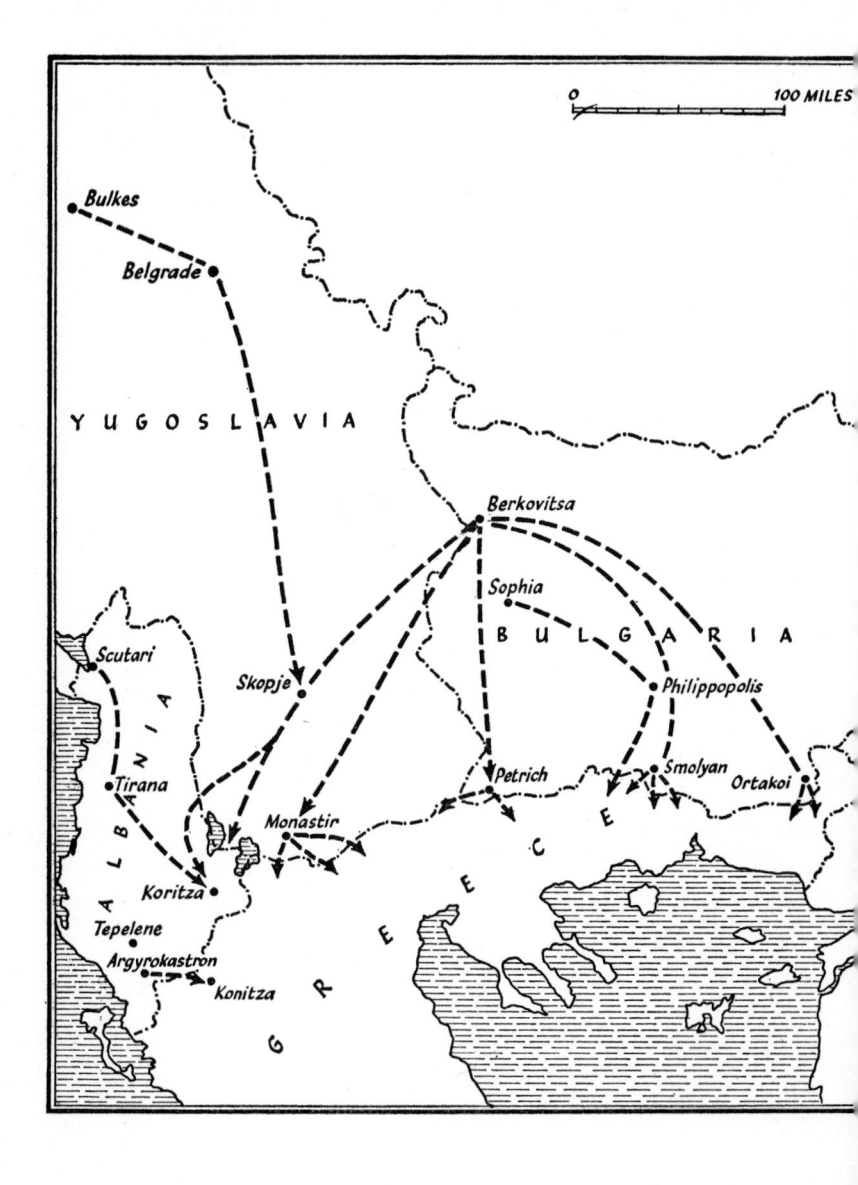

forces were unable to guarantee their security from Communist raids and reprisals on life and property. In these areas Communist rule was enforced, men were conscripted into the Democratic Army, taxes were levied and Communist law dispensed. This situation had come about because of lack of Government initiative and energy, rather than by deliberate planning, as the policy was not to take and hold villages.

Receiving less opposition from the Government forces than he had anticipated, General Markos began to think about selecting an area of mountainous territory inside Greece in which to set up his GHQ permanently. He chose a sector adjacent to the point near Lake Prespa where the Albanian, Yugoslav and Greek frontiers met, a sector which contained the Grammos, Vitsi and other mountain ranges. For convenience and clarity this can be loosely referred to in future as the 'Frontier Corner', and it was held, with qualifications, by the Democratic Army right until the end. It was wild, craggy, desolate country, easy to defend, but extremely hard to assault. In it a few determined men could hold up whole units.

During the winter, Markos concentrated upon improving his intelligence and supply systems, which were linked to the Communist underground that had spread into most towns and villages. He also had to train his 'conscripts' and his field commanders. This was mainly done at Bulkes, in Yugoslavia. Both Albania and Yugoslavia supplied rations, ammunition, explosives, small arms and mortars, and also some trucks, as well as training facilities. The latter included instructors and ranges for practice-firing of both guns and mortars. The policy of press-ganging men into the Democratic Army continued all winter, until by March 1947 Markos had over 13,000 armed men with some degree of training.

Noting how the bulk of the GNA was tied down in static defence, General Markos resorted to harassing tactics, playing on its communications and ambushing small parties and patrols. Prudently, he forbade his commanders to attack regular bodies of troops or strongly-held towns or villages, but to stick to avoidance tactics of the 'hit-and-run' type. The Democratic Army established a series of small bases in the mountains of Greece, especially in the Pindus Range, that were mobile in the sense that when hard-pressed they could hide their stores and move on elsewhere. Owing to the static dispositions of the GNA, the National Guard still had to bear the brunt of the fighting against the Democratic Army.

The morale of the Democratic Army fluctuated and it was not always so good or consistent as it was made out to be. The pressed men were often sulky and reluctant soldiers, and harsh punishments had to be meted out to those who failed in action or tried to desert, some being summarily tried and shot. Each unit had a political officer, who paired up with the military commander, and it was his job not only to spread the Communist word but to raise morale and keep it at a high level. The several minor successes encouraged the Democratic Army faint-hearts, but the comparatively heavy casualties inflicted on them by superior fire power whenever the insurgents ran up against the regular troops depressed them equally quickly. Often action was avoided because the Democratic Army unit could not be trusted to behave in the face of the GNA.

Democratic Army morale was bolstered by the constant rumour that International Brigades of foreign Communist volunteers were being formed in France, Belgium, Holland and even Britain, which would soon be coming out to help them, just as they had done to help the Republicans in the Spanish Civil War a few years previously. Their non-arrival caused morale to sag periodically. A camp, or headquarters of sorts, was set up near Toulouse, in France, with the idea of forming such International Brigades to send to Greece, but this never came to anything.

Democratic Army units were especially active throughout the winter in Macedonia, Thessaly and north-west Greece. A few spasmodic eruptions occurred in the Peloponnese, but these were not serious as the Democratic Army units there did not have such a free and easy time, mainly owing to the presence of armed groups of the X Organization, which, while rapidly losing their sting, were still a nuisance and a handicap to the Democratic Army commanders. Everywhere the Government forces were kept in a state of anxious alert; and owing to the policy of not allowing regular formations or elements of them to be moved without a lot of fuss, large sectors fell under Communist domination, as the hard-pressed, overworked National Guard, whose morale and discipline were strained to the utmost, was incapable of coping adequately. The spread of anarchy, or rather of calculated terror, in the countryside was such that it was unsafe to wander outside the towns. Frequent executions were carried out by the Communists, and both conscripts and hostages were carried off.

This unexpected aggressive and successful expansion of the

Democratic Army, unhalted by the winter snow and storms, and the spread of insecurity it brought in its wake, dismayed the Greek Government and had a depressing effect on the morale and spirit of the GNA, as well as the National Guard. At times officers were dubious of the loyalty of their men, as the Communist fifth column in the garrison towns became active amongst them. Periodically regular formations or units of the National Guard chased Democratic Army groups to the border, but they had to halt there while their quarry skipped over to safety, sometimes momentarily pausing to derisively fire back from diplomatically inviolate positions on the north of the frontiers.

During the winter initiative was generally lost by the Government forces, which had entered the lists too late. The Democratic Army had forestalled them by establishing mobile bases in the mountains of Greece, some of which were not dislodged for many months. Under the shrewd direction of General Markos, the Communists had completed the spadework for their plan to overthrow the Greek Government by force, by establishing an adequate and workable intelligence and supply system.

Amid this turmoil a UN Enquiry Commission arrived in Greece in the last days of January 1947, consisting of members from eleven countries. The EAM leaders in Athens, amongst whom were Siantos and Partsalidis, both of whom remained in the open, asked the Democratic Army to suspend field operations while the commission was investigating, but this request was ignored. General Markos fixedly carried on with his programme, and he was convinced that there was no prospect of gaining power by political action alone. He saw no point in surrendering any military advantage for something nebulous.

The UN Commission had absolutely no co-operation from Albania, Yugoslavia or Bulgaria, the requests to investigate being either ignored or refused point-blank, so it had to be content with gathering evidence in Greek territory only, or such of it as the Greek Government controlled. Ample was gained to give a clear picture as to what was happening.

Among many others of all parties and factions, EAM representatives were interviewed, but they merely demanded the withdrawal of British troops from Greece.[1] It was insisted that British troops only remained in Greece to counter-balance the Soviet forces in the

---

[1] About 16,000 British troops remained in Greece, a number progressively reduced to 5,000 by January 1948.

Balkan countries to the north,[1] and in any case they were being rapidly reduced in strength.

Another interesting point was that, despite discouragement from the Greek Government, the UN Commission arranged to meet General Markos.[2] Its members journeyed over the mountains on mule-back to his GHQ which was in a village in the Frontier Corner, but Markos was away when it arrived. The Commission was told that he was conducting operations in the field. After waiting for two days the Commission left without seeing him. However, two members, Polish and Soviet, remained and eventually saw General Markos on March 20th.

The Greek political situation deteriorated and the strong united government so badly needed to cope with the country's problems seemed always just beyond reach. In December (1946) Papandreou, Venizelos[3] and Kanellopoulos agreed to enter a coalition on the condition that Britain would give more arms, but this did not come to anything. Tsaldaris resigned in January 1947, and his government was followed by a coalition one, formed by Maximos, a Popularist, which contained Venizelos, Kartalis and General Zervas.

Zervas, late of EDES and now a general, was appointed, after a few days, Minister for Public Order and instructed to dissolve all semi-official armed organizations. This was obviously aimed at the X Organization of Colonel Grivas, and Zervas certainly took strong action against its members, many of whom he arrested. From this moment onwards, X as a force and power in the land began to decline. By the end of April 1947, after personally directing operations against X fighters in the Peloponnese, he declared that area to be free from all terrorists. He was almost right, as the Democratic Army elements were never very well rooted in the Peloponnese, where they seldom had the means or scope to cause insurrection to the same extent as they did on the mainland.

General Zervas took a tougher line against left-wing elements too, and early in March arrested over 500 for allegedly aiding the Democratic Army, either by recruiting for it, giving supplies or of helping in other ways. This number included many EAM members.

On March 23rd, Zevgos, a member of the Central Committees of

[1] There were about 100,000 Red Army troops in Bulgaria and another 10,000 in Yugoslavia. There was a Red Army training mission in Albania.

[2] General Markos had asked to be heard by the UN Commission. His request is alleged to have been transmitted to it by a British MP, Mr. George Thomas, who had visited the GHQ of the Democratic Army in the Frontier Corner.

[3] This was Sophocles Venizelos, the son of Eleutherios Venizelos.

both KKE and EAM, was shot dead in the streets of Salonika. His assassin was made out to be an escaped 'pressed man' from a Democratic Army camp in Yugoslavia, but it was a political murder. The left accused the right and vice versa. Zakhariadis declared it had been engineered by General Zervas. Zervas arrested many more Communists, and in riposte, the Democratic Army seized hostages and carried out a few impromptu executions.

On April 1st, 1947, King George II of Greece died and was succeeded by his brother, Paul I. Many hoped that the new King would be able to weld the political parties together, as he was generally popular and was not tainted with the Fascist Metaxas smear, as had been his brother.

The depths of the penetrations of the Democratic Army winter erosion made it obvious that the Greek armed forces would require large quantities of modern equipment, arms and vehicles to counter it. Britain, owing to her own acute economic problems, was unable to provide assistance on the scale required. Realizing this, Greece decided to turn to America, and on March 3rd formally asked for aid. The Greek armed forces totalled about 130,000 men in all three services, with the GNA at just over 110,000. An increase in numbers was necessary, which would involve more expense.

America thought that Greece and Turkey were suffering from a war of nerves brought on by the Soviet Union, the Communist ogre in world politics. Greece was suffering from internal stresses, while Turkey suffered from external ones. America felt that both deserved support, and to enable them withstand the Communist pressures, on March 12th President Truman asked the American Congress for $400 million economic and financial aid to help Greece and Turkey maintain their independence.

In April, concentrated Government offensives were made against the Democratic Army, having the object of clearing the insurgents from the Pindus, the Khasia and the Agrapha Mountain ranges. About 15,000 troops from the II Corps at Larissa[1] were used in the main part of the operation, and they consisted of elements of three divisions.[2] GNA divisions were predominantly infantry in character and fact, since they had little artillery, no armour and insufficient

---

[1] The GNA was grouped into three corps:
   I Corps—based on Athens and responsible for Attica and the Peloponnese.
   II Corps—based on Larissa, and responsible for Central Greece.
   III Corps—based on Salonika, and responsible for northern Greece.
[2] The 2nd, 8th and 9th Divisions, and an independent brigade group.

motor transport. They averaged between 10,000 and 12,000 officers and men, so it can be seen that elements of the divisions remained in their areas tied down by political pressures.

These operations jolted the Democratic Army plans and complacency, as the comparative passiveness of the GNA was becoming rather taken for granted by the insurgents, who were becoming cocksure and careless, as they were accustomed by now to being able to out-fight and out-smart the dispersed and overworked National Guard. A hard core of Democratic Army units was in the Pindus Range, between the road from Jannina to Kalabaka, by way of Metsovo to the north, and the River Achelous to the west, and to the north-east along a tributary of that river through Agrapha to Kalabaka. Within it were about 2,500 Democratic Army men in scattered, small pockets.

Starting on the 9th, after picqueting strategic bridges and roads, and putting out an incomplete cordon, the GNA formations moved into the mountains hoping either to kill or capture the insurgents, or to drive them into the waiting net. Briefly, one division advanced northwards from the Karpenisi area, another division moved from the west from the line of the River Achelous, and another moved in from the east, from the Larissa region. Each division had a few 25-pounder guns, and all the available aircraft of the Greek air force[1] were used. The operation was directed from Larissa, the GHQ of II Corps, which was responsible for Central Greece. Leaflets were dropped on the Democratic Army fighters, urging them to surrender, and then the aircraft took to more deadly means of persuasion, machine-gunning them and firing rockets.

Carried out amid alternate snow and hail storms, with snow at times lying several feet deep in some of the mountain passes, the operation caught the Democratic Army on one leg, as it had not anticipated that the GNA, which it had begun to despise for its inactivity, would move out in such bad weather, let alone carry grimly on regardless of discomfort. It is not always realized that insurgents and guerrillas are more handicapped by adverse weather conditions than regular troops who have a conventional line-of-communication to fall back upon to ease their physical discomfort. Hunted insurgents have no such support available and over 120

---

[1] The Greek air force had two squadrons of British Supermarine Spitfires, which were used as bombers, and some C-47s, which were also used in this role in a makeshift manner. The air force also possessed other aircraft, such as Airspeed Oxfords and Avro Ansons.

bodies of men who had died of exposure were found by the GNA within days.

For a fortnight the GNA troops struggled through the mountains with the Democratic Army units giving way before them, seeking to escape whenever they could. As they retreated the insurgents burnt the villages and forced the peasants to withdraw with them. On the 17th an assault was made on a strong Democratic Army pocket near Agrapha, which dissolved the following morning.

Next GNA troops were switched to the area between Grevena and Mount Olympus and the Khasia Mountains, but as may be expected, most of the insurgents slipped through the sieve-like net as it was not possible to cordon such a large mountainous area effectively with so few men and vehicles. By the 24th the operation was over. The GNA claimed, perhaps quite correctly, that over 1,200 Democratic Army fighters had been killed, wounded, captured or had surrendered, for less than eighty GNA casualties.

On the 27th the GNA troops, operating from Larissa, switched southwards and moved against Democratic Army elements in the Othrys Mountains which lay between Larissa and Lamia, but this time they were less successful, and while they netted a number of insurgents and inflicted casualties, most were able to escape by taking avoiding action.

When these clearing operations, grandly conceived and planned, ran down, the bulk of the GNA troops returned to their regions to revert to static defence. They undoubtedly needed and deserved a rest, and the politicians welcomed them back, being more loth than before to let them go away again. It was noticeable that after this for many months only a small proportion of troops of the field formations were available for mobile operations even in areas adjacent to where they were stationed. It was only with difficulty that seven or eight battalions, with artillery and transport, could be gathered together to take action against the Democratic Army.

After the April offensives, the Greek Government claimed to have cleared the mountains, especially the Pindus, the Agrapha and the Khasia ranges, but this was only partially true. The insurgents had given way at all points and sought to escape, fighting hard only when cornered, but they had not been defeated, only taken by surprise. They were surprised in the sense that they had underestimated the GNA's determination to operate in such foul weather. Owing to good intelligence, the Democratic Army units knew the scope and the extent of the GNA plans beforehand even to the dates and formations to take part, but they did not think they would materialize. Grandiose plans had been made on paper often before and had come to nothing, or hardly anything.

The GNA mistakenly read the Democratic Army retreats for defeats, not realizing that it was simply using typical guerrilla evasive tactics. As the GNA troops returned to their bases, Democratic Army units crept cautiously back to their former haunts.

Even so, these April offensives had been a hard blow which had shaken Democratic Army morale and confidence. During this month, over 600 insurgent deserters gave themselves up to the GNA. A hunted guerrilla, hungry and cold, soon loses enthusiasm and spirit. Had the cordon been better placed, had more troops been employed, had more transport been available, and had the operations been quickly followed by other similar ones while winter conditions remained, the hard core of General Markos' army might have been scooped up and the remainder scattered and demoralized. A chance was missed.

The opportune moment soon went, and once the reaction had worked off and the exhausted GNA elements had returned to their static defences, the Democratic Army recovered its spirits gradually and again became active in the mountains. The Government claim that the mountains had been cleared was no longer valid. There had been no attempt to reduce the Frontier Corner, or other mountain ranges in northern Greece, so it had never been very convincing anyway.

During the winter the Democratic Army had outpaced the GNA. The Democratic Army was expanding and preparing for a renewed phase of the fighting; while the GNA, after its one outburst of energy, was resting on its laurels and, under political pressure, sinking into lethargy. Lack of aircraft, transport, wireless sets and artillery made the Greek General Staff realize how ill-equipped the GNA was for the task that confronted it. GNA morale drooped again, just as that of the Democratic Army began to revive.

CHAPTER EIGHT

American Aid

The year 1947 was one in which the Truman Doctrine was translated into fact as US advisers took over much of the responsibility for helping Greece and guiding the GNA. By the end of the year quantities of American arms, vehicles and equipment began to arrive in the country. They came just in time, as the Democratic Army had increased to a strength of about 23,000 active fighters and had considerably extended its scope and areas of influence. As a riposte to American 'interference' the KKE set up a provisional 'Democratic Government of Greece'.

On May 22nd, 1947, President Truman signed the Bill authorizing aid to both Greece and Turkey. Greece was to have $300 million, of which $150 million was to provide the Greek forces with arms, equipment, clothing and rations necessary to deal effectively with the insurgents. $20 million was for agricultural rehabilitation and $130 million for industrial and financial reconstruction. Already in March Britain had given £1½ million worth of surplus stores then being used by the British army and RAF in Greece, but this was only a drop in the ocean to the poorly equipped GNA.

A US Mission was authorized to operate in Greece, and this became known as the American Mission for Aid to Greece, or AMAG. It was seen that the GNA had not only to be re-equipped but also retrained, its morale and fighting spirit raised and that the whole concept of its strategy and tactics would have to be drastically altered. It was obvious that this could not be done in a few days, or even weeks, so it was planned to keep the GNA active against the Democratic Army to hold the insurgents in check, under cover of which the GNA would prepare to undertake an autumn campaign. Failing that, a spring offensive was sure to do the trick.

A notable feature of the Democratic Army in 1947 was its increase in strength. In March it was probably about 13,000 strong, by May it had risen to about 18,000, and by July it had topped 23,000, at which level it roughly remained. These numbers represented fighting men in the field, either in the mountains inside Greece, or just over the border waiting to raid across it. In addition, there was always a number of recruits training in the several Democratic Army camps in Yugoslavia and Albania.[1] At one time there were as many as 8,000 men and women being trained. The Democratic Army expansion was due partly to voluntary recruiting; partly to semi-voluntary recruiting, the Communists putting moral pressure on young people to join it in the mountains; and partly to forcible recruiting. Whenever towns and villages were raided young men and women were persuaded to enlist in the Democratic Army, but if the required quota was not forthcoming, press gang methods were resorted to.

The intelligence and supply network was based on Communist 'cells' that were established in the cities, towns and large villages throughout Greece. These cells were small groups of varying size, of Communist workers, who styled themselves 'self-defence personnel', and the whole system became known as YIAFAKA. YIAFAKA took on the task of collecting information, supplies, money, recruiting and also occasionally carrying out acts of terrorism or reprisals, although the latter were frequently undertaken by OPLA. This secret organization, the YIAFAKA, which worked quite efficiently, swelled to huge proportions and, at its height in mid-1947, probably had as many as 50,000 active members. In addition, there must have been up to a quarter of a million sympathizers who gave occasional help in some way or another, several of whom were in positions of importance in the civil service and in other walks of life. Money, information, food and such items as medicines and drugs, flowed through the YIAFAKA to the Democratic Army units in the field. YIAFAKA also worked to undermine the confidence of the people in the Greek Government and to weaken the morale of the armed forces.

[1] Apart from the large Democratic Army training camp at Bulkes, in Yugoslavia, there were also others at Tirnovo, Berkovitsa, Pazardchik and Malkograditsa. In Albania there were training camps at Rubig and Nikolitsa, and there was one at Petrich in Bulgaria.

General Markos arranged with the Governments of Albania, Yugoslavia and Bulgaria to let him have more arms, equipment and training facilities. The arms were mainly small arms and light mortars, which were either Soviet surplus or confiscated German ones, but they also included a few field guns (Skoda 75mm) and some anti-aircraft guns as well. On May 22nd, for example, Democratic Army anti-aircraft gunners brought down their first Greek air force plane, a Spitfire, over northern Greece. The Yugoslav General Staff took a close interest in all Democratic Army operations, and a Yugoslav general, Dapchevic, with a small staff, was attached to the GHQ of General Markos.

The Democratic Army was organized into small units of between fifty and a hundred men each. These were scattered in the mountains, each being self-sufficient, responsible for its own fate and finding its own nook. Most, but by no means all at this stage, had wireless sets which enabled them to keep in touch with the GHQ in the Frontier Corner, or with the mobile tactical GHQ of Markos, wherever that might be. There were no higher or intermediate formations or headquarters, such as brigades or divisions. Whenever an operation was carried out, two or more Democratic Army units were brought together, each being given a particular part to play, after which they dispersed again to semi-independence. These small Democratic Army units were largely unidentifiable, there being no set system of numbering or naming them. Some did have numbers, but in rather a haphazard fashion, others were known by the names of their leaders, and some adopted designations that took their fancy.

In the harassing raids against villages, the Democratic Army units were instructed to employ the principles of surprise, shock and mobility. The progressive pattern of the insurgent war, as visualized by General Markos, was that first of all there was to be a spate of raids against unprotected villages over a wide area to obtain food and recruits and to carry out reprisals. These were to be gradually developed into larger undertakings in which several units co-operated. The next stage was to dominate large areas of the countryside, and to harass and sabotage GNA communications.

The Democratic Army made several raids in May, but in that month the GNA also carried out a few clearing operations against the insurgents. As these were disjointed, restricted in scope and only employed a limited number of troops, they did not achieve much success. The Democratic Army units were able to avoid the traps with comparative ease. The GNA was severely handicapped in this type of operation by lack of transport and the poor state of the roads.

On May 20th, 1947, Siantos died of a heart attack in Athens, and this event brought about a change of emphasis in KKE policy. Siantos with Partsalidis, the Secretary-General of the EAM, had stayed in the open in Athens, while other prominent Communist leaders, such as Zakhariadis and Markos, had gone underground or taken to the mountains.

Siantos had been in favour of political action, rather than insurgent war, and advocated stirring up economic unrest. He was also a nationalist. As deputy leader of the KKE, he did not favour the setting up of a Free Greek Government, either in exile or on Greek soil, as he thought that it might be the final straw that would cause the Greek Government to ban the KKE, and its satellite organizations, which would curtail or cut off so many open and fruitful contacts with Communist and left-wing parties and groups in foreign countries.

On May 15th, for example, a motion in the Greek Parliament to outlaw the KKE was postponed as the Government, while fully aware that it was the instigator of the insurrection, did not wish to drive it underground. It also feared that any such move might be misunderstood in Britain and America.

On the other hand, Markos had little faith that political action alone would ever bring the KKE to power, and he wanted to set up a 'Free Democratic Government', but not on Greek soil, as that would mean resorting to positional warfare to defend it. He knew that with so few heavy weapons at his disposal, his units would not be able to withstand the GNA artillery fire. Also, it would have meant prematurely turning his guerrilla units into conventional formations, which he did not want to do just yet as they would obviously not be fit, for a very long time, to take the field against the GNA and fight positional battles with it.

Zakhariadis, who spent much of his time at Bulkes in Yugoslavia when he was not travelling around different countries to solicit support, also favoured the proclamation of a 'Free Democratic Government' by the KKE, but he hesitated because he was not absolutely sure how much support it would command abroad. While most Communist Governments and Communist Parties in other countries were able to maintain a direct contact with EAM without causing international ruptures, Zakhariadis was not so sure that they would automatically switch their support to a KKE Government, as diplomatic and other pressures might be brought to bear to prevent this recognition.

Yugoslavia had been increasing its assistance to the Democratic Army, and was prepared to further increase it if the KKE would proclaim a 'Free Democratic Government', which would have given more validity for continuing support. Both Albania and Bulgaria also urged the KKE to set up a rebel government, but all these suggestions had been resisted while Siantos was alive. Yugoslavia had also separately encouraged the Greek Slav exiles as a body to think of forming an autonomous region in Macedonia.

At last, under Balkan pressures, General Markos agreed to consider taking a Greek town in which to set up his GHQ. He selected Florina. A practice raid had been made by 400 insurgents on the small Greek town of Doiran, near the junction of the Yugoslav-Bulgarian border, and the result gave confidence in the feasibility of such a plan.

Florina had a garrison of about 500 troops, but it was chosen because it was only about twenty miles from the frontier, was astride frontier mountain routes, and also contained a Communist and Slav fifth column which was expected to assist. On May 28th, employing about 650 men, General Markos sealed off the approaches to the town and under cover of a rain of mortar shells assaulted it. In the expectation of such an attack, many of the known and suspected fifth columnists had been arrested and so were unable to help the attackers. In short, after a five-hour battle the Democratic Army units had to fall back and give up.

This reliance on the Communist fifth column within towns and villages had been of great assistance to the Democratic Army units in several of their raids, and they had come to look upon it as a matter of course. They should have known better, for they had just previously been disappointed when on May 5th they assaulted the small town of Kastanoussa, in Central Greece. They had not learnt their lesson. The Government, having fallen for this ruse so many times, now took to arresting suspected fifth columnists, especially in the frontier regions.

Pressed again to take Florina if he could, General Markos moved in more of his units and made a second assault on June 1st, but in the interim period the Government had brought up reinforcements. The result was the same—failure for the Democratic Army. During these two attacks the Greek air force had been active, machine-gunning and firing rockets at insurgent troop concentrations. The Democratic Army units had not always shown up in the best light in these attacks against Florina, both of which had been personally commanded by Markos. Some units and men had gone to the wrong place, some did not arrive in time, the assaults were disjointed and were not driven home uniformly, and under fire some broke and ran away.

In the light of these experiences, General Markos changed a few of his unit commanders, and then made a somewhat hasty and ill-planned attack on the small town of Kilkis, in Macedonia to the north of Salonika in the Beles Mountains, which was overlooked by both the Yugoslav and Bulgarian frontiers. This was a failure too.

Markos, who had never been keen on attempting to take towns by assault at this stage, would have been content to let it go at that and revert to mobile insurgent warfare, but his Balkan advisers and sponsors would not agree, and persuaded him to move against Konitza, a town only eight miles from the Albanian border and just to the south of the Frontier Corner.

General Markos mustered about 2,500 men for the operation, the largest force he had assembled so far, which involved over forty units. Balkan staff officers had been lent to help with the planning as there was no Democratic Army infrastructure for command, communication or supply capable of handling this number of troops in battle. On July 13th, about twenty-five Democratic Army units, in three columns, moved on a wide front towards Konitza from the Albanian border, bumping the first strong GNA opposition at Borazani Bridge, about two miles from the town. The bridge over the River Aoos was taken and destroyed; and, having partially surrounded the town, the Democratic Army units moved into the assault.

The fighting went on for three days and altogether several attacks were made, but all were repulsed by the garrison GNA reinforcements were flown in to Konitza by commandeered Dakotas from the civil air lines, and a strong GNA force, with tanks[1] and covering aircraft, moved up from Jannina to deploy against the insurgent road blocks and picquets in the surrounding mountains.

There had been an initial delay in dispatching GNA reinforcements as the Greek General Staff thought this assault was a feint made to draw away GNA troops from other parts of northern

[1] The GNA had a number of British Centaur tanks, but the terrain in northern Greece restricted their use and value.

Greece, but once the magnitude was appreciated they were moved quickly and in strength. By this time the Democratic Army impetus was spent, and the assaults were discontinued for the simple reason that General Markos had lost control of his men. His communications had completely broken down and his troops faded from the battlefield.

This attempt to take Konitza had failed, partly because the collection of Democratic Army units was not used to working as part of a large formation, and partly because the defenders had better fire power. The insurgents were not trained to assault strong points and carry out sustained actions, and although there was in the Democratic Army a brave and aggressive element prominent in all the fighting, there were many more who were cautious and even reluctant in battle. Insurgent units failed to respond to orders, they were slow to move to their battle positions, they turned up in the wrong places and gave ground prematurely and dispersed under heavy fire. The fault was mainly lack of good communications. The units had old wireless sets which did not always work.

General Markos, commanding personally in the field as ever, tried to take Kastoria a few days later, using fresh insurgent units raised in and around that area. GNA troops had been thinned from this district to take part in the Konitza battle, and he hoped to jump in and strike hard before they could be reinforced. Kastoria was easy to isolate, but easy to defend. Markos was unsuccessful.

Then, on the 25th, he had a try at taking Grevena, mustering over 1,200 men, some of whom had taken part in the battle for Konitza. This project also failed, as the GNA was able to move forward sufficient troops to block the attempt in time. The towns of Konitza, Kastoria and Grevena were cut off from one another, and only heavily armed convoys or patrols could make contact through insurgent-infested terrain.

On the 31st about 600 men of the Democratic Army unsuccessfully attacked Alexandroupolis, in Thrace. This was one of the few operations of any size that was not personally directed by General Markos.

Although in control of most of the countryside, it was now obvious to the Balkan staff officers—as it had been to General Markos from the start—that the Democratic Army, which was nothing more than a collection of small, semi-independent insurgent units, was not capable of waging positional warfare, or of taking defended towns. Insurgent casualties in killed, wounded and deserters, had been heavy, and morale had been shaken, especially by the setback at Konitza, where once again the mythical International Brigades had failed to turn up to help as promised.

Markos persuaded his Balkan sponsors that the only sound solution—for the time being, at any rate—was to revert to widespread guerrilla insurrection to wear down the GNA. He would disperse his units throughout Greece to pinprick the Government forces and dominate the people. He knew he neither had the means nor the operational or administrative machinery to enable his units to take on the GNA in a series of straight battles. A long training period for officers and men would be necessary to precede a gradual welding together of the Democratic Army units into field formations. General Markos was convinced that a victory in the field could only be achieved when the still-hoped-for International Brigades arrived.

As Minister for Public Order, General Zervas took extremely repressive measures against the Communists in Greece. Zakhariadis' utterances had forewarned him of the KKE plans, and in July he made wholesale arrests, alleging he had proof that the Democratic Army GHQ had transmitted orders to the EAM in Greece to call up all reservists and to prepare for general insurrection and sabotage. Within days he had detained about 2,500 in Athens, and others in Salonika, Volos, Larissa and Kavalla, until the total exceeded 3,000. Amongst those arrested were Partsalidis, the Secretary-General of EAM, most of the EAM Central Committee and the majority of the staff of the remaining Communist newspaper, *Rizospastis*. This curtailed the activities of YIAFAKA. Several members of OPLA were also detained.

OPLA, the terrorist wing of the KKE, had been periodically active, and amongst its several acts of violence it had murdered some air force officers. Of the OPLA men arrested, over twenty were eventually condemned to death for this crime.

Uneasy political instability persisted, and Maximos was unable to broaden the basis of his government to include moderate parties, as both Britain and America would have liked him to do. They insisted that to have any chance of quelling the insurrection the Greek Government must have the support of a much wider section of the population than it had. Maximos resigned on August 27th over criticism of the severe measures taken by Zervas against the Communists. Neither Zervas nor Gonatas, another member of the Government, was liked by the Americans. It was said that Zervas had deported over 15,000 people to the Aegean Islands. Tsaldaris tried, but failed to form a government; but eventually on September 7th, Sophoulis,[1] then over eighty years of age, managed to form a coalition.

In the diplomatic sphere relations between Greece and the Communist states became more strained. The Soviet Union had withdrawn its ambassador in April, and he was still away. In August the Yugoslav Chargé d'Affaires and his staff left Athens.

On August 16th the Democratic Army Radio[2] declared that a 'Free and Independent Republic' would be formed, and went on to say that local elections would be held in the 'liberated' areas. Two months previously, Zakhariadis and Porphyroyenis (of the Central Committee of the KKE) had attended the Congress of the French Communist Party at Strasbourg, where they tentatively put forward the idea of setting up a 'Free Democratic Government' of Greece, to see what the reaction would be and what support they might expect to get for it from fellow Comrades. They were encouraged by the reception the suggestion received.

In riposte, the Greek Government offered an amnesty to insurgents who gave themselves up, and the Greek air force dropped thousands of leaflets over territory held by them. This again did not quite have the effect that was hoped, although it caused the Democratic Army leaders some anxiety. The political officers of the units clamped down strictly and no one was allowed to read the leaflets. Men caught doing so were severely dealt with, while a few who discussed the contents were executed.

The Greek Government held an unduly and indeed unwarrantedly optimistic view of its supremacy over the Democratic Army. The period of the amnesty, which should have terminated on September 14th, was extended for another month. During this time the Government claimed that just over 5,000 insurgents surrendered, of whom over half were 'pressed' men. This number, although slightly exaggerated and including the normal toll of deserters, was a disappointment as the Government had hoped that with the winter coming on the bleak prospect of being hunted in the mountains

---

[1] Sophoulis was born in Samos. He had organized a revolt against the Turks in 1908, was sentenced to death, but escaped to Greece. He was then active in Greek politics. He was interned by the Axis Authorities during the Occupation, and was released by the Allies.

[2] The Democratic Army Radio station, situated near Tirana, in Albania, at first, had been opened for broadcasting on July 17th, 1947. It was later moved to Yugoslavia. Before this the Democratic Army had used both the Albanian radio station at Tirana, and that at Sophia, in Bulgaria, to make its announcements. Facilities were still allowed to both the KKE and the Democratic Army on these two state radio stations.

would cause wholesale surrenders.[1] During the year the Government had released about 10,000 from exile or detention, but almost at once the younger ones had gone off to join the Democratic Army and many of the others had gravitated to the YIAFAKA.

Military agreements had been re-negotiated at Bled in Yugoslavia between General Markos and representatives of the Yugoslav, Albanian and Bulgarian General Staffs, with Soviet officers looking on. It was decided to provide the Democratic Army with technical stores, such as trucks and wireless sets, as well as more weapons, and to increase training facilities. A Balkan Joint Staff was formed of officers from Yugoslavia, Bulgaria and Albania, on which Yugoslav officers predominated, to assist the Democratic Army in its insurgent campaign. The three Balkan countries also agreed to have troops ready near their frontiers to support the insurgents in case the GNA tried to force its way across the frontiers after them.

In return, the price extracted was that the Democratic Army should be guided and advised by the Joint Balkan Staff, which was to co-ordinate operations and supplies. No senior member of the Democratic Army was to be removed or changed without its approval. This Yugoslav domination (as in fact Yugoslavia controlled the Balkan Joint Staff) took some time to implement and was resisted by Markos and the KKE leaders, but Markos had to frequently fall in with Yugoslav plans, often against his will and better judgement. It was realized that Yugoslav aims and those of the KKE did not always coincide.

The formation of the Cominform in October 1947 when the Communists of nine countries[2] set up an Information Bureau to co-ordinate the activities of the Communist Parties and to exchange information and experiences did not help Greece. The Cominform was established at Belgrade in Yugoslavia and the KKE of Greece was excluded, probably on the insistence of Tito who was busily intriguing for Trieste and because of the proximity of the UN debate on Greece. Albania was not included either, but at once applied to join.

---

[1] In November 1947, it was alleged that the Greek Government was encouraging 'head hunting', and photographs were published in foreign newspapers of members of the Greek Government forces carrying or exhibiting human heads. On November 13th, Rentis, the Minister of Public Order, explained to foreign journalists that the insurgents were 'criminals', with a price on their heads, and that it was an old Greek custom to 'produce the head' when demanding payment. However, he said he had ordered the custom to stop.

[2] The founder countries of the Cominform were the USSR, Yugoslavia, Poland, Rumania, Hungary, Czechoslovakia and Bulgaria, and the founder Communist Parties were those of France and Italy.

During the summer the Democratic Army strengthened its hold on the countryside, especially in the region of the Pindus Mountains and in northern Greece generally. Forcible recruiting was carried on wherever the insurgents could expect to obtain conscripts, and the underground YIAFAKA used blackmail and the threat of reprisals to procure men and women for the Democratic Army ranks. These recruits were first of all sent to one of the training camps just over the borders outside Greece for a four-week basic course, before being posted to one of the field units. Courses of instruction at the training camps were run for both unit commanders, officers and political officers. The system of command by committee, or 'dual command', was retained in all units.

The strength of the Democratic Army remained about 23,000 men and women, although some authorities insist that it rose to 25,000. These figures include the fighters in the units, the staff and ETA, but not recruits under instruction in the training camps. The recruits fluctuated considerably in number, varying between 3,000 and 7,000. As far as can be roughly estimated, from about this period onwards women amounted to about twenty per cent of the total numbers. All the women were armed and trained to fight, but they were largely employed on logistic tasks. A small proportion of women were always to be found in the ranks of the Democratic Army fighting alongside the men. These women were invariably young and convinced Communists, and as such were a big morale and propaganda asset to the insurgents. The Democratic Army, like ELAS, had a romantic appeal to many young people.

The size of the insurgent battalions in the field increased until many had a strength of between 200 and 250. It is estimated that in mid-1947 there were between sixty-five and seventy of these battalions inside Greece, of which just over half were in and around the Frontier Corner and in Epirus. About twenty battalions, consisting of over 5,000 of the best insurgent fighters, were actually in the Frontier Corner, guarding the passes and the GHQ. Another twenty-four battalions were in Macedonia and Thrace, and the remainder were in Thessaly and the Peloponnese. There were a few additional battalions, usually those in the process of forming or being re-formed after being knocked about in battle, in the border areas just outside Greece.

Towns such as Konitza, Florina and Kastoria, which were set amid insurgent-dominated territory, were almost literally besieged, and strong armed convoys were the chief means of distributing food and supplies to them. Aircraft were also used whenever they could be spared from operational sorties. Airstrips were constructed at some of the frontier towns so that reinforcements could be flown in at a moment's notice in case of attack by insurgents.

During the summer the ETA (the quartermastering organization) was re-cast. Some of its functions had been blurred by YIAFAKA, but now tasks and duties were more clearly defined. YIAFAKA was made responsible for recruiting, obtaining money and supplies from towns, for controlling the Communist underground and for sending information to the Democratic Army. OPLA still operated and occasionally carried out acts of terrorism and reprisal.

As the Democratic Army increased in size and settled on large sections of the countryside, so conventional lines of supply were required, and ETA became almost entirely a field supply organization for the insurgent units in the field, although it continued to work closely with YIAFAKA. The supply system was on a territorial basis as far as possible, and small ETA units were established in certain convenient places, and were made responsible for forwarding food and ammunition on to the insurgent units in their areas. The distribution was carried out mainly at night, and mules were extensively used. YIAFAKA still produced a small proportion of the food and most of the medicines and drugs, but by mid-1947 the bulk of the rations and all the ammunition for the Democratic Army came from beyond the Greek frontiers, thus providing ETA with a more or less straightforward job of distribution in the field under battle conditions.

The ETA supply units, consisting of between fifty and sixty men and women, remained static; whenever Government forces swept through a region the unit hid its stores and mules and split up, the personnel either temporarily taking to the mountains or going underground, until it was safe to emerge and re-form again. The Democratic Army fighting units took guerrilla-like avoiding action when faced by superior bodies of the GNA and moved elsewhere whenever necessary, but the framework of the ETA stayed put. ETA units were also responsible for the setting up of small supply caches at strategic points and for evacuating the wounded.

The insurgents' armaments improved, and soon most units possessed a variety of mortars, anti-tank weapons and machine-guns, as well as small arms and grenades. This multiplicity of different types of weapons caused a complex ammunition problem. Ammunition was inevitably scarce and the Democratic Army never had enough, so it had to be hoarded and expended carefully, even in battle. The mountain guns provided by Yugoslavia were either kept in the Frontier Corner or just outside the Greek frontiers. This was partly because an artillery piece is hardly a guerrilla weapon as it is a drag on mobility, partly because of the problem of transporting ammunition, and partly so that the gun could be quickly withdrawn to diplomatic safety if threatened by a superior GNA force.

It was estimated that about seventy-five per cent of the small arms in use by the Democratic Army, and all the mortars, anti-tank weapons and artillery, had been obtained from Balkan sources. The remaining twenty-five per cent of the small arms were British, German or Italian models, which the insurgents had possessed for some time. Precise numbers of arms were difficult to assess at any particular stage, but all members of the Democratic Army, including recruits under training, were armed with some sort of weapon. Reports that the insurgent recruiting was geared to the number of arms available may have been largely true, as the KKE view, and that of General Markos in particular, was always that an unarmed insurgent was of little use in the field.

It was now fully realized that Greece was in the throes of a deadly civil war, and to dispel any lingering doubts the Greek Government issued some figures alleging that between October 12th, 1944, and September 25th, 1947, the Communist forces had killed over 45,000 civilians. Allowing for a slight exaggeration and any miscalculations, this must have been broadly correct and it showed the enormity of the conflict. The Greek Government admitted that in the same period over 3,000 gendarmes and 1,000 soldiers had been killed by the Communists. Also there were over 400,000 refugees who had been displaced from the battle areas, and who were now crammed into the towns, causing a gigantic feeding and accommodation problem.

The first shiploads of American military aid to Greece arrived at Salonika in August 1947 and others followed in the ensuing months.[1] This enabled the Greek armed forces to be re-equipped and increased in size. During the summer AMAG had been taking stock of what was required, and by the end of the year the Greek military forces were entirely supported by American aid. The British Military Mission remained, but was reduced in size and influence as the Americans made their presence felt.

---

[1] During the next five months the US shipped some 74,000 tons of military equipment to Greece.

Under American guidance a drive was made to repair and improve communications. Work on the reconstruction of docks, railways, roads and bridges was given first priority. Also, airstrips were scratched out near many garrison towns, if this had not been done already, to facilitate communication and physical contact. The US aid, which was not all military, was timely as UNRRA supplies had ceased in June 1947.[1]

In conjunction with the Greek General Staff, plans were drawn up to expand the Greek armed forces, and in September it was announced that the Greek National Army (GNA) would be increased to 200,000. The regular army proper, which had reached a strength of about 120,000, was to double its field force of about fifty battalions, and would call up another 30,000 men to enable this to be realized. The GNA consisted basically of eight infantry divisions and three independent brigades, all organized on the British pattern: that is, with three brigades in each division and three battalions in each brigade. However, some divisions had only two brigades, and some brigades only two battalions. The extra infantry battalions were required to fill out the framework of the eight divisions.

It was also planned that special commando units, which became known as LOK units, were to be formed and trained in anti-insurgent warfare, while the infantry units generally were to be made more mobile and their fire-power increased.

The Greek air force was to receive US dive-bombers and napalm bombs, and the Greek navy was promised six naval patrol vessels to facilitate coastal co-operation with the land forces.

The National Guard, which had been badly knocked about, was to be re-formed with a strength of 50,000. It was to consist of 100 battalions, each of about 500 men under regular officers, and was to be composed of army reservists, gendarmes and local defence volunteers. Its task was to patrol the countryside and to deal with small groups of insurgents, thus leaving the GNA free for offensive operations against larger Democratic Army concentrations.

So far the GNA had used 'selective' conscription, although this was publicly denied, not taking anyone with known Communist views or connections, which meant that such young men were left free either to push off and join the Democratic Army in the mountains if they wished, or to work underground for the YIAFAKA.

---

[1] UNRRA had supplied Greece with 2,667,500 tons of supplies, mainly food, since 1945. This was second only in bulk to the amount given to Italy by UNRRA.

This policy was changed and all conscripts, regardless of political affiliations, were scooped up and compelled to serve in the GNA whenever their age groups were called up. Left-wing personnel conscripted were segregated and given political instruction. Extremists who did not respond were sent to island corrective camps[1] where more serious attempts were made to wean them from their political convictions. The really hard cases were simply isolated and kept apart in groups.

The KKE tried a political manœuvre in September 1947, when the Democratic Army offered to cease-fire[2] provided an all-party government, which would include the EAM, was formed in Greece. It also asked to be allowed to lay its case before the General Assembly of the UN. This was taken as a sign of weakness by the Greek Government, which did not bother to reply.

The Greek Government also declined to be drawn on a memorandum sent to it by the EAM, demanding the restoration of constitutional liberty, the release of political prisoners and the abolition of security committees that had the power to imprison and deport. The EAM stressed that it had no connection with the Democratic Army; but Sophoulis, the Prime Minister, would not hear of any conditions being imposed by the Communists. The EAM also insisted that the Government disarm and disband the Local Defence Volunteers, whom the Communists referred to as 'bandits of the right'. The Government refused to do this as they were about to be incorporated into the re-formed National Guard.

The Americans took a much tougher line than had the British, who had been cautious and reluctant to interfere in Greek domestic politics or to hurt Greek susceptibilities. On October 18th, for example, on American insistence, the Communist newspaper *Rizospastis* was closed down.[3] In December, the right to strike was abolished, and then there was a purge of all Government employees who were Communists, suspected of Communist sympathies or had been engaged in disseminating Communist propaganda. The Americans said that all this should have been done months before.

---

[1] The main camps were on the islands of Makronnisos and Yioura.

[2] Strangely enough this offer was made through the columns of *The Times* (London), to which General Markos sent a letter, extracts of which were published in that newspaper on September 10th, 1947.

[3] On August 6th, 1947, *Rizospastis* had published a proclamation from General Markos, urging the Athens Communists to murder certain ministers, who included Zervas, Gonatas and Papandreou. Despite this and its general vindictive outpourings, it had been allowed to continue publication.

On November 18th, a Joint Greek-US Army Staff was formed, which was to be responsible for planning, equipping and supplying all operations that were undertaken. It overshadowed the British Military Mission which merely retained the responsibility for training and organization of the Greek forces. The US military mission was enlarged from sixty-two officers and men to over ninety officers and eighty men. Apart from staff duties, a number of American officers were employed as observers with headquarters and divisions. American officers did not command formations or units, but were in a position to ensure that joint formulated plans were pushed through and not side-tracked, avoided or ignored.

So far the operational direction of the campaign against the Democratic Army had been left in Greek hands. Like the British, who had not pushed their suggestions too hard, the Americans, too, had in the first instance confined their activities to the logistic spheres, but this policy changed when it was seen that the Greek generals did not seem to be able to formulate a constructive and successful strategic plan.

The GNA counter-measures in 1947 had been so unsuccessful because of its piecemeal deployment in static defence. To obtain the release of infantry battalions for field operations, or for any re-deployment of units, no matter how small, the approval and permission of the Greek General Staff had to be obtained. Owing to political pressures at high level in Athens this was not freely given and was often delayed. This political drag militated against economy of manpower, dampened the offensive spirit and retarded manoeuvre of the GNA, factors so vital in view of its small size and the gigantic task it had to accomplish.

In December 1947 a Joint US Military Advisory and Planning Group, JUSMAPG, was formed to co-ordinate operations and to give logistic advice. US tactical experts were brought in, and battle plans were hammered out by the Americans, although it was all done in the name of the Joint Staff. JUSMAPG took a tough line and insisted that all its recommendations be carried into effect, at once and in full. This attitude of urgency was something new to Greece, its Government, its General Staff and its politicians.

During the autumn, the Democratic Army continued its policy of guerrilla insurrection, attacking small towns and villages, and committing acts of sabotage.[1] The main trouble spots were: around

---

[1] The Greek Government alleged that in the month of October 1947, for example, the Democratic Army had attacked and pillaged 83 villages, destroyed 218 buildings, blown 34 bridges and wrecked 11 railway trains.

Konitza; Delvinakion, adjacent to the Albanian frontier; the Kaimakchalan, Kroussia and Vermion Mountains, near the Yugoslav frontier; and the Souphli region, adjacent to Bulgaria. There were eruptions in the Mount Olympus Range, around Mount Parnassus and in the Kandilion Mountains, and also outbreaks in the area of the Taygetus and the Parnon Mountains in the Peloponnese.

In northern and north-western Greece, the Government troops had concentrated in the towns since the battle for Florina (May–June 1947), when all isolated outposts had been withdrawn, thus virtually handing over large stretches of the terrain to the insurgents. For example, the whole region from the Grammos Mountains to the Aliakmon Valley lay unprotected and at the mercy of the Democratic Army.

During the last week of October and the first week of November, there were several sharp clashes between the insurgents and the GNA in the area of the Metsovo Pass, where General Markos was again personally directing operations in the field. There was also spasmodic fighting in the district of Grevena and towards the Albanian frontier, but that died down by early December when there was a lull as the snows began to fall and block the mountain passes.

Under American urging, the field battalions of the GNA were more active in chasing the insurgents in the autumn. In June it had been declared impossible to spare any of the twenty battalions of the II Corps, based on Larissa, from Central Greece to help in the north. Now the majority of the Greek infantry units were moved into the northern part of the country, and grouped into what became known as the Northern Greek Command.

General Markos would have been content to continue his satisfyingly successful erosive insurgent tactics, but his hand was again forced. Both Albania and Bulgaria loudly pressed for the early proclamation of a 'Free Democratic Government' to be established on Greek soil. From a political point of view, local elections had been held in 'Free Greece' in October, on the familiar Communist one-party pattern, and a Communist form of government and administration had been imposed on a large number of villages. On the military side it was pointed out that the insurgents held the Frontier Corner, where so far the GNA had not dared to attempt to penetrate, and that the Democratic Army should now be ready and capable of successfully assaulting a town. Some training in conventional warfare had been given to both officers and men.

Yugoslavia remained cautious, being of the opinion that support of a Greek Communist Government on Greek soil might provoke the Americans into giving all-out military aid, instead of merely restricted help, perhaps to the extent of sending American-manned aircraft and American ground troops. Yugoslavia wanted to see a Greek Communist Government, but not necessarily on Greek territory. Yugoslav aid, which now included heavy artillery,[1] was conditional on parts of Greece being detached into a Yugoslav federation, and Tito was not quite sure how America would react if this became commonly known.

The KKE leaders were now ready and willing to proclaim a Communist Government. Markos felt somewhat snubbed by the negative reaction to his cease-fire offer, and others were bitter about the rejection of the EAM suggestions that it take part in an all-party government. Zakhariadis was especially in favour, owing to the warm reception of his suggestion at the French Communist Congress and the promises he had received there. He thought any such government would at once be recognized by all Communist countries; but like Markos he was dubious of the wisdom of seizing and holding a Greek town as a provisional capital. Markos knew this would provide an irresistible target for the Greek air force and the GNA guns to hammer away at. General Markos, while feeling confident of his ability to take such a town, doubted the ability of his men to hold it against the concentrated might of the GNA.

However, it was decided that this course should be taken, and on December 24th a 'Free Democratic Greek Government' was proclaimed over the Democratic Army Radio, and the next day, the 25th, General Markos launched his units into a large-scale assault on Konitza. Why the two events took place in that order is not absolutely clear. The most likely explanation is that it was the intention to take Konitza first, and then announce a Free Democratic Government from the captured town, but that owing to the lack of adequate infrastructure there were delays and the attack could not get under way on time – being, in fact, several days late.

The broadcast from the Democratic Army Radio in Albania, announcing to the world the formation of a Provisional Democratic Government of Greece, declared that the first object was to establish diplomatic relations with friendly disposed states; but to the dismay and chagrin of the KKE, despite promises, not a single foreign government recognized it, not even that of the Soviet Union, or those

[1] In October 1947, 45 75mm guns and 15 105mm guns had been sent to the Democratic Army from Yugoslavia and Bulgaria. Most were in the Frontier Corner.

of the three Balkan countries that had pressed the Greek Communists so hard to take this step. While in all Communist newspapers in all countries the new Government was welcomed, no official comments were made at all by any of the Balkan Governments. The only visible reaction was that in Sophia in Bulgaria a committee was set up to give moral and political support to it.

Markos was appointed Prime Minister and Minister of Defence, and he called for a strong army, air force and navy to resist aggression. His Government consisted of eight members,[1] all Communists except one, all of whom had been prominent in the resistance movement against the Axis Occupation. A ten-point programme[2] was announced.

Zakhariadis, still the Secretary-General of the KKE and the top man in the Greek Communist hierarchy, was not included in the new 'government', preferring to remain in the background. The reason for this may have been that he thought General Markos, the insurgent leader in the field, might make a better public figure, at home and abroad, to rally everyone to continue the fight that was by no means won. In fact, victory was not even in sight. Also, Zakhariadis probably thought that when the insurgent war was nearly over and won, he could come forward and take the leading political office, when he would be in a position to repudiate all the unfavourable agreements that Markos had made and might be

---

[1] The Free Democratic Government was listed as follows:

Markos Vaphiadis—Prime Minister and Minister of Defence.

Ionides—Deputy Prime Minister (Member of the Central Committee of the KKE)

Roussos—Member of the Central Committee of the KKE. (He had been a representative of the KKE in wartime Cairo).

Porphyroyenis—Member of the Central Committee of the KKE. (He had been acting Secretary-General of the EAM, since Partsalides had been detained.)

Barzotas—Member of the Central Committee of the KKE.

Stringos—Member of the Central Committee of the KKE.

Vlandas—Member of the Central Committee of the KKE. (A Cretan.)

Kokkalis—A former PEEA Member. The only non-Communist.

[2] The Ten-Point Programme was:

1. Mobilization of popular forces to liberate Greece.
2. Establishment of popular justice.
3. Nationalization of foreign assets and heavy industry.
4. Agrarian reforms.
5. Reconciliation amongst Greek people.
6. Reorganization of the country on democratic lines.
7. Friendly relations with democratic states within the UN framework.
8. Recognition of full equality amongst minorities.
9. Creation of armed forces to resist aggression.
10. Holding of elections.

compelled to make in the future to obtain sufficient aid to carry on the war.

The Greek Government took the announcement as Communist bravado, but nevertheless arrested over 500 people in Athens alone.

On December 25th, fourteen battalions of the Democratic Army, numbering over 2,000 men, under the command of General Markos, moved southwards from the Grammos Range in the Frontier Corner towards Konitza, while another 1,000 insurgents caused havoc elsewhere in Thessaly and Epirus. At first they settled on the heights overlooking the town and then took Borazani Bridge, over the River Aoos, which controlled the approaches on the most vulnerable side.

The insurgent attackers had a profusion of mortars, two batteries of mountain guns and three or four heavy guns (105mm), which were used to shell Konitza preparatory to moving into the attack. Some of the guns were sited in Albanian territory, but the smaller ones, such as the Skoda 75mm, moved right forward and got into a good position from which they were not dislodged until January 4th (1948). Several assaults were made from different angles, but all were repulsed by the defenders, who amounted to about 900 GNA troops.

Argyrokastron, a large village just over the Albanian frontier, was a supply-collecting centre for the insurgents from where rations, ammunition and men were sent by truck down the road to the frontier, and then towards Konitza. The volume of fire, both small arms and artillery, surprised the GNA, and also the fact that the firing continued day after day. This showed that Markos and the Balkan Joint Staff had stockpiled ammunition ready for such a battle. The battle headquarters of General Markos was at the village of Kastaniani, near the border.

Heavy rain retarded the dispatch of GNA reinforcements, and it was not until the 30th that strong columns from both Jannina and Grevena arrived and made contact with the Democratic Army units on the outskirts of the town. Under cover of both air and artillery support, the Government troops, in a series of disjointed battles, cleared the insurgent units from the high ground. The Borazani Bridge area held out longer, which prevented the GNA detachments from entering the besieged town. The new weapons provided by America, which included some automatic rifles and mortars, were brought into use, and the Greek air force strafed with machine-gun fire and rockets. The American idea of the more liberal use of fire-power, which was now able to be adopted by the GNA, caused many insurgent casualties.

The constant hammering from shells, bombs and bullets drove back the Democratic Army attackers, but they gave ground reluctantly at first. As casualties mounted panic set in amongst some units, which began to withdraw on January 1st. Withdrawal became more rapid, but even so several insurgent units clung fast to their positions in and around Konitza, and the two artillery batteries carried on firing. It was not until January 7th that the GNA stood triumphant in Konitza.

Democratic Army units only retreated as far as they were forced, remaining watchful and wary just outside shell range. Kastaniani, where Markos had his command headquarters, remained in his hands.

Once again the Democratic Army had failed to take a defended town. This time the failure had been costly, as its casualties were over 1,200 in killed, wounded and deserters. The newly proclaimed Democratic Government was still without a provisional capital on Greek soil.

During 1947 Democratic Army units had spread out to dominate large areas of Greece, but they had failed in all their attempts to seize towns. In the first part of the year, the GNA had been outclassed by insurgent tactics and its morale began to fall. The GNA policy of concentrating troops in the frontier town rather than in the countryside gave them a defensive mentality.

By the end of the year American aid was arriving in quantity, and this arrested the deteriorating situation. American drive prodded the GNA into action; which, while not accomplishing a great deal from a military point of view, did at least help to confine the Democratic Army units to the mountains, especially in Thessaly. On the whole, despite superiority of manpower, weapons and transport, the GNA failed to resume the offensive.

CHAPTER NINE

A Year of Stalemate

The successful repulse of the Democratic Army attack on Konitza gave both the Greek Government and JUSMAPG hope that a spring offensive would break the back of the revolt and pave the way for a large summer clearing operation that would put a satisfactory end to the civil war. This did not happen, and despite more American aid there came the dull realization as the year wore on that hardly any real impression was being made on the Democratic Army, which was holding on to all its gains by the skilful use of insurgent tactics.

After his failure, General Markos went off to Belgrade to confer with the Balkan Joint Staff and to thrash out future policy. Disappointed at the defeat, Tito withheld recognition of the Democratic Government, which it is believed he had promised should Konitza be taken. Markos convinced the Balkan Joint Staff—which in effect meant the Yugoslav staff officers on it—that his original idea of widespread insurgent mobile warfare designed to disperse and wear down the GNA was the best method in the circumstances. He seems to have had his way, which was also endorsed by his 'Government' and most of the members of the Central Committee of the KKE, although Zakhariadis and others were impatient and doubtful. There was a gradual shift of Democratic Army units from Albania to Yugoslavia, and Yugoslavia assumed a more proprietorial air over them. The Democratic Army Radio moved to that country: the Markos Government was already there.

Partsalidis had escaped from a detention camp on December 25th (1947), and with other prominent Communists made his way to

Yugoslavia. He too, having ELAS experience, supported the 'Markos Plan' to revert to insurgent operations and to leave strongly defended towns alone.

It was agreed that Balkan aid to the Democratic Army would continue on much the same scale, to enable it to wage insurgent war against the Greek Government. General Markos, in his negotiations, had asked for material aid on a grander scale, and indeed his pronouncements envisaged a 'strong air force and navy'. He hoped that Albania might provide him with some small ships and the use of certain harbours, and Yugoslavia and Bulgaria some aircraft and the use of airfields. Neither Yugoslavia nor Bulgaria did this, perhaps for the obvious reason that they were not prepared to become openly involved in the Greek Civil War for fear of provoking America into taking military action against them. They could not be absolutely certain that Stalin would help them in such a contingency. Two airstrips were scratched out in the Frontier Corner, near Lake Prespa, and this caused some alarm, especially as the Democratic Army Radio appealed for pilots and air crew. However, the Democratic Army remained without aircraft, and in fact never possessed any at all.

A few small sea-going ships were obtained from Albania and used to transport men and supplies. ELAN, the old naval counterpart of ELAS, was revived and became active around the Gulf of Corinth and along the west coast of Greece. In March (1948) an old Italian submarine was acquired by ELAN, and it was used to ferry stores and personnel across the Adriatic Sea by night.

Heavier arms of sorts still flowed to the Democratic Army, including numbers of mortars, anti-aircraft and field guns. On February 8th, the insurgents used flame-throwers in a spectacular raid on a train in northern Greece, and on May 10th two Greek air force planes were shot down in the fighting over Grevena.

Had the KKE been able to establish a Democratic Government at Konitza perhaps these Balkan countries may have been prepared to assist more freely and openly, but as it was caution and wariness were the watchwords.

For the first three months of the year (1948) there were spasmodic clashes between the GNA and the Democratic Army in several parts of Greece, especially in the frontier areas. The Democratic Army concentrated upon damaging communications so as to isolate GNA garrisons in towns, and also embarked upon a deliberate policy of destroying villages in order to drive the inhabitants into the towns

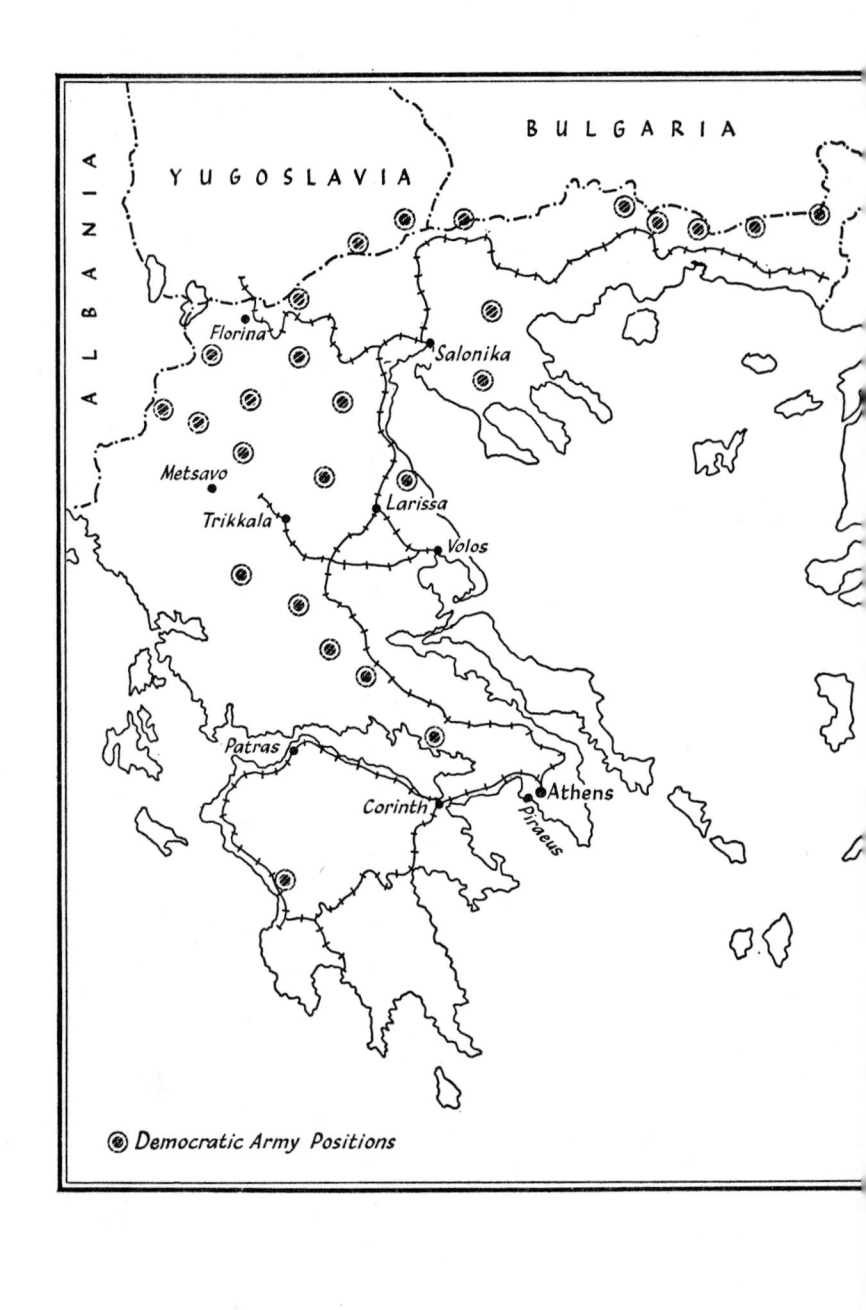

® Democratic Army Positions

to exacerbate the already acute housing and feeding problems. The insurgent units continued to assault villages and small towns generally over a wide area, but this time the main objects were to recruit forcibly, to further terrorism and to spread the feeling of insecurity by showing the people that Government forces could not protect them.

Owing to a combination of GNA fire power, faulty Democratic Army tactics and poor leadership of units, the insurgent casualties in the field were exceptionally heavy. The Greek Government estimated that in the twelve months ending March 1948 the insurgents lost 20,284 killed, captured and deserted, of whom over 9,000 were killed. The strength of the Democratic Army had sunk to about 21,000, and an energetic recruiting campaign was carried out in the first three months of 1948, bringing its strength up to over 26,000. There was no longer any question of merely taking a 'quota' to replace casualties or to increase strength consistent with the quantity of arms available; now all were swept into the net and none allowed to escape. A few still volunteered, as the idea of being an insurgent fighter at large in the mountains had its romantic attraction to Greek youth, and a few more were half-persuaded and half-dragged in by YIAFAKA, but the large majority of those taken in 1948 were reluctant and protesting men and women. Women had always been accepted by the Democratic Army since its formation, but they had been volunteers or, perhaps at the worst, semi-volunteers. However, from the autumn of 1947 they were also recruited forcibly on a grand scale.

Under American prodding, elements of the GNA, amounting to the major part of six divisions and a few LOK (Commando) units, were active in the mountains during the first three months of the year against the insurgents, and on the whole these operations were fairly profitable. They were conducted during bad weather, and the Government claimed that in this period 754 insurgents were killed, 571 captured and 289 surrendered. The Democratic Army fighters hated being harried amid the bleak, inhospitable, snow-bound mountains.

Determined to finish off the Civil War in 1948, JUSMAPG insisted that the GNA make full preparations quickly for a strong spring offensive. There were over 250 American officers in Greece, of whom over fifty were attached to Greek formations and units in the field. More American arms, including 75mm guns, were promised. In January, the GNA was given over $25 million-worth of ex-German war material; early in February the first US aircraft were delivered;[1] and at the end of that month 35,000 British rifles, purchased partly by Greek residents in the UK and partly subsidized by AMAG funds, were sent to Greece.

AMAG had been compelled to increase the military aid programme at the expense of the economic one, and already an additional $14 million had been allocated towards equipping the re-forming National Guard. By mid-February it was announced that enough small arms and equipment had been received to increase the National Guard battalions from fifty-four to sixty-six, and by the end of March America had delivered over $71 million-worth of military equipment, which included 75,000 weapons of all types, 7,000 tons of ammunition and 2,800 trucks and vehicles, together with 'large numbers' of aircraft, probably trainers. The exact number of American aircraft delivered to the Greek air force was not made public, and it is believed that they included some on temporary loan from time to time.

On February 7th, General James A. Van Fleet was appointed to command JUSMAPG; and a week later, to further the more efficient and energetic prosecution of the war, both he and the officer commanding the British Military Mission (Major-General Rawlings) joined the Greek National Defence Council in an advisory capacity. They were thus able to baulk political pressures to some extent. The British Military Mission retained responsibility for training, while the Americans took over advising on operations and supplying equipment to the Greek armed forces.

An attempt was made to reorganize the GNA at the top to decentralize command and to encourage greater initiative on the part of the commanders in the field. General Ventiris, the commander of the Northern Army, was brought in as Chief of the General Staff, and the Northern Army as a formation disappeared. The field army was organized into five corps, instead of three, all of which now came under the direct control of the Chief of the General Staff. Formerly, each corps commander had been directly responsible to the National Defence Council for operations, and the troops in the Peloponnese had come under the Minister for Public Security. General Ventiris was later retired, and replaced by General Yiandzis.

In May 1948, authorized increases were made in the strength of the Greek armed forces. The air force was increased from 6,500 to

---

[1] There was still a small RAF training mission attached to the Greek air force, but apart from this the RAF had only one flight (of 6 aircraft) remaining in Greece.

7,200, and the navy from 13,000 to 14,300. An extra 15,000 men were authorized for the army. This brought the total authorized strength for all the armed forces to 168,000.

The Greek Government took strong action in the civil sphere to back up the GNA in the field, and many convicted of subversion against the country were tried and executed. For example, twenty-nine persons were shot on February 7th for aiding the insurgents, another nineteen on the 22nd, and seventeen more on the 27th, some of the latter for their part in shelling Salonika a fortnight before. On March 1st sixty Greek sailors were arrested and accused of conspiring to seize control of the Greek navy, and on the 13th fourteen prominent Communists, who included two members of the Central Committee of the KKE and the editor of *Rizospastis* the Communist newspaper, were seized while attempting to leave the country.

The police successfully broke up a number of YIAFAKA cells in Athens, Piraeus and Salonika, arresting over 200 members of this underground organization in the south in February, and another fifty in Salonika the following month. Although not so many were caught in northern Greece the police detected and seized quantities of YIAFAKA transport in that part of the country, including several buses, many trucks and some small boats, as well as locating a few small 'factories' that made equipment, uniforms and boots for the Democratic Army.

For quite a time arrests averaged not less than fifty a week, and this tearing inroad into YIAFAKA personnel soon had a damaging effect and hampered its smooth functioning, while the fainter-hearted fellow travellers were deterred from so freely giving voluntary aid by the frequent Government executions of convicted Communists. After having an easy run for several months, YIAFAKA began to run into difficulties on many sides, and fear had to be increasingly used as a lever to enforce active help.

In spring 1948, the GNA, having about 132,000 men, with artillery, armour and two squadrons of aircraft to support them, together with about 50,000 National Guards, faced approximately 23,000 Democratic Army troops, who had little artillery, no armour and no aircraft. On April 15th the GNA began its planned spring offensive,[1] and the first part was aimed at clearing an area of about 2,000 square miles in the 'waist' of Greece, in the region of the Roumeli Mountains. About 20,000 GNA troops, consisting of three

[1] Known as Operation 'Dawn'.

divisions and a few LOK (Commando) units, were deployed against about 2,500 insurgent fighters. The National Guard battalions had been deployed to free the GNA units for this operation.

Greek naval ships bombarded insurgent positions and concentrations along the coast of the Gulf of Corinth, and the Greek air force flew in support overhead. There was hard fighting in the Mornos Valley and around the town of Artotina, but the hard-pressed Democratic Army units, abandoning mules and hostages, took guerrilla-like avoiding action and escaped towards Agrapha. The LOK (Commando) units then made raids up the Karditsa Valley towards that town.

By May 7th the insurgents had been squeezed from that section of the Roumeli Mountains.

The GNA felt quite pleased with this accomplishment, as well it might, for at the cost of a total of 145 casualties it had accounted for 641 insurgents killed and 1,368 captured or surrendered, but it did not exploit the success. After concluding this satisfactory clearing operation, instead of quickly bringing up fresh troops to launch a new offensive elsewhere without giving the Democratic Army any respite, the GNA paused and rested. The Greek General Staff was not able to switch its mind or its men so swiftly from one operation to another, and the opportunity was lost. Apart from some disjointed attacks on insurgent units, the remainder of the month of May was comparatively quiet.

Meanwhile, on May 1st, a member of OPLA, the Communist terrorist organization, murdered the Minister for Justice, Ladas, in Athens. The assassin was captured and many OPLA personnel were arrested.[1] After this tragic event Government executions of convicted Communists increased to such a point that they aroused protest from both Britain and America, and other foreign countries too. The Greek Government admitted that since December 1944, 2,961 persons had been sentenced to death for 'murder with their own hands', of whom 157 were executed up until May 1st, 1948. Between May 4th and 9th, another sixty-one people were executed.

A close surveillance was kept on all Communists and those suspected of left-wing activities. All were now drafted into the armed forces, and those of doubtful reliability were sent to Makronnisos Island for screening; those who would not repudiate the Communist revolution were retained there. In May 1948, there were

---

[1] On June 28th, 1948, six men were executed for being implicated in the Ladas murder.

about 15,000 conscripts on Makronnisos Island–about the average number for some months–in various stages of screening and political instruction. The Greek Government insisted that only about 500 were die-hard Communists[1] who had to be kept apart in detention.

On March 3rd, in Belgrade, at a meeting of the Balkan Youth Conference, it was decided that children between the ages of three and fourteen years living in 'Free Greece' should be taken away and 'cared for' in Cominform countries. Later this territorial restriction was extended, especially around Florina and other regions adjacent to the frontiers. Many children were taken away without their parents' consent, or without their parents properly understanding what was being done, and sent off to 'safety' in Communist countries.

This action caused widespread and deep-felt bitterness, and loud protests were made within Greece and also by foreign countries. It was also alleged by the Greek Government and its supporters that not only were these children abducted, but that they were 'brainwashed', and as soon as they were old enough were recruited into the Democratic Army and sent back into Greece to fight. The extreme youth of some of the insurgents gave colour to this allegation, and a UN Balkan Commission[2] was asked to investigate and report. Both Britain and America urged the Communist governments concerned to return the children to their homes, but usually there was no answer. Yugoslavia openly refused, saying that the children had been given shelter for 'charitable reasons'. On the other hand, the Greek Government took children from certain fringe areas and put them into colonies for care and education, both on the mainland and in the islands. These, in 1948, amounted to about 14,700.

The General Assembly of the UN had taken over the Greek problem in October 1947 when, as the result of the Soviet vetoes, its Security Council was unable to take any action at all. UNSCOB (United Nations Special Committee on the Balkans) was set up and directed by the General Assembly. It went to Greece but received absolutely no co-operation from any other Balkan country. It

[1] There had been a mutiny on Makronnisos Island in February 1948, during which some Communists had been killed.

[2] Eventually, in December 1948, the UN Balkan Commission issued its report, announcing that it had been informed by the Red Cross organizations that 23,696 Greek children had been retained in East European countries. The breakdown of the figure was quoted as being 10,000 in Yugoslavia, 3,801 in Rumania, 3,000 in Hungary, 2,660 in Bulgaria, 2,235 in Czechoslovakia and 2,000 in Albania.

remained, ineffectually hovering near the scene of strife in Greece, occasionally issuing a report.

On May 31st, 1948, General Markos broadcast a peace offer on his Democratic Army Radio, saying that he was willing to discuss pacification proposals if a 'democratic way of life' in Greece was ensured and that the country's independence was guaranteed without foreign intervention. This had been prompted by the deepening Yugoslav-Soviet dispute, which both Zakhariadis and Markos watched with anxiety. On June 28th, the Cominform expelled Yugoslavia for 'retreating from Marxism'.[1] The dilemma of the KKE leaders was to decide which country to support in this Communist quarrel. If they supported the Soviet Union, the fountainhead and leading exponent of Communist thought, would Tito be prepared to continue his help to the Democratic Army? If not (which was most likely), what then? The Soviet Union had not produced anything worthwhile for the Greek insurgents, and Albania and Bulgaria had either more limited means or were less enthusiastic towards the Greeks than the Yugoslavs. The Central Committee of the KKE decided to try to negotiate with the Greek Government if possible, but such a brazen face was put forward that Sophoulis, the Prime Minister, rejected the proposal out of hand.

Nationalist emotion came to the surface, and the Yugoslav attitude to Bulgaria was one of accusing that country of wanting to expand southwards to incorporate Eastern Macedonia and Salonika, an area that Yugoslavia also had designs upon.

About this time there was a changing attitude on the part of many in Greece over the country's relations with other Balkan countries. Some Greeks were in favour of resuming normal diplomatic relations to see if this would ease friction, while others were bitterly and firmly against such a course. On June 7th, the Greek Government said that it had decided to enter into negotiations with Albania for a peace treaty, and on the 13th a Bulgarian offer to resume diplomatic contact was accepted by Greece.

In June, the largest GNA operation of the war was launched, involving nearly 40,000 men. It was a three-pronged advance on to the Grammos Range, and had the object of eliminating the insurgents there, who amounted to about 8,000 or more. A total of six GNA divisions of both the I Corps, in Western Macedonia, and II Corps, in Epirus, took part, three of which were to assault and three to be used to block escape routes.

[1] On July 2nd, 1948, the Cominform headquarters moved to Bucharest.

At the commencement of the Grammos Operation the Democratic Army strength was roughly 24,000 field fighters, being distributed as follows: about 8,000 were in the Grammos and Smolikas Ranges and along the Albanian border as far south as Konitza; about 5,000 were in the Vitsi part of the Frontier Corner; about 5,000 were spread out elsewhere along the Yugoslav and Bulgarian frontiers; 2,000 were in Epirus; about 1,500 were in Central Greece and 2,500 were in the Peloponnese. There were also about 4,000 recruits in training, and wounded waiting to be sent back to their units, making an overall total of about 28,000. This was a maximum, and from this moment onwards the strength of the Democratic Army steadily shrank.

Starting on June 19th (after several days' intense air and artillery bombardment, in which for the first time American 250lb incendiary bombs were used) the main thrust of two divisions advanced from north of Konitza towards the Grammos Range. Two other divisions moved from the Grevena–Metsovo line and made their way towards the objective, while the other two advanced from the region of Nestorion to cut off and block all contact between the Grammos Range and the main part of the Frontier Corner to the north around the Vitsi Range. The object was to isolate the gigantic pocket and prevent its retreat into Albania.

On the 20th, the GNA troops succeeded, after hand-to-hand fighting, in seizing some heights overlooking the Aliakmon Valley, thus settling on one of the main insurgent supply routes.

By the 22nd GNA units had reached the fringe of the Grammos Range and had even penetrated a little way in some places, but they ran up against hard resistance, and despite artillery and air support they could not make any headway at all. The insurgents held grimly on to their heights and the GNA could not budge them. Coming up against this blank wall of rigid opposition, the largest GNA operation so far planned ground ignominiously to a halt, and a stalemate set in which lasted for about six weeks. Only the lower half of the pocket had been partially surrounded. This forced a change of plan.

After these initial gains, the GNA paused while reinforcements were brought up and further artillery and air bombardment carried out. Napalm was dropped on insurgent positions. Democratic Army reinforcements were also rushed in until the total of insurgent fighters in the pocket exceeded 12,000.

The stalemate was costly as both sides strove to oust the other, and there was particularly heavy slogging around a mountain known as

Mount Prophitas, over 5,000 feet high in the Smolikas Range, across the valley to the south and south-east of the Grammos Range. The GNA eventually seized the key position in the Smolika Range: Mount Klephtis, over 6,000 feet.

During the first week of August, the GNA offensive was resumed and the insurgent units were forced backwards one by one under the pressure of heavy fire power. On the 5th, the frontier heights of Golio, Kardari and Steno, all over 6,000 feet, were seized by GNA troops, who fought magnificently, and other similar successes followed in the ensuing days, thus blocking off a section of the Albanian frontier to the insurgents. These positions were not lightly abandoned, and the Democratic Army units put in frequent counter-attacks. Soon the insurgent-held salient into Greece, adjoining Albania, was reduced in size to less than 250 square miles, and parts of it were less than fifteen miles wide. The main bastion of insurgent defence was around Mount Grammos itself, which was over 9,000 feet. This was taken on the 17th. In the meantime, Mount Kamenik in the Smolikas Range had fallen to the GNA soldiers, and these units also had been switched to the Grammos massif.

General Markos, who was conducting the battle, saw the position clearly. He had been inveigled into positional warfare. If he carried on and fought to the last man, his position would be gradually surrounded and some of the best troops in his army eliminated. His men – and women – were being badly shaken by the continual bombardment and the GNA assaults, and a few of his units had broken under the strain. Morale was not all it might have been and other units were on the point of giving way too. His casualties were terrific, and he had about 3,000 wounded with him in his defensive area, as it was difficult to evacuate them. Markos had frantically called in Democratic Army units from other parts of Greece, drafting in over 7,000 extra fighters in all, but they were still not sufficient to hold back the steadily encroaching GNA troops.

The guerrilla instinct of Markos came to the fore and he decided to break out of the position before he became enclosed in an iron grip. But this was easier said than done. He managed to keep open a small gap at the northern end of the Grammos Range, near Slimnitza, but even this became partly choked by GNA units. On the night of August 20th he made a strong assault on the GNA troops blocking his exit route, and succeeded in breaking clear, taking with him his guns, of which he had over forty-five in the position, his men and his 3,000 wounded, together with the bulk of his other equipment. This was a masterly break-through and withdrawal, and much credit must go to General Markos for organizing and conducting it. Markos, the guerrilla fighter, had been successful again. He later, over the Democratic Army Radio, paid tribute both to his women fighters and supporters and to his male soldiers, and also expressed thanks for the help given by his Balkan allies.

Despite fluctuating morale, his insurgents had fought amazingly well, many units holding on to their positions literally to the last round and the last man. With only sketchy communication and command structure, the semi-independent units clung to their positions in the mountains until they were ordered to withdraw and break through the surrounding ring.

The GNA claimed a victory in taking and clearing the Grammos Range, but it had been an empty one, as most of the insurgents had escaped the cordon which had neither been strong nor tight enough to hold them in. After a brief rest, most of the insurgents regrouped in Albania and then began to infiltrate back into the Vitsi area, just to the north, to stiffen up its defences.

The Grammos operation had been a hard-fought one on both sides, as the casualties testify. During the eight-week campaign, the GNA lost 801 killed, about 5,000 wounded, and 31 missing, the highest totals in the war for an operation yet. On the other side, the Democratic Army losses were far heavier, there being an estimated 3,128 killed, 589 captured and 603 deserters, with the wounded being put at over 6,000. A large proportion of these casualties had been caused by artillery and air action.

While the battle for the Grammos Range raged, insurgent units elsewhere were somewhat restricted in their activities as many were taken as reinforcements, but they kept up an aggressive façade, raiding and committing acts of sabotage. In particular, they took to damaging the water supply systems of the towns. On August 25th, for example, insurgent units attacked Trikkala and penetrated the town, burning buildings and battling with the National Guard, before being driven out again.

The American advisers saw that there was no universal system of either individual or unit training in the GNA, and so the JUSMAPG introduced US methods and doctrines during the summer. All training methods and programmes were revised, revitalized and tightened up. The GNA soldier was largely tired and inefficient by British and American standards, and as many men and units as possible at a time were withdrawn from operations to retrain them.

GNA units were given instruction in commando tactics, mountain warfare, communications and transport techniques. There was a special emphasis on weapon training, and a number of units were equipped with modern US weapons. American trucks and mules were now being received in number.[1] The National Guard increasingly took over static defence duties to release the GNA units for operations. Also, the GNA embarked upon a programme of arming anti-Communist civilians for local defence.

After a pause the GNA, on August 29th, launched a somewhat smaller and less ambitious operation against the hard core of the Frontier Corner–the Vitsi Range–but this at once ran into hard resistance near Florina. Markos had begun to reinforce the Vitsi area on August 24th, and the majority of the insurgents who broke out from the Grammos encirclement made their way there until the Democratic Army strength exceeded 12,500. This GNA offensive abruptly ran down and then hung fire for a week, when a surprise attack by insurgent units forced the GNA troops sharply back for at least five miles. The fighting spirit of the Democratic Army was still strong, and other smaller counter-attacks followed.

Another small GNA operation was mounted against the Murgana bulge on the Albanian border, where there was a pocket of about 1,500 insurgents. This lasted from September 6th to the 16th, but ended inconclusively, although 259 insurgents were killed or captured.

On September 20th, General Markos brought into action about thirty of his field guns, and collecting eight of his best battalions moved up from Kastoria to hit the GNA formations that were halted before the Vitsi Range, hard in the flank. This time the GNA was prepared, and the Democratic Army did not come out of the fighting so well. Markos lost several unit commanders and officers early in the battle, and before long he had to call off the attack and withdraw, leaving over 400 dead on the field. Activities then died down in the Frontier Corner until mid-October.

Markos spent the month of September preparing for large-scale insurgent activities that would recover the territory he had so recently lost in north-west Greece. He disbanded some units that had not done so well in battle, merged others, and formed completely new ones by shuffling personnel from one to another. He now had for his seventy-five to eighty battalions ample officers who, in the

---

[1] By June 30th, 1948, the US had prepared for shipment 8,330 trucks, 4,000 mules, some 75mm pack howitzers and some trainer aircraft.

fighting, had proved themselves to be both reliable Communists and brave and skilful leaders in the field. He promoted the best to lead the units, and ruthlessly weeded out the faint-hearted, the battle-fatigued and the incompetent. A few he shot for failing in action.

Both Markos and Zakhariadis had been acutely disappointed by the lack of response from the people in the cities and the towns to their Communist cause. They had expected bigger and better things, and had instructed the KKE leaders remaining in Athens, who formed a Politburo, to support the Democratic Army in the field by instigating a general rising of the people. If this had not been possible, they had at least expected general insurrection and wide-spread civil disobedience in the urban districts. This had not happened, and they expressed their disappointment and displeasure over the Democratic Army Radio by dismissing the complete Athens Politburo, ordering its members to leave Athens, take to the mountains and report to GHQ in the field.

The Athens Politburo was alleged to have failed on a number of scores, mainly because it had not effected a mass exodus of people from the capital to join the insurgents in the field. It was also said that it had not sabotaged the US-controlled services to the Greek Government, as instructed, nor had it infiltrated Communists into the civil service, the trade unions or the factories, nor had it organized a strong subversive core in all towns. Clearly this was a big and vital failure. Had insurrection and exodus occurred in support of the Democratic Army then the KKE might have been able to plunge the country into chaos and so enable itself to seize control. The KKE and the Democratic Army never gained the support of the majority of the people, and so were never able to realize their ambition to cause the GNA, the National Guard and the civil service to disintegrate. This was their downfall. By fear they extracted a certain obedience and compliance, but few minds were permanently won over.

This rattled the Communist leaders, as did the reports that foreign Press correspondents sent back to their newspapers about the Communists and their activities. On October 11th, the Democratic Army captured Mr. Matthews, the BBC Correspondent in Greece, and held him until the 27th, to 'educate' him and to show him that the Democratic Army men and women were not as bad as some people said they were. Fortunately Mr. Matthews was returned safely, but not so Mr. Polk, the Correspondent of the Columbia

Broadcasting System, whose body was washed up on the shores of Salonika Bay on the 18th. He had been murdered by OPLA.

The Central Committee of the KKE appointed a new Athens Politburo and ordered it to take advantage of favourable conditions to foster a general uprising of the people of the capital.

Refreshed, reorganized and with new battalion commanders in many cases, General Markos flung several of his units into action in the Frontier Corner against the GNA formations that had been halted on the edge of the Vitsi Range. On October 18th, LOK (Commando) units had stormed Mount Vitsi, but the fighting was inconclusive. During the following two weeks the insurgent fighters struck hard and tumbled the GNA troops back, recovering most of the territory they had formerly dominated in that area. The GNA resisted well, but showed signs of fatigue and were slow to respond to situations. The result was further withdrawal. By the end of the month, these Democratic Army offensive operations died down for the simple reason that the impetus ran out due to sheer exhaustion, casualties, loss of good leaders, lack of heavy arms and shortage of ammunition, thus allowing the GNA formations to rest where they were.

Elsewhere, to create diversions in support, insurgent units had been undertaking sabotage, especially of roads, bridges and railways. At this period about 100 people were being killed daily in Greece because of the civil war. On October 29th, martial law was extended to the whole of the country. Previously only certain parts had been under this restriction.

The US Government and AMAG were extremely disappointed that the civil war had not been satisfactorily concluded in 1948, as had been anticipated. Although the GNA had won a series of actions in the spring and summer, by the autumn it was suffering reverses, which only the winter snows prevented the insurgents from exploiting. The seemingly so successful Grammos operation had been an empty triumph, as the majority of the trapped fighters managed to escape to fight again a few days later. The blunt fact was that despite superiority in numbers and fire power, and the possession of aircraft, the GNA had been pushed from the Vitsi Range in the Frontier Corner by a far smaller Democratic Army force. The insurgents in the Vitsi region had numbered less than 13,000 men and women, while the GNA had employed about 50,000 men. The Democratic Army recovered far more quickly from the Grammos fighting than had the GNA.

In mid-October, the US Secretary of State, Mr. Marshall, went to Athens, as did the Secretary of the US Army, who inspected the GNA. A searching inquest was held on why the war had not been won, and what was to be done to bring it to a speedy end. The GNA was sharply criticized for not immediately switching to assault the Vitsi Range in strength after its Grammos success.

For the Democratic Army it had been a splendid, but hard, year, and General Markos had accomplished much of what he had set out to do. His policy of continuing widespread insurgent warfare from mobile bases had paid off, but the cost had been heavy, and according to Greek Government estimates, the insurgent casualties for the year of 1948 were about 32,000. GNA casualties over the same period were about 20,000. Despite the nature of the GNA harrying tactics and the intensive air bombardment, and the fact that the Democratic Army remained a collection of semi-independent units with hardly any command infrastructure, with faulty intercommunication and a shortage of ammunition, its morale and aggressiveness were amazingly high.

Despite such terrific losses, the overall strength of the Democratic Army was in the region of 21,000,[1] and it was remarkable how General Markos managed to replenish his ranks. This was partly accounted for by the return of wounded to the battle, partly by scouring the camps and depots for all fit personnel (Markos also faced the problem of the faint-hearted who had to be dug out from the rear areas) and partly by stepping up voluntary and semi-voluntary recruiting, but mainly by an energetic and ruthless campaign of brutally enforced conscription. A large proportion of the Democratic Army intakes for 1948 were conscripts, who were estimated to number about 24,000 for that year. The means by which these pressed men and women were trained, persuaded to fight against the GNA—which so many did exceptionally well—and to remain loyal to the alien Markos Government and the Communist cause, was a fascinating but deadly combination of leadership, political indoctrination and fear.

The Democratic Army tactics were based both upon defence for a 'limited time' and hit-and-run raids. In the Frontier Corner, the Pindus and other mountain ranges, the insurgent mobile bases that had been established did not automatically move out of the way when GNA units came up against them, but held on and fought

[1] About fifty per cent were along the northern frontier areas, and fifty per cent were scattered in the interior of Greece and the Peloponnese.

M   *177*

back for a short period. These mobile bases had an outer covering screen which was drawn in when it had temporarily halted the GNA units and forced them to deploy, and an inner, and harder, core with stronger defences. In the event of the GNA pushing forward, the inner core fought back and only when it saw overwhelming GNA reinforcements moving up against it, or that the GNA seemed determined to eliminate it, did the insurgent fighters slip away.

These prickly spikes forced the GNA to bring up all arms, including aircraft and artillery, and deploy them individually against each one, which was time-wasting, exhausting and ill-rewarding. This policy of defence for a 'limited time' was often successful in itself, as when it was thought that an insurgent position might be firmly held, the GNA had to consider whether or not sufficient troops were immediately available, or whether a large-scale operation was worthwhile. Because the answer was frequently no to both propositions, the Democratic Army bases were often left alone.

Many successful raids were made on towns and villages throughout the country by the insurgent army, the main objects being to obtain recruits and to instil fear. For these raids two or more insurgent battalions, usually 'roving units', worked together, and the routes along which GNA reinforcements could be rushed were first of all blocked by ambush parties. Sometimes bridges were destroyed, thus isolating the town or village. Then the insurgent fighters rushed in to overpower the defenders, retiring again when they had achieved their purpose.

The two main reasons for the success of these raids were good intelligence and surprise. The YIAFAKA, until it was nearly smothered, usually provided reliable information as to strengths, arms, dispositions and defences, while surprise was obtained by the insurgent units making long forced marches over the mountains by night through country where they were not thought to be.

The year ended in Greece on a note of disappointment. The war-weariness of both the people and the Government was obvious. Despite the seriousness of the situation, the Greek politicians were discontented, distrustful of each other and squabbling amongst themselves. The Liberal politicians attacked the Populists, and the Populists the Liberals; none could agree to work together. It was all Sophoulis could do to hold his coalition together, while the US advisers breathed down his neck urging him to broaden the basis of his government.

CHAPTER TEN

Communist Defeat

The year 1949 was the one of final victory in Greece, during which the GNA changed its strategy and began systematically clearing areas one at a time, removing sections of the population when necessary so that the Democratic Army was deprived of all contact and information. This, together with the defection of Yugoslavia from the Moscow orbit and the gradual closing of its frontiers to the insurgents, were the main causes of the Communist defeat.

The actual defeat of the Democratic Army can be dated from November 1948, or slightly before, when after a considerable amount of argument and controversy, the KKE leaders decided that its strategy and tactics must be completely changed. This decision was taken against the background of the Yugoslav-Soviet split, and the possibility of Balkan aid and facilities being completely or partially cut off, the fact that there was no prospect of International Brigades ever appearing to fight in Greece, and the general tense international situation.

Although his rupture with the Cominform had occurred some months earlier and his quarrel with Stalin was becoming more intense and bitter, Tito, even when he saw the KKE veering towards the Moscow line of thought, did not immediately restrict his aid or the use of his facilities to the Democratic Army. Things went on pretty much the same for many weeks, the Democratic Army personnel using camps and hospitals (of which they had great need), being fed with Yugoslav food and firing Yugoslav ammunition. The freedom to cross and recross the Yugoslav border into Greece as and when it wished was similarly unrestricted for the time being. It seemed as though Tito was deliberately exercising patience and understanding in the hope that this attitude might influence the KKE to support his views.

From an ideological point of view the Greek Communists leaned towards the Stalin line of thought (still the fountainhead of world Communism to the KKE) but practical politics and inherent nationalist feelings caused differences of opinion as to whether it was wisest to be so open and frank at this critical juncture. Most of their eggs were in the basket held by Yugoslavia, and they would be difficult to retrieve, place elsewhere or replace. If they did not back Tito, the nationalist-minded Communist, he would cut off all help and close his frontiers, which would cripple Democratic Army activities. If they opted for Yugoslavia, they would be cut off from other Balkan aid; and, while Albania, Bulgaria and Rumania's share of assistance to the Democratic Army was not as great in volume or as immediately vital as that of Yugoslavia, it was quite appreciable, and if deprived of it the Democratic Army would again also be heavily handicapped. If Albania and Bulgaria closed their frontiers to the Greek insurgents, the GNA would be in an immeasurably stronger position, and would be better able to localize the insurgent units in Greek territory.

The hope that foreign Communist International Brigades, on the Spanish Civil War pattern, would come rushing to their rescue was no longer seriously entertained by the KKE leaders, although it occasionally featured in their propaganda outpourings. The international situation of 1948 was of such acute friction and tension that the threat of war between the West and the Soviet Union was never far below the surface. This was the year of the Berlin Airlift, and such momentous events inevitably underlay the decisions of the KKE. The Greek Communists calculated that the USA would not risk war by physical intervention with combat troops in Greece, but would restrict her aid to measures just short of this.

Therefore, the KKE leaders decided to support the Cominform, and not Yugoslavia, in the Tito-versus-Stalin dispute. They decided to remain friends with Tito as long as they could, so that Yugoslav aid and facilities could be utilized while they were available. This decision was by no means unanimous, and in fact caused the fatal split in the KKE leadership which hastened its defeat.

So far, under the insistence of General Markos, the Democratic Army had remained a collection of small insurgent units practising mobile guerrilla tactics, and he had resisted all persuasion to organize his army in larger military formations and to embark upon conventional operations. He reckoned that if his policy was adhered to he would gradually wear down and exhaust the GNA, when at an opportune moment he could convert his army into a conventional one and close in for the kill, precisely as Mao Tse-tung was doing on the other side of the world in China at the time. Markos was sure that premature conversion would be dangerous, not to say fatally disastrous, and that only all-out American combat participation could destroy him while he stuck to such tried and successful insurgent tactics. Time, the essential factor for an insurgent, he insisted was on his side.

On the other hand, many did not agree with this analysis and conclusion, being of the opinion that time was not on their side but was in fact running desperately short for them. Led by Zakhariadis who was impatient for power, a faction overruled Markos, and decided that the Democratic Army must be turned into a conventional field army to move against the GNA as soon as possible. Zakhariadis, who differed from Markos on political matters, also differed with him on military ones. Zakhariadis calculated that time was running hard against the insurgents. He saw that America was embarking upon a greater than ever material aid programme to the GNA, and he estimated that it would be best to move out in strength to destroy it before such quantities of arms, aircraft, vehicles and equipment were fully absorbed, by which time it would most probably be too late. The successful Democratic Army counter-offensive of October 1948, in the Vitsi Mountains, had profoundly influenced Zakhariadis as to its capabilities, and he reasoned that if unco-ordinated units could achieve such an impromptu victory over larger, better armed GNA formations it should, if properly welded together as a united army, be able to smash the GNA in one or two gigantic hammer blows.

Zakhariadis felt that this course should be taken as soon as possible, and he differed with Markos over the time factor. He deduced that there would be a limit as to how long Yugoslav territory and support could be relied upon, and he was also concerned about the Democratic Army manpower problem. The rate of insurgent losses had reached alarming proportions, and it was no longer possible to continue replacing them as the conscription potential was being drained dry. From this time onwards a gradual decrease in strength was inevitable.

General Markos was suspected of favouring Tito's nationalist line, while Zakhariadis was known to be an old Moscow-faithful. If the Democratic Army could quickly strike blows that would cause the GNA to stagger, in the ensuing chaos and panic the KKE might have a chance to seize power in Greece, when Zakhariadis would receive (he hoped) appropriate rewards for remaining faithful to Stalin's policy of international Communism. Zakhariadis was sure of this and he had no confidence in Tito's ultimate success in a long-term struggle against the might of the Soviet Union; nor did several others, who were later proved wrong.

Accordingly, overriding Markos' protests, Democratic Army units were hastily grouped together into brigades, each of three and sometimes four battalions. The strengths of the brigades varied considerably, being between 1,000 and 2,000, dependent upon such factors as whether units were up to strength, or whether the formation had a priority or not. Next, the brigades were formed into five small divisions. The principle of 'dual command' was retained, each military commander being paired with a political officer. Officers had to be taken from the fighting battalions and promoted to fill new positions. Also, officers had to be found to man the necessary command and communication infrastructure.

This switch from insurgent to conventional warfare also meant—although this was not at first comprehended–that the Democratic Army now required ordinary lines-of-communication, and that the ETA and YIAFAKA were no longer adequate for the operational procurement and distribution requirements of an army in the field. Again, more officers had to be taken from the fighting battalions, and invariably the best and most experienced were selected for command and staff posts. This meant that the units were milked of their most capable officers, and there was a consequential lowering of efficiency. Zakhariadis had not seemed to appreciate this aspect.

The business of reorganizing the Democratic Army was put into gear and the month of November 1948 was fairly quiet as the new insurgent formations took shape, but by the following months the new brigades had been formed and were anxious to test themselves in action. Medium-sized towns were selected as objectives but on the whole the assaults that were mounted were not always a marked success. They highlighted the inexperience of the commanders, the lack of competent staff officers, lack of practice in working together and the lack of conditioning for this kind of warfare.

On December 1st, a Democratic Army brigade of over 1,000 men and women attacked the town of Serres but was repulsed by the defending GNA troops. Battered by the Greek air force using high explosive, incendiary and napalm bombs, the insurgent formation left behind 183 dead, and lost 206 prisoners and deserters who gave themselves up.

On the 12th, a larger brigade of about 2,000 men and women mounted an attack on Karditsa, overwhelming the garrison of about 400 soldiers. The insurgents put out strong road-blocks, ambushed approach roads and destroyed a bridge on the Trikkala-to-Larissa road, which delayed the arrival of reinforcements. When GNA troops reached the town a battle, lasting over eighteen hours, was fought among the houses. Once the fight was joined the Democratic Army brigade headquarters lost control of its units, and although many of the sub-units resisted well, the insurgent fighters were ejected with heavy loss.

Another, smaller insurgent brigade, which was ordered to assault Karditsa from the east at the same time, was slow in starting off. It was ambushed by GNA troops and had to withdraw. In this battle a mounted detachment was used, but it was strafed by the Greek air force and dispersed before it could reach the town. There were in Thessaly three or four small mounted units which had been used fairly successfully for foraging, but this was the first time one had been included in an assault operation.

On the 21st and 22nd, another Democratic Army brigade attacked both Edessa and Naoussa, liberally using both machine-guns and mortars. After confused fighting the insurgent formation was forced to withdraw, leaving 177 dead and 70 prisoners and deserters behind.

On the 28th and 29th, a more successful attack was made by a Democratic Army brigade in the Vitsi Mountains, when the GNA troops were pushed back a little way and a village and a small valley were seized. The insurgents used over a dozen guns in this fight, and the GNA estimated that over 4,000 shells were fired at them during those two days.

The policy of assaulting towns continued, it being anticipated that experience would improve technique, and on January 12th, 1949, a brigade again attacked Naoussa, a small industrial town of about 11,000 inhabitants, where the GNA garrison had been increased to about 900 men. The insurgents successfully overpowered the garrison. The town was sacked, several executions were carried out and over 500 people, including 200 women, were abducted. All medicines and drugs were taken from the hospital.[1] Heavy snowfalls and deliberate damage to the approach roads delayed GNA reinforcements, and it was not until the 16th that they arrived in sufficient numbers to oust the Democratic Army brigade.

During this period the Democratic Army, having no aircraft, used its guns to shell towns and villages indiscriminately. The guns were quietly brought within range, usually at night, and a number of shells fired into the town. The guns were then withdrawn before the Greek air force could locate them, and the same process was repeated somewhere else the following night. This was the insurgent counter to the Government air raids over their territory.

The Greek air force took very effective action against insurgent troops in their conventional attacks, bombing and strafing their concentrations and positions. The insurgent troops, now that they were expected to keep in formations and work to an operational plan, came to dread the Government aircraft that flew overhead. As guerrilla fighters, they had been used to take cover automatically and disperse whenever aircraft appeared above them. Regardless of orders to the contrary, some insurgent units still went to ground when aircraft were about and stayed there until they had all gone. This problem was aggravated by the lack of good, experienced officers in the sub-units, which severely hampered the type of operations that the Democratic Army was trying to undertake.

Next, on January 21st, a Democratic Army brigade took Karpenisi and held it for sixteen days.[2] This town, in the Agrapha Mountains, in Central Greece, was selected because large stocks of food for refugees had been accumulated there. Apart from thoroughly ransacking the town, the insurgents seized 500 hostages[3] and also conscripted all the eligible males between fifteen and forty years of age, who amounted to 1,300. The GNA field force was widely dispersed at this moment, and troops had to be brought in from as far away as the Peloponnese to form relief columns to march to Karpenisi. In addition, several days of blinding snowstorms delayed the retaking of the town.

Although the insurgents were eventually driven from Karpenisi,

---

[1] Hospitals, medical centres and surgeries were always thoroughly ransacked for medicines, drugs and medical equipment, which showed how desperately short of these items the insurgents were.

[2] A US officer, Lieut.-Col. Edner, was shot down when flying over the Karpenisi battle area on January 22nd. On February 18th, his mutilated body was discovered.

[3] The Greek Government estimated that the insurgents had abducted over 7,000 persons between October and December 1948.

the action devolved into a long-drawn-out one. Up to 4,500 insurgents were moved into the area to help block those GNA forces in pursuit of the Democratic Army brigade that had taken Karpenisi, and to try and keep the escape routes open for it. The melting snows and heavy rains hampered the GNA units, and the last action in this protracted operation was not fought until March 25th (1949) against a Democratic Army brigade, about 1,500 strong, that was temporarily trapped in a pocket against the swollen River Achelous. After some fighting the insurgents escaped to the east side of the river. The insurgent casualties for this Karpenisi operation were estimated by the GNA to be over 2,400, and this figure excluded the wounded.

Tito began slowly, but progressively, to reduce his assistance to the Democratic Army, and in view of this it was decided to throw out another feeler to see if there was any possibility of the KKE coming to some agreement with the Greek Government. On January 27th, the Democratic Army Radio announced that the KKE offered to co-operate with it on the usual conditions, which included the departure of foreign missions, a cease-fire, an amnesty, free elections and so on. This time the KKE offered to send representatives to Athens to discuss proposals, but Sophoulis was adamantly opposed to the idea, and the offer was not taken up.

The Fifth Plenary Session of the Central Committee of the KKE was held somewhere in the Frontier Corner on January 30th and 31st, 1949. Policy was thrashed out, but Zakhariadis dominated the meeting and forced his proposals through. Briefly, Markos was dismissed, both as Head of the Democratic Government and as commander of the Democratic Army, it being later given out that he had been relieved of these two posts on the grounds of ill-health. General Popovich, the Yugoslav adviser to General Markos, was dismissed at the same time.

Ionides replaced Markos as Head of the Democratic Government, and Zakhariadis took over the command of the Democratic Army, at the same time retaining the all-important position as Secretary-General of the KKE. A new Politburo, under Zakhariadis, was formed, composed of members who subscribed to his views on the military strategy to be adopted, the attitude to be taken towards Yugoslavia and also how to deal with the Slav-Macedonian problem. In due course, General Markos and his supporters were expelled from the Central Committee of the KKE.

Zakhariadis took direct charge of the Democratic Army. He had decided ideas on what should be done. It was to move over to the offensive to smash the GNA before the large quantities of US arms and material could be absorbed and used against it. He also wanted a Greek town in which to establish a provisional capital for the Democratic Government. The results of the scattered operations carried out by the new Democratic Army brigades in December and January, despite the lack of success and the heavy losses incurred, had by no means discouraged Zakhariadis, who felt he now had a good knowledge and grasp of military strategy. Operations so far had only been experimental and had been directed by the reluctant Markos, but in them the insurgent officers and troops, both men and women, had acquired the necessary experience in positional warfare – or so he reckoned. By now the units had shaken down well in their larger formations.

He noted the general slowness of the GNA to react to these Democratic Army attacks, and the fact that it was widely dispersed and had difficulty in quickly mustering reserves and moving them into battle. Reshuffling a few military and political commanders, Zakhariadis set to work to plan for large-scale activities which he hoped would knock the GNA out of action. In the meantime pressure was kept up against towns such as Florina, Serres, Kastoria, Konitza and Jannina.

In the Tito versus Stalin dispute, Zakhariadis came out on Stalin's side, carrying the KKE with him, and having thus declared his position could hardly expect Yugoslav assistance for much longer. He had burnt his boats. Time was now running against the Democratic Army.

The projected Slav–Macedonian state, which was to contain some 80,000 Slavs and 1·5 million Greeks, had been pushed by Communists generally, but differences arose over whose sphere of influence such a state would fall into.[1] Tito wanted a Greek Macedonia to become part of the Yugoslav Federation, while Bulgaria intended that it should form part of Greater Bulgaria. Nationalist-minded Greek Communists wanted it to remain Greek. The Cominform, now that it had split with Tito, favoured it being detached from Greece and put under Bulgarian influence. Zakhariadis, a disciplined Moscow-man, was prepared to support this, but held

---

[1] In 1947, Tito and Dimitroff met at Bled and agreed to work towards a federation of southern Slav peoples. They agreed that the Bulgarian Slav area (of Pirin) and the Yugoslav one (of Vardar) should merge with Greek Macedonia, but the two leaders fell out almost immediately over this.

off making any pronouncement lest it incite Yugoslavia to abruptly cut off all assistance, or cause an even deeper rift within the KKE.

On the Government side, the military stalemate stirred the discontent and frustration that were mounting in the uneasy coalition. Greek party strife became acrimonious and bitter, and on January 19th, Sophoulis again resigned. The politicians could not agree to sink their differences, nor could any single party gain a sufficient majority to govern strongly. The confused situation was such that the King had to step in and firmly tell the politicians to find a government quickly or else he would find another solution. This had the desired effect, and on the 20th a five-party coalition took office under Sophoulis. On February 1st the sittings of the Assembly were suspended until June.

During January and February there was a reshuffle of senior Greek officers, involving the gradual replacement of less efficient and energetic divisional and brigade commanders, and also of some staff officers. But more than this was required, and it was decided that the best plan would be to appoint a Commander-in-Chief, who would have absolute authority in the armed forces. General Papagos, the general responsible for the Greek victories in the Albanian Campaign of 1940, was asked to accept this position, but he hesitated. The reason was that he thought the National Defence Council (which consisted of thirty-six members) too unwieldy. His objection considered, General Papagos became the Commander-in-Chief of the Greek armed forces on February 25th. A much smaller National Defence Council, which was really a small War Cabinet, of which General Papagos himself was a member, was given supreme authority over all economic and military resources.

The Chief of the General Staff, who was responsible for field operations, was given more authority over the troops under his control. Formerly, he had been hamstrung by the National Defence Council and he had been unable to impose strict discipline on field commanders. The new Chief of the General Staff was General Kosmos, who had commanded a Greek corps in the Albanian fighting in 1940. General Ventiris was recalled and appointed Inspector-General of the Army.

Revitalized at the top, the GNA looked forward to finishing off the war in 1949. US military material was being received at a satisfactory rate, but General Papagos reckoned that the army should be stronger, which in turn would call for more aid still.

The Greek armed forces, including the air force and the navy, but excluding the National Guard, had risen to about 168,000 all ranks, to which America had already delivered some $170 million-worth of arms and equipment. The approximate strength of the army was 132,000 and General Papagos proposed that it should be increased to 150,000 as quickly as possible. It was organized into eight divisions, three independent brigades and four LOK (Commando) units.

The US military experts were not so sure that this increase was necessary, and instead favoured the conversion of infantry units into LOK (Commando) ones. JUSMAPG was of the view that the GNA was too thinly and openly spread over the country and still had a defensive outlook; and that it would be more profitable to have Commando units, which were having outstanding success in the Peloponnese, to search out insurgent formations. It was necessary to develop a more aggressive attitude and Commando-mentality might help. It was not yet realized by the GNA or the JUSMAPG that the Democratic Army was changing its guerrilla character.

So far GNA operations against the Democratic Army had been mounted haphazardly, sometimes dictated by political pressures, sometimes by the whims of the local GNA commander and some-times by necessity. Lip-service had been paid to a central plan, but often little more. Now General Papagos was able to issue firm directives, to lay down priorities and to insist that targets be reached. The country was to be treated as a whole and to be swept through from south to north.

A start had already been made in the Peloponnese, where an estimated 4,000 insurgents operated in the mountains in small groups. They were supported by a small section of ELAN, and an underground organization, known as Autoamyna, which was the equivalent of YIAFAKA, but was neither so well-organised nor so efficient, although it was believed at one time to have had over 20,000 members. The Democratic Army troops in the Peloponnese were poorly armed and clad, and short of ammunition.

A complete infantry division, together with the four LOK (Commando) units, was lifted from the mainland to the Peloponnese by the Greek navy.[1] Between December 19th and January 6th, 1949, over 4,000 Autoamyna members were arrested, and this did much to dislocate the insurgent support. By mid-January, all sabotage had ceased in the Peloponnese, and the GNA was able to get to grips with the Democratic Army units in the mountains.

---

[1] The Greek Navy consisted of about 115 ships, three-quarters of which were on loan from Britain. There were 1 cruiser, 10 destroyers and 2 submarines.

On January 23rd, LOK (Commando) units drove insurgent fighters from the town of Leonidion, killing over 120 and taking over sixty prisoners and deserters. After this the insurgents kept to the mountains. The GNA operated in small units, which searched out the insurgents by moving at night and getting in amongst them. Heavy snowfalls blocked the Democratic Army escape and supply routes. The Greek navy covered the coastline, preventing both supplies and reinforcements reaching the insurgents.

These energetic GNA tactics continued throughout February, and in that month some 1,500 Autoamyna underground workers surrendered to the Government forces, thus hamstringing the insurgent intelligence and supply service. GNA operations were so successful that by March 16th the Greek Government was able to announce that the Peloponnese was completely clear of insurgents, and that Government troops could be released for operations on the mainland. During this time, the GNA claimed to have killed 1,686 insurgents in the Peloponnese operations, captured 1,722 and that 1,104 surrendered or deserted: the remainder faded away, some escaping to the mainland. The Autoamyna was dissolved, over 1,200 members, including the principal organizers, being arrested. The GNA casualties were 235, of whom fifty-eight were killed.

Meanwhile, Zakhariadis had marched his best division, amounting to over 4,000 men and women, against the frontier town of Florina. This Democratic Army division was well clothed in khaki battle-dress and greatcoats, and was well shod. The insurgent depot at Mikrolimi, near Lake Prespa in the Frontier Corner, had obtained cloth from YIAFAKA factories, and was busily making up uniforms. The first phase of Zakhariadis' plan was to seize Florina and then advance swiftly across Macedonia to take Salonika, when he calculated that all northern Greece would be his. Florina stands at the head of the Pisoderi Gorge, which runs south-west for about twenty-five miles into Albanian territory.

On February 12th, the Democratic Army division moved down the Pisoderi Gorge from Albania, and its guns, which were both 105 mm and 75 mm, were pushed forward and put into positions from where they could bombard the town. The artillery shelling began at 3 a.m.[1] and continued until daylight when, under the cover of this fire, the leading brigade of the division was able to get into the southern part of the town, where it was checked by the garrison. The other insurgent brigade (there were only two in this division)

[1] The GNA estimated that the insurgents fired over 1,500 shells prior to the attack.

took up positions in the surrounding mountains overlooking Florina and blocking the routes leading to it.

As the roads and passes were snowbound in many places, GNA reinforcements were slow to arrive. The Greek air force came into action, dropping high explosive and napalm and using rockets against the Democratic Army fighters.

Although they had succeeded in entering part of the town, their progress was then blocked. On the second day the insurgent assaults began to flag, and on the third day the sting had completely gone out of the attack. The insurgents had not been able to make any headway. By this time GNA reinforcements were arriving, and in a series of battles pushed the insurgents from the town. Then, using a combination of heavy mortar fire and counter-attacks, the GNA managed to dislodge the insurgents from the heights surrounding Florina.

By the fourth day the Democratic Army command and communication structure had broken down completely, and Zakhariadis lost all control of his men. Tired and panicky, they streamed back down the Pisoderi Gorge, along which his wounded had been taken back into Albania during the battle and his ammunition and rations brought forward. In this four-day battle for Florina, the Democratic Army division lost 783 killed and 350 taken prisoner or deserted, while the GNA casualties were given as 44 killed, 220 wounded and 35 missing.

This failure to take Florina was a major setback to Zakhariadis, who had hoped for a great victory. As self-styled general and commander of the Democratic Army, he had lost his first battle. The plan had been sound and all had gone reasonably well during the first two days, but after that his men (and women) had had enough. They had not been trained for prolonged fighting. Also, they had been subjected to very heavy bombardment, both from the air and from artillery and from mortars. Zakhariadis had over-estimated the capabilities of his Democratic Army and under-estimated those of the GNA. Again, the Greek air force had played a big part in turning the tide of battle.

The Democratic Government had been reshuffled against the background of the Slav–Macedonian project and Tito's defection from the Soviet orbit. Under Cominform prompting, the NOF (Autonomous Macedonian Movement) came under Bulgarian influence and Yugoslav claims were rejected. Accordingly, to support the Moscow line of international Communism, Zakhariadis had to openly pledge to support this decision, which was not popular in his own Party. This was a complete reversal of policy, as before the Tito-Stalin split the KKE had advocated 'equal rights' for all Macedonians within a Greek Republic. Zakhariadis broadened his Government (he had taken over the Premiership from Ionides) on March 30th to include an Albanian and a Bulgarian. He also promised that Slav-Macedonians would be given senior appointments in the Democratic Army.

On April 5th, Zakhariadis stepped down from the job of Prime Minister in favour of Partsalidis (the Secretary-General of the EAM, who had escaped from Government detention), retaining command of the Democratic Army and of the KKE Party machine.

On May 3rd, the Democratic Government broadcast yet another peace feeler,[1] saying that it was willing to negotiate cease-fire terms and that it would welcome mediation. This time the demand for the removal of the US and British Military Missions was omitted, and it was suggested that a general election be held under UN supervision. This was rejected by the Greek Government. Later that month the Soviet Union urged Greece to consider the Democratic Government's peace proposals, but the Greek Government insisted that as the first essential preliminary the Democratic Army must lay down its arms.

General Plastiras wanted to go to Paris to discuss the Soviet suggestion but the Greek Government refused to issue him with a passport. The USA also rejected a Soviet proposal for a joint agreement on Greece by the Soviet Union, Britain and America.

Yugoslav aid decreased and restrictions on Democratic Army movements caused it to transfer many of its troops and installations to Albania or Bulgaria; and it was from Albania in the first days of April that a Democratic Army division, newly equipped with the latest Soviet-type automatic weapons, entered the Grammos Range, seizing and occupying peaks and passes, many of which were unoccupied as GNA units had withdrawn from them during the winter months. This insurgent division was over 3,000 strong and also had ample mortars and mortar bombs.

Too late a GNA division moved back to try and forestall the invaders. There was some indecisive fighting for about a week in which the GNA did manage to retrieve a few heights, but at great cost. The insurgents remained solidly in possession of a large sector of the Grammos Range, having successfully slipped back into the

[1] This was the twenty-first such proposal the insurgents had put forward since 1946.

area from which they had been squeezed the previous year. During this fighting the GNA estimated that the insurgents lost 825 killed and 995 captured or deserted, while the GNA had 67 killed, 132 wounded and 48 missing.

The Democratic Army casualty figures caused its leaders great anxiety, as its recruiting resources had been drained practically dry. During the winter the Democratic Army had scooped in over 6,000 new recruits, the majority by force, but now it was no longer able to replenish its losses, as its former recruiting grounds were systematically sealed off from it by the strict preventive measures taken by the Greek Government as the GNA began to clear the mainland. In March 1949 the approximate strength of the Democratic Army was just over 19,000 men and women, and the proportion of women in the ranks had increased from twenty per cent to over twenty-five per cent. From this moment onwards there was a steady decrease in strength.

Figures issued by the Greek Government indicated that between June 1945 and March 1949 the Democratic Army losses had totalled 70,027. These were broken down as being 28,992 killed, 13,105 taken prisoner and 27,931 surrendered. No figures were issued for the wounded, but they must have been twice as many again.[1] The tide of manpower was now turned against the Democratic Army.

Having cleared the Peloponnese of insurgent elements, the GNA began to do the same on the mainland, working slowly northwards, dealing with the mountain ranges to the north and north-west of Athens first. The units of the GNA seized and held the peaks and passes, while LOK (Commando) units and other infantry battalions trained in anti-insurgent warfare spread outwards probing for insurgent fighters.

The success of these tactics in the spring and early summer was partly due to intensive police action in arresting and detaining all Communists and suspects[2] in towns and regions where clearing operations were about to take place, so that they could neither aid

[1] The GNA casualty figures for the same period were given as 10,927 killed, 23,251 wounded and 3,756 missing, which included the gendarmerie and police. They also indicated that the GNA had a deserter problem too, although it was not of the same proportion as that of the Democratic Army. Also quoted for the same period were 3,156 civilians executed by the Democratic Army and EPON, and 731 killed by mines and other similar causes.

[2] Already, in January 1949, supervisory censorship over the Greek Press had been brought in, especially to prevent mention of GNA troop movements. These had always been freely and fully reported in the Press. They were obviously quickly passed on by YIAFAKA to enable the insurgents to take avoiding action.

nor give information to the Democratic Army, and partly due to moving whole sections of the population to prevent 'back infiltration'. This deprived the insurgents of their 'eyes' and 'ears'. Suddenly the Democratic Army was deprived of its most valuable asset, a fifth column amongst the population that could quickly pass on intelligence. The insurgents were now completely in the dark over future GNA operations and their units on the mainland were surprised, out-manœuvred and trapped with increasing frequency. YIAFAKA was almost completely nullified. The Democratic Army no longer knew when and where the GNA was going to strike next, and its morale declined as its troops became nervous and jittery.

Largely freed from political stresses and interference, and under the more forceful leadership of General Papagos, the GNA was skilfully deployed in the field. More troops were brought to bear against the decreasing number of scattered insurgent units. The GNA preponderance of manpower was for the first time producing results.

On June 24th, 1949, Sophoulis, who had been the Prime Minister since September 1947, died. He was aged eighty-eight years. He was succeeded by Diomidis, who formed a Government that was much the same sort of coalition in essence. The Greek Government and the people began to feel more confident, and hopes rose as the end of the war at last seemed to be in sight. The successes the GNA were having in Central Greece and the eradication of the YIAFAKA and EPON caused a feeling of relief which boosted morale.

The GNA descended upon Roumeli and Thessaly in April, determined to drive the insurgent units northwards.[1] Held by the 2nd Democratic Army Division, which was about 4,500 strong, its units were systematically attacked and decimated by the GNA, so that by the end of May they were in a desperate condition, being short of ammunition and food. Sections of the population had been moved so there was no support they could rely upon, and they were remorselessly hounded from ridge to ridge. The object was to drive them northwards over the River Aliakmon. The insurgents were guerrillas without people, and like fish without water they gasped helplessly and hopelessly.

Leaflets were dropped on the survivors, urging them to surrender, and many did so. The Democratic Army sabotage-instructional-centres, of which there were eight or nine in the mountains of central and northern Greece, were disbanded and the personnel formed into

[1] This was known as Operation 'Rocket'.

small units that were sent to operate in Southern and Central Greece. Their task was to gain intelligence, to recruit and to commit acts of sabotage. They worked on stony ground and only had limited success.

On June 21st the Democratic Army divisional commander and some of his staff were killed in Roumeli, after which the insurgent resistance in Central Greece came to an end, thus freeing more GNA troops for major operations farther north. A few insurgents, both men and women, remained at large in Central Greece, but they were now fugitives rather than fighters.

Meanwhile, in Eastern Macedonia and Thrace, Zakhariadis had been urging his divisions to take aggressive action and they had a few minor, temporary successes. On May 5th two insurgent brigades, totalling just over 1,000 personnel, took the village of Neon Petritsi, and remained in control for twenty-four hours.

On the 15th another brigade, numbering about 700 men and women, took the village of Metaxades and held it for three days until driven out by GNA reinforcements. On June 20th another insurgent brigade captured a GNA frontier post in the Beles Mountains but lost it again the next day.

Zakhariadis' problem, now that he was feeling the pinch in man-power, was to concentrate a large enough force to successfully attack small towns and large villages.

In preparation for summer offensives several changes were made in senior posts in the GNA. General Ventiris, who had been the Inspector-General of the Army, was appointed to command a new large formation of GNA troops in Epirus and Western Macedonia. In other words, he was given the job of clearing the Frontier Corner. His place as Inspector-General was taken by General Kalogeropoulos, who had just cleared Central Greece. This was the pattern of several other changes of senior commanders of both divisions and brigades, and of staff officers too. The successful and the intelligent were given positions of responsibility and decision by General Papagos, who had a reputation for being able to pick subordinates and to place the right man in the right job.

In May 1949 Tito had protested to the Soviet Union about the assistance given to Yugoslav 'traitors' and for encouraging acts hostile to Yugoslavia. In riposte, the Soviet Union alleged that Tito had conducted secret negotiations 'behind the back of the USSR' with Britain in 1947 over Yugoslav claims on Austria. In June Yugoslavia's claim for Trieste was turned down.

Also that month the Cominform, which had broken with Tito a year previously, loudly denounced Yugoslavia for various political heresies, and this was followed by a spate of violent propaganda from Moscow and the satellite capitals. Trade relations were successively severed with Yugoslavia by Czechoslovakia, Hungary and Poland, and before long the Soviet economic blockade of Yugoslavia was complete.

On July 10th, at Pola, Tito made his famous speech in which he said he intended to progressively close his frontiers with Greece, owing to the numerous violations and the many Yugoslavs who were being killed. He also alleged that the Democratic Army Radio had said that he had allowed GNA troops to cross into Yugoslavia to deal with the Greek insurgents, which he flatly denied. A few days previously the Democratic Army Radio had said that there had been consultations between Yugoslavia and Greece, and the US and the British Military Missions in Greece. This was also denied by Tito.

The closing of the Yugoslav–Greek frontier was a deadly blow to the Democratic Army. During the spring, Greek insurgent movements, both in Yugoslavia and over that border, had been increasingly restricted; but even so, Yugoslavia had continued to supply the Democratic Army with food and ammunition and to allow it to use Yugoslav camps and hospitals. Perhaps Tito thought that this magnanimous attitude might win the KKE over to his side, and it can only be wondered why he was so patient for so long and did not clamp down on Greek insurgent activities sooner. It was only when the KKE leaders came out openly in support of Stalin against him, and also agreed to accept the Bulgarian-sponsored Slav–Macedonian state, that he took this action. Tito intrigued against the KKE over the Slav–Macedonian state, which he wanted to be joined to Yugoslavia, and indeed two members of the Central Committee of the KKE defected to him over it.

More military assistance was given to the Democratic Army by Bulgaria, probably on Stalin's instructions, and the amounts received from Rumania were increased. In particular, Bulgarian camps and hospitals and Rumanian hospitals were placed at its disposal. Otherwise, the main centre of the Democratic Army activity was concentrated in Albania, adjacent to the Frontier Corner.

At the beginning of July the GNA launched an offensive against the Democratic Army brigade about 1,200 strong that was holding the Kaimakchalan Mountains, which stretched eastwards from the Monastir Gap on the Yugoslav border. After a week's fighting the insurgents were driven from their positions. They lost over 400 dead, but the remainder managed to escape into Yugoslavia, where a few days afterwards they were disarmed.

This GNA action drove a wedge into the Democratic Army, physically separating the main body, which was in the Frontier Corner, from the division in the Beles Mountains on the Bulgarian frontier. This meant that the insurgent army had to fight from two widely separated bases, which brought about a multiplication of supply, liaison and communication problems.

Zakhariadis had completely turned from insurgent tactics and had fully committed himself to positional warfare. The summer months were spent constructing a strong bastion in the Frontier Corner, around the Vitsi massif, which was to be a spring-board for offensive operations into Greece. This area took up about 250 square miles, backed on to Albania, touched Yugoslavia, and presented to the GNA a 'front' about forty miles in length. This part of the country consisted of precipitous mountains, rocks and forested valleys, and was most decidedly defensive terrain. The insurgents built concrete emplacements for their guns, surrounded them with barbed wire and supporting machine-gun positions, many of which were also concrete. Zakhariadis declared that this defended base was impregnable.

GNA forces moved up against this defended sector, and to prevent the insurgents breaking through into Greece they also constructed a strong containing line around that part of it which was in Greek territory. There were soon daily exchanges of gun-fire between the two sides.

Zakhariadis had about 7,000 troops in the Vitsi Range bastion, and another 5,000 just to the south, in the Grammos Range. Separated from him physically were another 1,200 in the Beles Ranges, and there may have been up to another 1,500 scattered in small pockets in the mountains of Northern Greece, adjacent to the frontiers. A total of perhaps nearly 15,000 in all. The proportion of women was still about twenty-five per cent. The GNA was now over 160,000 strong.

The plan[1] was that after the bulk of the GNA field force had been deployed against the two Democratic Army strongholds in north-west Greece, a diversionary attack was to be launched against the Grammos positions, and then the full weight suddenly switched to the Vitsi Range, just to the north. When Vitsi fell, the GNA

[1] Known as Operation 'Torch'.

formations were to turn back again to envelope and crush the Grammos pocket. The Beles pocket, to the east, was to be dealt with separately.

As most parts of Greece, other than those just mentioned, were now clear of insurgent units, General Papagos was able to concentrate six of his eight field divisions. His I Corps (of three divisions) was to clear the Vitsi Range, and his II Corps (also of three divisions) the Grammos Range, while the III Corps (of two divisions and two independent brigades) was to eliminate the Beles pocket.

The diversionary attack on the Grammos Range began on August 5th and lasted nearly a week. It made little progress.

Next, on the 10th, I Corps, supported by heavy aircraft bombing and artillery fire, moved against the Vitsi Range position, the main fortified bastion, making a three-pronged attack. This ran into stiff resistance. There was hard fighting, and the insurgents clung grimly on to their positions in the mountain-sides and wooded valleys. The morale and fighting spirit of the Democratic Army in these trying circumstances remained high.

On the 14th the insurgents launched unsuccessful counter-attacks from the direction of Konitza, but the pressure was telling. Soon the heavy pounding from the air and from the GNA guns was too much for the insurgents and they began to give way. By the 16th the last organized resistance in the Vitsi defended area was overrun.

Once again the victory had not been complete, as the majority of the Democratic Army fighters had slipped away at the last minute, over 4,000 crossing the border into Albania, where they re-formed and began to filter into the Grammos position just to the south. Nearly 1,000 insurgents escaped over the Yugoslav border, but they were disarmed and interned. In this battle for the Vitsi Mountain bastion, which Zakhariadis had declared to be impregnable, the Democratic Army had lost at least 2,000 killed, captured or surrendered.

Some Albanian soldiers took part in the Vitsi fighting, and over twenty were found dead on Greek territory and another seven were captured. These were individual Albanian soldiers whose enthusiasm had caused them spontaneously and unofficially to join in and fight with the Democratic Army. There is no firm evidence that Albanian units as such took any part in this series of final battles along the Albanian border. Albanian units took up positions along the line of the frontier to bar GNA troops should they attempt to cross it to get at the Greek insurgents, but at the same time they allowed escaping

Democratic Army troops to slip over as they had always done. Guns were fired from Albanian territory at the GNA in Greece, but again there is no certainty that they were Albanian gunners firing them.

The GNA strictly kept to its own side of the frontier, and the reports of UN observers who were with all GNA divisions substantiate this. By this time Albania was becoming alarmed and anxious as the GNA now had the ability to invade Albania. Owing to Tito's split with Stalin, Albania could no longer rely upon the Yugoslav army coming to her assistance in such a contingency.

On August 19th III Corps, with aircraft support, launched its attack against the Democratic Army brigade in the Beles Range, and after a four-day offensive cleared it. Only sixty-three Greek insurgents were found, and as many more prisoners and deserters taken. Of the remainder, about 1,000 escaped into Bulgaria, being helped to slip over the border by Bulgarian troops who stood firm on the frontier in the face of the GNA, and the rest infiltrated into Greece. In this fighting, Bulgarian guns fired from Bulgaria at GNA troop concentrations on Greek territory.

The Grammos stronghold held fast and it was obvious that it would be a hard nut to crack. To help do this the Americans supplied the Greeks with fifty-one Curtiss Helldivers to replenish their air force, which had pretty well worn out most of its machines. The Helldivers were armed with cannon, machine-guns and rockets, and carried about two tons of bombs. They were also capable of pin-point bombing, which was essential if the insurgents were to be blasted out from their caves and prepared positions in the mountain-sides.

These new Helldivers were unleashed on August 25th when the GNA began its final offensive with three divisions on to the main Grammos bastion. The weight of fire-power and men slowly, but surely, bore the insurgents backwards, prising them from their positions. On the following day (the 26th) several 'frontier' heights were seized by the GNA, which had begun to make a pincer movement round the Grammos Range, a division each closing inwards from the north and from the south, along the Albanian Frontier.

On the 27th Mount Grammos itself was taken by the GNA, after which insurgent morale and resistance went to pieces. Several Democratic Army units stood their ground and fought back well, while others, ignoring commands and appeals, had lost heart and abandoning the fight were streaming back into Albania. The heavy rains of high explosive and incendiary bombs, and the accuracy and efficiency of the new US dive-bombers had proved to be too much for them to withstand.

On the 28th the GNA troops seized and blocked the two main passes from the Grammos Range into Albania, the Starias and the Baroukas, which had been used so extensively by the Democratic Army during the previous few months that they had been nicknamed by it the 'Twin Boulevards to Athens'.

For three days longer a few insurgent pockets held out stubbornly, but one by one they were overrun or withdrawn when it was realized how desperate their situation was, until on the morning of the 30th the GNA could at last correctly claim to dominate the Grammos Range.

During this last week's fighting about 1,000 insurgents had been killed or captured. Hardly any had given themselves up, as the defenders were the hard-core Communists, who expected small mercy from the Greek Government should they surrender. This meant that the remainder, nearly 8,000, had once again made good their escape into Albania as the GNA had not been able to seal off the Democratic Army pocket in time. Indeed, it would have been virtually impossible to cast a watertight cordon around this insurgent stronghold as so many men would have been required to do the job properly.

Since Yugoslav assistance to the Democratic Army had begun to dry up, Albania had become the main source of food, supplies and ammunition for the main body of the insurgent army. Albanian territory had been freely used by the insurgents, both to escape when GNA pressure became too heavy (as in both the Vitsi and the Grammos battles) and for base, training and hospital camps. This aid and use of facilities, although blandly denied, was given because the Communist Hoxha régime was bitterly opposed to that of Monarchist Greece. In the first place Hoxha knew that for long the GNA was in no fit condition to look after its own territory, let alone invade Albania, and also he believed he was sheltering securely under the Soviet umbrella. He thought that if the GNA lost patience and marched into Albania, Soviet troops and those from other Communist Balkan countries would rush to his aid. He counted on the USA and Britain restraining Greece from invading Albania, because it might bring the Soviet Union into the conflict and thus perhaps ignite a world war.

Suddenly the situation had changed, and with US aid the GNA had been converted almost over-night from an ill-equipped, dispersed and not-too-efficient army, into a formidable, well-equipped, competently led fighting force with guns, trucks, tanks and over fifty modern aircraft. If Greece chose to swoop into Albania to try and encircle the Greek insurgent elements sheltering there, there was nothing the tiny, rag-tag Albanian army could do to stop her, and now Hoxha was not so sure that the Soviet Union or Bulgaria would step in with combat troops to help him, or that the USA or Britain would be able to restrain Greece should she be determined to take such a course. Yugoslavia could no longer be counted on at all.

Also, on the horizon appeared a group that was attracting world notice: Albanian exiles of differing views who had banded together to form the 'Committee of Free Albania'. This committee originated in Paris and then moved to America. It never came to anything, but at this moment of international tension in Europe it gave Hoxha some uneasy moments.

From a strictly realistic point of view—and all successful Communists are extremely practical and realistic—General Hoxha saw that the Democratic Army was beaten in the field, so he decided to stop aiding it. On August 26th he announced that all armed Greeks found on Albanian territory would be disarmed and detained. For some time he did not carry this into effect as his small army was incapable of doing so, but he restricted Democratic Army movements wherever he could and curtailed supplies. The Democratic Army was disintegrating anyway, and in September Hoxha was in fact able to disarm several small elements of it in his territory, and to concentrate the larger bodies into camps and to keep them passive by threatening to cut off their rations. As he began to put this policy into practice the many Greek insurgent fighters dispersed and tried to make their way, either in small groups or independently, across Yugoslavia or Greece to Bulgaria.

Zakhariadis managed to keep the main body together for some time. He tried to restore some order and discipline to what was left of his army, and to arrange for it to be moved to Bulgaria, but the difficulties were insurmountable. Zakhariadis simply had to fall in with Hoxha's instructions, or get nothing to eat.

In fact the war was over, but neither the Greek generals (nor the US advisers for that matter) realized it, and during the month of September GNA formations were held ready to block any expected insurgent invasion or large-scale infiltration into Greece. Other GNA units were used, together with the National Guard battalions, to deal with small parties of the Democratic Army, it being estimated that there were still up to 5,000 armed insurgents scattered in the various mountain ranges inside Greece.

When no insurgent moves were apparent it was thought that the Democratic Army was reorganizing, refitting and waiting for the winter to set in before infiltrating back into Greece in strength. The GNA deployed to deal with such a situation.

This contingency never arose, although the fighting spirit of the Democratic Army remained fairly strong, and a few hundred hardened insurgents were prepared to continue the war using guerrilla tactics. The Democratic Army had not been extinguished completely and Zakhariadis did not consider that its future was completely hopeless, although the way ahead was hard and dis-couraging. Yugoslavia had closed its borders and interned the Greek insurgents within its territory, and now Albania was trying to do likewise, but Bulgaria remained friendly and helpful. Bulgaria had a joint frontier with Greece, over which she was prepared to allow the Democratic Army fighters to pass and repass, and Rumania, lying just back from and adjacent to Bulgaria, was prepared to provide food, ammunition and supplies, and to allow the use of certain facilities.

It is believed that Zakhariadis, his Democratic Army generals and the Central Committee of the KKE were readjusting themselves to a prolonged insurgent struggle waged from Bulgarian territory against the Greek Government, when Stalin stepped in and forced the Democratic Army to declare a cease-fire.

On October 16th, 1949, the Democratic Army Radio announced that its army had decided to 'cease-fire' to 'prevent the complete annihilation of Greece'. It declared that this did not mean that the Provisional Government of the Democratic Republic had renounced the fight for the people's rights, but that it had been forced to retreat in the face of material advantage and Tito's defection and treason.

The timing of the cease-fire announcement was Stalin's idea of embarrassing the Western Powers on the eve of the final meeting of the Balkan Conciliation Committee at Lake Success, by putting the Greek Government at a political disadvantage. It is also believed that Stalin toyed with two other plans, neither of which came to fruition. One was to set the Democratic Army against Yugoslavia to stir up insurrection and rebellion in Tito's domain, especially in the Vardar (Macedonian) sector, and the other was to insist on an amnesty for all Democratic Army fighters and their repatriation to Greece, where they would be able to carry on the struggle by open political means.

At the time of the cease-fire about 8,500 personnel were in Albania, over 3,500 in Bulgaria and about 1,000 remained at large in Greece. There may have been far more than 1,000 armed insurgents inside Greece, but there was probably only that number remaining in any organized and disciplined groups. The remainder had disintegrated and gone into hiding.

General Papagos[1] and the Greek General Staff were extremely suspicious of the Democratic Army cease-fire statement, and they doubted its motives. In the past the insurgent army had proved so resilient that they could hardly believe they had at last battered it to its knees and knocked it out. They thought this was a ruse to cause the GNA to relax its guard and to withdraw formations away from the frontier areas so that insurgent units could again slip into the country. They were almost sure that the Democratic Army was merely seeking a breathing space in which to recover to fight again another day, as it had done so often before.

This time it really was the end, and the Greek Civil War terminated at last. The cost in human lives alone was over 158,000 dead, of whom about half were militant Communists and the remainder Government troops, security forces, police and civilians.

In Greece the Communists had lost their insurgent war, while on the other side of the world Mao Tse-tung, having won his, had entered Peking in triumph. Why was this?

[1] General Papagos was promoted Field Marshal on October 27th, 1949.

CHAPTER ELEVEN

Analysing the Communist Defeat

Finally, a brief analysis of why the Communists were defeated, why the Greek National Army won, and why it took so long.

When there is no chance of a sudden *coup* to enable the Communists to seize power quickly, as they did in Russia, and they decide upon war, there is a definite progressive pattern which they apply—or try to apply—stage by stage as opportunities occur. By now this pattern is recognizable. But it was not so familiar, nor was its course so predictable, in 1945 or even in 1949; so perhaps there are excuses for the mistakes of those responsible for conducting the fight against the Greek Communists.

The Communist offensive pattern begins with the idea, or perhaps the ideal, that a Communist government and form of society are the answer to all social evils and injustices that exist in a country or a region. This attracts devotees and binds them together. The next step is to form an official Party organization which eventually throws up a leader. Forming a national Communist Party is not so difficult, as young Communists inevitably gravitate together—in the open if possible; if not, in secret. Clandestine help sometimes, but not automatically, may be given by Moscow.

The selection of a national Communist leader may be a longer and more painful process, as ambitious, ruthless candidates cut, thrust and intrigue amongst themselves for the dominant position. It is only when one outstanding figure emerges as the leader, often, but not always, the one backed and secretly supported from Moscow, that the new Party can stabilize itself and impose discipline on its members in preparation for the next step forward.

Those who believe that Communist Parties are always, and have always been, solidly united from their inception, and that a split such as that between Tito and Stalin, or Khrushchev and Mao Tse-tung is a highly unusual event in a disciplined Communist world, have obviously not studied the history of practical Communism. The bitter, fratricidal struggles that often attend the birth of a new National Communist Party are conveniently forgotten, denied or whitewashed as soon as possible. The whole history of Communism and the Communist Parties seethes with heresy and counter-heresy, as rivals use every twist and turn to grasp power and the means of enforcing their own particular interpretation of Marxist doctrine upon the people.

A party with a governing Central Committee having been established on the conventional pattern, a cadre of followers is trained to infiltrate trade unions, the civil service, the armed forces and moderate and left-wing political organizations, guilds and youth clubs. Secret 'cells' are formed then. At first, quality rather than quantity is the aim, while men and women are selected and groomed for key posts in the coming war. The Communist emancipation programme is very attractive to young women, especially those in the backward countries, and they usually form hard-core militant groups. Only after a measure of infiltration has been achieved and the cells established, does a wider recruiting take place to swell the Party numbers and gain converts. The cells are the basic framework.

Where there is political freedom, as in a democracy, an attempt may be made to compete openly for power, and Communist candidates appear at elections. This is not usually successful as few ordinary people will freely vote for a Communist programme. The Communists make little headway and are banned if they are thought to be potentially dangerous; or ignored if they are thought to be incompetent and of no general appeal; or allowed to stay in the open but under surveillance. Harsher and less tolerant régimes do not allow them to function openly at all, and so they have either to work underground if they can or in exile.

If war is thought to be the only means to achieve power and the prospects seem favourable, even if only in the long term, a subversive movement is begun. To obtain the support of the people, a popular cause is espoused, such as land reform or the eradication of some particularly oppressive social evil that is burdening the community. This will ensure that people are sympathetic to and will help the Communists, thinking that they are working to rid them of their burdens. In certain conditions, this develops into a guerrilla movement and this can be long and difficult. Communist guerrillas appear, band themselves together in small groups and live in the mountains and other less readily accessible parts of the country, or even partly underground in the towns and villages. Government forces are avoided and their primary concern is survival.

As arms, material and recruits are obtained and the guerrillas gather strength, experience and confidence, the guerrilla stage merges into one of protracted warfare. The guerrilla fighter becomes more aggressive and his object, by using mobility and avoidance tactics, is to harass, weaken and distract. Pin-prick attacks on Government forces, installations and police stations develop into larger hit-and-run raids and ambushes.

Next comes the mobile warfare stage. By this time the small bands of the guerrilla army have been converted into larger, better armed and trained formations. Pitched battles with Government troops are still avoided. While the Communists march and countermarch about the country, the Government troops, trying desperately to catch up and bring them into combat, become dispersed, worn down and exasperated.

The last stage is that of positional warfare, when the Communists are ready to move into the kill. A culminating fatal blow is planned and executed. The ground is chosen, the Government troops are drawn into a trap and the waiting Communist divisions hurled against them. The Government forces, so long dispersed to combat insurgency tactics, are unprepared and surprised by the unsuspected strength of concentrated opposition. When this battle has been won the way is clear for the Communists to take over the country.

This has come to be recognized as the standard pattern of Communist insurgency; underground cells; bands of hunted guerrillas; mobile warfare; positional warfare; the final set-piece battle. The persistent motive throughout is lust for power and the ruthless determination to achieve it. All means are bent to that end. Occasionally a stage is shortened or lengthened, according to circumstances, the efficiency of the Communist leaders, the amount of support they have, and the effectiveness or otherwise of the Government countermeasures. Sometimes a stage is skipped and sometimes, having over-reached themselves, the Communists have to retract and go back to the one before.

It is the guerrilla stage that has been the most publicized, and rightly so, as it is both the most vital and the most vulnerable one for the Communists. It is invariably the longest and toughest, and until it is won the Communists cannot move on to the next. The guerrilla stage is one that cannot be skipped; however much a guerrilla can harass and disrupt, he cannot conquer, and he has many problems to contend with. It is during the guerrilla phase that Government forces have the best chance of defeating the Communist insurgent.

The guerrilla fighter is often pictured as roaming the countryside freely, nonchalantly eluding Government forces as he raids, ambushes and seizes arms and supplies. Unencumbered by a top-heavy general staff and without restricting supply lines or base camps to protect, the guerrilla is thought of as being capable of marching long distances by night over difficult terrain, of living off the country and keeping always one gay step ahead of the ponderous Government troops, whose officers are hopelessly outclassed in quick thinking and intelligent anticipation.

In fact the guerrilla has most people's hand against him; forever apprehensive of death or capture by betrayal or mistake and dogged perpetually by hunger and exhaustion. He lives in the mountains and remote forests only because they are the only places where he can hide away. He would much rather be in comfort underground in the big cities near the seats of power which his leaders covet so much. It is all the average guerrilla fighter can do to evade government troops and to feed himself, let alone effortlessly lead them a dance for the fun of the exercise.

Unless there are several major elements in the guerrilla's favour he cannot survive long, let alone thrive and become a conventional soldier in a large conventional formation. Perhaps the five most important essentials are an ideological motive, people, space, supplies and bases. While the guerrillas are poorly armed, poorly equipped and in the minority, all five—not just one or two of them— are needed to survive, while to prosper additional ones are desirable.

An ideology—a cause—is necessary to give him something that will attract and hold his attention, energy, loyalty and faith. The dogma and doctrine of Communism provide this; and its articles of faith (suitably keyed to local conditions) keep alive cohesion, discipline and morale. Without this motivating reason, the guerrilla would be no better than a scavenging bandit—thinking only of loot, pillage and the spoils of war—who would not hesitate to change sides tomorrow if that would be to his personal benefit.

The next essential is people: the more numerous, the poorer and the more discontented the better, as the guerrilla must have them to support and protect him from the probing of Government security forces. If there are no people about the guerrillas become little more than gangs of criminals in open country, who can be sighted and hunted down like packs of wolves. The guerrilla lives on the people and relies upon them to give him food, fill his ranks with volunteers and provide information that will enable him to keep out of danger and avoid traps. He must have a local population to harbour his underground supporting organization and to merge into whenever hard pressed. If the people are sympathetic to his declared ideals he has these advantages; even if the people are hostile, neutral or indifferent, he may be able to terrorize, win over or otherwise press them into compliance.

Next the guerrilla must have space—plenty of it—where he can take avoiding action and keep out of the reach of Government troops. If space is restricted, he can be cornered, surrounded or 'beaten' into the open. In this respect China, with her huge expanses, is ideal for guerrilla warfare. Greece is less so, although she does have some twenty-six separate mountain ranges in which looking for small bodies of guerrillas is like searching for needles in haystacks.

There is, however, an alternative to space, which the Greek Communists possessed, and that is an adjoining country with a government sympathetic to the aims of the guerrillas, prepared to help secretly and allow her territory to be used as a sanctuary and base. If the frontier is long, mountainous and rugged, it is practically impossible to seal off unless unlimited Government troops are available, and this is seldom the case. For a time the land frontiers of Albania, Yugoslavia and Bulgaria were closed to the GNA but open to the Greek insurgents, who could slip across them to escape pursuit, and this made up for the lack of the essential space factor. As long as guerrillas could choose their time and place to cross these frontiers, the Democratic Army had the full advantage of space.

A guerrilla needs supplies just as much as any other type of fighting soldier. He has to eat just as regularly, and he requires ammunition for his weapons. This elementary premise seems always somehow to surprise many military experts and students, who often seem to believe that Mao Tse-tung's guerrillas could march for days on end and fight any number of hit-and-run engagements on a bandolier of rice. It is possible that a handful of guerrillas may be able to live off the country for a short time, being fed by the peasants, but as they must increase in numbers, to adhere to the insurgency pattern, the problem of supplies, arms and ammunition becomes just as great as that of a conventional army. In fact, owing to the Government control of roads and main centres, and its possessing a preponderance of soldiers, vehicles and aircraft, the guerrillas have correspondingly greater difficulties, handicapped as they are by the lack of wheeled transport and not being able to use the roads freely. As a matter of interest, when General Giap, the Viet Minh guerrilla leader in Indo-China, took to mobile warfare on emerging from the guerrilla stage, in his operations his human porters always outnumbered his fighting soldiers.

Another indisputable fact is that supplies must have a source, and unless a guerrilla movement has one it will soon be starved out of existence. The source can be external, internal, or a mixture of both. In Greece it was a mixture of both. During the Axis Occupation, for example, arms and ammunition were dropped by British aircraft and the food was obtained from villages in the mountains. This was possible because the Axis Authorities were largely indifferent to what went on in the interior as long as the main communications were not interfered with. Quantities of arms were seized from the Italians and Germans on their respective surrenders, and a certain amount of food was taken from the villages while the Democratic Army was in actual control of large areas, but there was a limit to the amount of food which could be confiscated owing to the poverty of war-ravaged Greece. Later, sympathetic Communist countries sent both military supplies and food.

Another fact that tends to raise eyebrows is that guerrillas must have bases in which to muster, to organize themselves, to train, to rest, to recuperate from wounds, and to store reserves of food, arms and ammunition. This surely must dispel the theory that a wandering guerrilla has no static cares, and can therefore run rings round the Government forces that have to rely upon normal lines-of-communication, and have installations, wireless stations, airfields and towns to protect.

Smaller guerrilla bands can make do with small mobile bases in the mountains and forests for a short period, but these can only offer extremely limited facilities and have always to be ready to decamp at a moment's notice when Government troops locate them and make a move to ferret them out. During the Axis Occupation of Greece the guerrillas had bases in the mountains which were largely undisturbed, but this was only because the Occupation Forces were not interested. Whenever punitive sweeps were made into the interior these bases had to be moved quickly and the stores hidden.

Several were overwhelmed before they could be moved and quantities of material lost, which could only be replaced with difficulty.

In the latter part of the Civil War, the Democratic Army had its bases in adjacent foreign countries (especially Yugoslavia) where they were immune from GNA counter-action. The GNA in pursuit had to stop short at the border, so the Democratic Army was fortunate in that it had all the advantages of firm bases without the usual corresponding guerrilla disadvantage of vulnerability.

As guerrilla forces increase in strength according to the master plan, larger—and therefore less mobile—bases are required in larger numbers to complement the lines-of-communication that have to be formed to supply the guerrilla army. Bases eat up manpower and attract reluctant warriors. Communists are no exception to this tendency and both General Markos and Zakhariadis were faced with the problem of guerrillas who had to be prised away from the security and comfort of the bases and packed off, almost at pistol point, to fight in the field.

This was especially true when morale was low (which with all guerillas is fairly often) and at times there were more troops in base camps in Albania, Yugoslavia and Bulgaria than fighting in the field in Greece. It may be said that many of these were wounded who were convalescing, which was true, but many were not, and time and time again they had to be winkled out whenever reinforcements were urgently needed.

Those are some of the favourable factors that have to be present before guerrilla forces can operate with any degree of certainty of survival, let alone success. If any one factor is countered and nullified, the guerrillas cannot carry on for long. Examples of the effect of depriving the Democratic Army of vital essentials can be seen when the Greek Government decided to move whole sections of the population, when Democratic Army bases were lost (when the Yugoslav frontier was closed to it) and when space became cramped.

There are several other factors that can work to the guerrillas' advantage, but none are individually essential to bare survival. To quote a few: good morale, good planning, good training, good leaders, modern weapons, foreign recognition; in the country as a whole, a discontented people, an agricultural economy, a despotic government, social evils, restrictive laws, a stretch of coastline. The list is long and there are many others. All are helpful, but none are vital, and if anyone, after having been available, is suddenly

o

eliminated, this will not cripple resourceful guerrillas but merely inconvenience them.

There were perhaps half a dozen major related reasons why the Communists lost the war in Greece, of which no single one alone brought about defeat. Also, several subsidiary reasons helped in some small measure to hasten the final result.

The major cause was the failure to win over the minds of the people—or at least a sizeable slice of them. In China, Mao Tse-tung was most careful on this point, and it was always the most important factor in all his calculations and plans. His treatment of prisoners, for example, was considerate and just (with exceptions), and as a result he won the majority to his cause. The KKE never appreciated the importance of this, and thought that terror would be a sufficiently powerful substitute. At one time the Communists were in effective occupation of four-fifths of all Greece. This was their big chance to win over the hearts and minds of the mass of the population. They did not take it.

Instead of just, considerate treatment and skilful propaganda, the people were given brutality and terrorism, so that they feared the Communists and fell in with their wishes because they dared do no other; but they never respected them nor were many wholeheartedly converted to Communism. Prisoners taken by the Greek Communists, including hostages, were viciously and often sadistically treated, and the executions and torture of those suspected of helping the Government to the detriment of the Communists bred hatred of Communism that was suppressed only by fear. Once the fear was removed, the hatred rose to the surface. The Greek Communists had neglected the primary principle of insurgent warfare: that of winning the minds and hearts of the majority of the people.

The most widely recognized cause of failure was the closing of the Yugoslav frontier, and there is no doubt that this was very significant as Yugoslavia had been the mainstay, refuge and principal supplier for the Democratic Army. Until that moment the Democratic Army had plenty of space, or the equivalent, secure bases and ample arms, ammunition and food. In one move practically two-thirds of these three essentials had been wiped out. The Democratic Army still had the support, space, bases and supplies from Albania and Bulgaria (and also Rumania to some extent), and could have still fought on, but with lesser strength and venom.

The faulty judgement of the KKE leadership was another major cause of the Communist failure, as it made at least two disastrous decisions. In 1945 it misjudged British reaction to the bid by ELAS to take over Greece by armed force, and in late 1948 it decided to back Stalin instead of Tito.

British military intervention in 1945 broke up ELAS, and set the KKE almost right back to the beginning again after having very nearly snatched the prize. The KKE had seen the British back the Communist Tito in adjacent Yugoslavia, which gave it hope and anticipation that while Britain might not quite so fully approve of a Communist régime in Greece, she would at least be neutral in any conflict between ELAS and the Greek Government. Also, it was thought that Stalin would probably persuade Britain not to take military action against ELAS, if such a course were contemplated. Communists everywhere, Greece included, had great faith in Stalin, and that Stalin would unstintingly aid the Communist cause to his utmost ability.

Still blindly believing in Stalin and his goodness, the KKE made a greater misjudgement in 1948 when it decided to opt for him instead of Tito. Tito was looking for allies at this critical juncture and would have welcomed the support of the Greek Communists, when in return he would have almost certainly continued to assist the Democratic Army. Yugoslavia was far too big a proposition for Greece to take on, so there was little chance of the GNA losing patience and marching over the Yugoslav frontier in pursuit of the Greek insurgent fighters. Had it done so it would have probably been annihilated by the much stronger Yugoslav armed forces.

This KKE decision had fatal repercussions as, once the Tito–Stalin split occurred, Albania was in a delicate and vulnerable situation, being small, militarily weak and physically cut off from other Cominform countries. The Albanian army was incapable of stopping the GNA should it decide to cross her frontier to eliminate Democratic Army elements in Albania. Seeing the red light just in time, Albania ceased aiding the Democratic Army as soon as she could, thus forcing it to contemplate moving the bulk of its troops and stores to Bulgaria. But this was a long way round, and the alternative but more direct route across Greece was highly dangerous.

Had the Democratic Army not ceased fire when it did, it is more than probable that Albania, although she was a Cominform country by this time, would have come to some arrangement with the Greek Government. Those who scoff at such a probability have not fully realized that national survival often overrides the principles and theory of international Communism.

The decision to back Stalin instead of Tito was not unanimous and caused considerable argument and controversy in the Central Committee of the KKE. Those in favour, led by Zakhariadis, carried the day, no doubt anticipating protection, support and material assistance in quantity from the Soviet Union. They sadly misjudged Stalin, who held a low opinion of the value and ability of the Greek Communists, and they in return for their loyalty received little or nothing.

The divided leadership of the KKE was another major reason for the Greek Communist defeat, as the difference between the two contending factions reflected on the morale of the political officers and on the Democratic Army generally. One faction was led by Zakhariadis, who favoured international Communism as prescribed by Moscow, and who put his trust in Stalin as the acknowledged fountainhead of Communism. The other faction was led by General Markos, who favoured a form of national Communism and collaboration with Tito, and was wary and probably disillusioned by the non-fulfilment of Moscow promises.

Personal feelings sharpened this dispute, and Zakhariadis, who had spent the years of the occupation of Greece in a concentration camp in Germany and so had no hand in the rise and activities of ELAS, and therefore no first-hand experience of guerrilla and subversive warfare, was inclined to be jealous of General Markos, who had extensive experience in this field. Although still the leader, being the Secretary-General, Zakhariadis had to take a back seat and allow Markos to form the Democratic Army and conduct the war against the Greek Government in the first place, but his jealousy and impatience gradually got the better of his common sense, causing him to eventually assert his views and authority.

The doctrinal difference between these two factions, or in effect between the two prominent personalities, extended to other matters such as the Slav-Macedonian problem, the use and siting of the Democratic Army Radio and how the propaganda machine should be operated. It also extended into the sphere of strategy and tactics. For a long time the façade of unity was maintained and presented to the world by the KKE, and everyone assumed that strict Communist discipline smothered any personal disputes or rivalries.

The switch from guerrilla to conventional warfare seemed on the face of it to be such a colossal mistake that one can only wonder what impelled Zakhariadis to force his decision through the Central Committee. It is usually ascribed to his impatience to seize the power that he felt was slipping from his grasp by the cautious guerrilla methods of Markos and the fact that he thought he could achieve much quicker results. Many felt that personal animosity and the desire to outshine Markos as a fighting general motivated his decision; that Zakhariadis wanted to become in effect a Greek Mao Tse-tung. This was not necessarily so, although these personal ambitions and considerations may have tinged his thinking. The real reason most probably was that Zakhariadis' information was faulty.

Greek Government counter-measures were strangling the YIAFAKA, which was not able to pass information as freely and as quickly as before, nor was the information it gleaned so accurate. Zakhariadis' intelligence was out of date in most respects, and badly so in some. According to the information he had, he estimated that he stood a good chance of knocking out the GNA if he acted fairly promptly, and that to continue guerrilla warfare would cause this splendid opportunity which was unlikely to return for many, many months – if ever – to be missed. In early 1948 the morale of the GNA left much to be desired: its equipment was old and insufficient, the conscripts were unwilling, its commanders defensive-minded, and its medium-grade officers not adjusted to anti-insurgent warfare. Zakhariadis knew this, and he also knew that American material aid was beginning to be fed into the GNA.

On this information he calculated that if he massed his troops the Democratic Army would be able to knock out the GNA while its morale was low, its state of training poor, and before the influx of American arms and equipment could be absorbed. That is most likely to be the real reason for the sudden switch from guerrilla to conventional warfare. Unfortunately for Zachariadis, his information was stale, and he did not fully appreciate the change that had been wrought within the GNA in the summer and autumn of 1948, the amounts of American material absorbed, the improved state of training, sounder planning, better staff work and a more aggressive policy and attitude generally.

Those perhaps are the major factors that together brought about the Communist defeat in Greece. There are other subsidiary ones that also helped, such as the failure of the Democratic Government to obtain recognition abroad, heavy casualties, the drying up of recruiting sources, the denial of space because of the systematic GNA sweeps through the entire country, and the loss of so many experienced military and political officers in the fighting.

On the Greek Government side there were also several major factors that contributed greatly to its victory, of which perhaps the most important was the timely aid given first by Britain and then by America. British military intervention defeated ELAS in battle and saved Greece from a Communist take-over, but the Varkiza Agreement was circumvented by the Communists, and the Democratic Army rose from the ashes of ELAS.

In 1946 and 1947, the GNA did not have much success against the rising might and penetrative powers of the Democratic Army. While this could partly be put down to the economic state of the country, lack of firm political direction and political influence on the GNA, the main factor was lack of sufficient modern arms, vehicles and finance to equip and train the Greek defence forces adequately for the task and to increase their size. Britain had provided some assistance, but owing to her own economic difficulties was unable to let Greece have as much as was required.

The Truman Doctrine, which authorized American aid to Greece and Turkey, was undoubtedly one of the major causes of the GNA victory, as American material, which began to arrive in late 1947, saved the day. Had it not arrived when it did, or been delayed, or been more restricted in volume, the GNA might well have been defeated. It brought new hope and gave the essential material supremacy over the Democratic Army. During 1948 the GNA was re-equipped and retrained so that its standard of efficiency rose to that required to give the GNA soldier confidence that he was a better man than his opponent on the field of battle. Perhaps if the fifty-one American Helldivers had been delivered earlier the war might have been shortened, as the small Greek air force was practically worn out; but this is the only criticism that can be levelled against the magnitude and promptness of American aid to Greece.

Under American insistence energetic counter-measures were taken against the Greek Communist guerrillas, and one of the most effective of these was the systematic removal of whole sections of the population. This was more far-reaching than is usually realized. It removed the people, it demarcated a 'front line', it prevented 'back infiltration' and it caused a blanket of silence to descend. Without population to support and succour him, the guerrilla is a fish out of water; he might as well be fighting in a foreign and hostile country. From being an indigenous fighter, fighting for his people, he finds himself alone and an unwanted invader.

The guerrilla abhors a 'front line', which a 'no man's land' tends to produce; he likes to be able to move about amongst, in and behind the areas where the Government troops and the people are. If he cannot do this, and instead runs up against a front line every time he wants to hit out, he is little better than, if as good as, poorly armed, second-rate infantry. The front-line effect caused by removing sections of the population also prevents 'back infiltration', which plagued the Government forces for so long, nullifying their sweeps. Once squeezed out from among the people, the guerrillas could not get back in again.

The separation of the guerrillas from the people also caused a cessation of the stream of reliable speedy information that had flowed through YIAFAKA to the Democratic troops, often in advance of orders being issued to the men themselves. The guerrillas now had to fight with their eyes shut; and they were more handi-capped than the Government troops had ever been, as they had no reconnaissance aircraft.

The harsh policy of displacing thousands of people was a difficult decision for a democratic country to take, even in wartime, and the Greek Government hesitated for a long time. However, once this policy was put into effect it paid handsome dividends, as was seen when the southern and central parts of Greece were cleared of Democratic Army fighters with amazing speed.

From the tactical point of view, one feature is deserving of men-tion. The GNA operations in the mountains in bad weather contributed considerably to its success in the field against the Democratic Army battalions. At first the GNA was reluctant to get out and about in the mountains in the depths of winter, which gave the advantage to the insurgents, who are particularly vulnerable when the elements are against them.

In Greece in winter the mountainous parts of the country are bleak and barren, with passes blocked by deep snow, villages cut off from each other, and many miles of roads and tracks made impassable even to mules. In such conditions it is difficult, un-comfortable and extremely hard going even for tough, well-trained regular troops to have to comb through the mountains in alternating blizzards, hail storms, mist and fog, but they do have the benefit of certain facilities, such as blankets, regular rations, hot food at intervals, a change of clothing and a rest in warm billets when they return from operations or patrols—as well as aircraft to control operations, drop food when necessary and to search for any soldiers who may get lost in the snow.

Guerrillas have few facilities; and if villages are made unsafe for them in winter by continual aggressive military action and patrolling, they are forced out and turned into hunted refugees, cold, miserable, and in danger of death by exhaustion, exposure or starvation. There is no friendly aircraft to search for the guerrilla lost in the fastness of the mountain snows, or to drop him hot food, blankets or medical supplies. He is left to perish or survive alone, like a wild animal. The value of this aspect of anti-guerrilla warfare cannot be over-emphasized in any country with a harsh winter, or even in a tropical one with a heavy monsoon season.

It is often asked why the Greek Civil War lasted so long, and why more than 150,000 men could not defeat a mere 30,000 or so. The answer is not just the simple one that it takes a preponderance of conventional troops of over ten to one to eliminate them (although this was largely true, of course), and that this is a slow process. The other main contributory reasons for the length of the war were the Democratic Army's adherence to the guerrilla warfare stage, the time-lag in the arrival of American aid and the National Defence Council.

General Markos kept his troops in small, semi-independent units right up until the autumn of 1948. Had this policy been continued the war would have lasted longer, although it would have been won by the Government eventually. Once the guerrilla stage was abandoned and the Democratic Army turned almost overnight into a conventional army, expected to fight positional battles, the end was in sight, as it could not stand up to the overwhelming GNA fire-power.

The time-lag in the arrival of American aid has been mentioned briefly. Had it come earlier the war would almost certainly have been correspondingly shortened.

The existence of the large National Defence Council, representing several political parties and diverse interests, was a drag, because before an important decision could be made, too many people had to be consulted, too many opinions sought and too many objections listened to. By the time a decision had been forced through the opportune moment had often gone, and its effect was nullified or muffled. An example was the removal of sections of the population to cut off the Democratic Army fighters from the people; although this had been put forward on many occasions, it was not finally agreed upon until late 1948.

The lack of a centralized field command, free from local political influence and with complete authority over all the formations, has been frequently mentioned, and many attempts to correct this fault were frustrated and delayed by the National Defence Council, to which individual field commanders had to report direct. The mistake was that always the attempts to rectify this bad structure and chain of command were made at the bottom—or at the best, half-way up—instead of starting at the top. It was only when General Papagos was appointed Commander-in-Chief, and the National Defence Council reduced to a small War Cabinet (which was the condition that General Papagos made on accepting the appointment) that things got moving. Had a small War Cabinet, with full control and the power to issue and enforce directives, been established earlier, and the large, often dissenting National Defence Council abolished, the war would have been shortened.

It may be of interest to glance briefly at the structure and tactics adopted, first by ELAS and then by the Democratic Army, against the fuller background of the war as a whole. In the first instance, the guerrillas in occupied Greece were in a primitive confused state, scattered in small bands, motivated by hurt nationalism, vaguely determined to embarrass the Occupation Authorities. The strongest and best organized were Communist-inspired, but they were far more concerned with eliminating or absorbing all other bands than taking action against the authorities. The Communists were already planning for the future.

On to this scene came British officers charged with the task of encouraging the guerrillas to sabotage and commit insurrection with the object of tying down as many Axis troops as possible. They tried to bring the various guerrillas under their direction, holding out a carrot in the shape of arms and ammunition. As has been seen, in the case of ELAS the response was only partial; it grabbed all the arms it could, while at the same time doing the least in return for them. The Communists planned to create a proper army, and lacking an able organizer with experience, they were compelled to co-opt General Saraphis for the purpose. He formed the bands into battalions and subsequently the battalions into larger formations. Brigades and divisions followed, and even a corps appeared in Macedonia as ELAS expanded its army structure. The British officers were not alarmed by the growing organization of ELAS but only at its lack of activity against the Occupation Forces. Few understood guerrilla tactics at that time.

ELAS made a few raids on communications (usually initiated by the British officers in the manner of Lawrence of Arabia in World War I) but only enough to back up their demands for more British arms. Instead of practising good guerrilla tactics ELAS concentrated almost entirely upon becoming a conventional army ready to fight positional battles. In short, it had barely touched the guerrilla stage and had entirely skipped the protracted and mobile warfare ones, when it marched against the Athens Government. It was a gamble that would have succeeded but for the intervention of British troops, rather than a calculated progression on the Communist pattern of insurgency.

The Democratic Army, when it was formed under General Markos, was more of a guerrilla army using guerrilla tactics and formations. Markos understood the pattern of Communist subversive warfare better than the other ELAS leaders, and he insisted that the Democratic Army should consist of small, semi-independent units. He would not permit the formation of brigades or divisions. He had a GHQ staff, which gradually became larger, and also the ETA (the supply organizations) but that was all. He concentrated upon raids and sabotage against the Government forces, and also terrorized the population.

No ex-regular officer, with a conventional military background and his head full of staff tables and neat military formations, exerted any influence in the Democratic Army, and for fully three years General Markos had his way and fought a successful guerrilla warfare stage. The only change was that, as more sophisticated weapons were received, the units increased in strength, from about fifty fighters to about 300.

By the end of 1947 these guerrilla tactics had the GNA tottering. It was over-extended, riddled with fifth-columnists, operating with worn-out equipment and frustrated at every turn it took. The Democratic Army held four-fifths of Greece, and Government supporters could not move far outside the towns in safety. All this had been achieved by well-organized and well-controlled guerrilla tactics. General Markos was under some pressure to move on to the protracted warfare stage and to start forming brigades and divisions, but he resisted, as he estimated the time was not yet ripe. He was wary of the British troops still in Greece and remembered how quickly British reinforcements had been brought in in 1944.

In 1948, US military material was pouring into the GNA, improving its aggressive ability, but as General Markos continued to wage guerrilla warfare the Democratic Army held its own and lost very little territory. Democratic Army units gave way before GNA advances and then infiltrated back when the way was clear again. It was not until the end of the year that the Greek insurgent intelligence services began to fail, when the Government started moving sections of the population and stifling YIAFAKA, thus presenting the KKE with a false picture. Zakhariadis forced a change of strategy and structure, and later took over the command of the Democratic Army himself. The story and the result have been told. The Democratic Army, hastily put together as a conventional army of five divisions, was no match for the GNA in positional combat.

Had the KKE listened to General Markos, there would have been no pitched battles with heavy, irreplaceable losses, or attacks on defended towns, as the GNA would have had little to hit out at. In tiny, mobile groups, the Democratic Army could have survived much longer.

A few remarks in conclusion centring round the word 'if'. A popular generalization frequently voiced about this war is: 'If Yugoslavia had not closed her frontiers, the Communists would have won'. This is not true, and does not take into account certain facts. It is true, though, that if the closing of the Yugoslav frontier had never happened, the war would have been prolonged. Of course, if active hostilities had broken out between Yugoslavia and Greece, the insurgent element would have been submerged.

The Democratic Army had committed itself to conventional warfare; and as it could not match the GNA fire-power there was obviously a limit to the number of its brigades that would have been able to return to the battle. Positional combat meant tremendously heavy casualties every time the two sides clashed, and as the Democratic Army recruiting sources had practically dried up there was little prospect of replacements. This policy meant eventual extermination.

Another 'if'. 'If the Democratic Army had reverted to guerrilla warfare it could never have been defeated.' This again is not true, if it is assumed that the insurgent army, as a true guerrilla body, continued to be supplied by Yugoslavia, or other Balkan countries, and could use that territory as a sanctuary and a base to raid freely over the Greek frontier as it chose. Greek Government counter-insurgency measures were just getting into their stride and becoming really effective. They would have prevented the revival of YIAFAKA, which had been nearly nullified. It had been infiltrated by Government agents and the periodic waves of arrests tore huge gaps in its ranks. This stopped reliable intelligence being fed through to the Democratic Army, causing a blank curtain of silence to descend. Its remaining free members remained passive for fear of detention, or worse.

A guerrilla needs information more than anything else. The YIAFAKA had provided this for so long and so promptly that the Democratic Army could not manage without it, and as it stood little chance of constructing a similar organization in its place, even if the insurgent army had reverted to guerrilla tactics it would have had to operate in the dark. False information would have been fed to it, its guerrillas would have been tempted over the frontier into Greece, traps would have been laid for them, and they would have stumbled blindly into ambush after ambush. There is nothing so demoralizing and depressing as when men go out on operations or patrol never to return, and no one knows whether they have been killed, captured, deserted or turned traitor. The statement that if the Democratic Army had reverted to guerrilla tactics it would still have been able to carry on fighting for an indefinite period should be treated with reserve.

Reverting to the first 'if', a related one is, 'If the Yugoslav border had remained open to the Democratic Army, and it had reverted to guerrilla warfare, the war could not have been won by the Greek Government.' The answer must be the same, despite the length of the Yugoslav frontier. The guerrillas would have been tempted into Greece and eliminated small group by small group.

Another 'if' – 'If Zakhariadis had backed Tito instead of Stalin he would have won' – can also be discounted, because of the efficiency of the Government counter-insurgency measures.

In fact most of the 'ifs' that can be thought of, short of open war between Greece and any of the Balkan countries, would have made little difference to the ultimate result. Perhaps some may have caused the war to last a little longer – but that is all.

The plain fact was that in Greece the Communist guerrillas had been defeated, while on the other side of the world those in China had been triumphant. The completeness and magnitude of Mao Tse-tung's victories awed the world and caused military experts to become thoughtful. They overshadowed the smaller, and less spectacular triumph over militant Communism in Greece, where the weaknesses in the Communist pattern of insurgency to seize power had been demonstrated to all who cared to look.

Initials used in the Text

A few sets of initials are unfortunately essential to this account to identify groups, parties and organizations. They are all formed by the initial letters of a group of Greek words, which, unless you read modern Greek fluently and understand it colloquially as well, will mean little to you in themselves. It is convenient to use them as no short, apt descriptive name can be given in place of the initials. For example, ELAS is formed by the initial letters of Ellinikos Laikos Apeleutherotikos Stratos, which means loosely the National Popular Liberation Army. This is a brief reference list, quoting the most generally accepted English translation of the Greek words.

AAA   The Liberation Struggle Command. A Republican organization, headed by Papandreou. General Saraphis was the leading military personality in it before his defection to ELAS.

EA   National Co-operative movement.

EAM   National Liberation Movement. A Communist initiated and controlled organization, at first consisting of a coalition of six left-wing parties. This organization controlled ELAS, and sometimes is referred to as EAM/ELAS because the two were so closely intertwined.

EDES   National Republican Greek League. The guerrilla army controlled by Colonel Zervas.

EEE   Greek Fascist Party.

EEAM   Workers' National Liberation Front. An underground

Communist organized body that was in opposition to the Axis-supported Trade Union Confederation. Responsible for many strikes.

EES   National Greek Army. A local organization in Macedonia, armed by the Germans, located around the Mikhalagas group of valleys.

EKKA   National Socialist Liberation Group. A Republican organization and guerrilla force, led by Kartalis and General Psaros, during the Occupation, operating mainly in the Roumeli area.

ELAN   National Popular Liberation Navy. The naval section of ELAS.

ELD   Union of Popular Democracy. A Socialist Party in the EAM coalition until it broke away in January 1945.

ELAS   National Popular Liberation Army. The Communist guerrilla force, controlled by EAM. Sometimes referred to as EAM/ELAS.

EOA   National Organization of Officers. An underground organization during the Occupation, strongest in the Peloponnese.

EOK   National Organization of Crete. A Republican organization that dominated Crete during the Occupation.

EP   National Civil Guard. The police organization of EAM.

EPON   National Panhellenic Organization of Youth. The youth organization of EAM.

ERGAS   Workers Anti-Fascist League. A Communist organized body.

ES   Greek Army. An officers underground organization during the Occupation, strongest in the Peloponnese.

ETA   The supply organization of ELAS, which was revived for the Democratic Army.

KEN   Seamans Partisan Committee. A Communist controlled body.

KKE   Greek Communist Party.

KOEN   Communist Organization of Aegean Macedonia.

KOSSA   Communist Organization of the Army and the Security Corps. This provided Communist cells that infiltrated the Greek National Army.

MEEN   Educated Union of National-Minded Youth. A Royalist youth organization.

NOF	Macedonian National Liberation Front. A Communist body that supported the idea of an autonomous Slav-Macedonia.
OENO	Maritime Organization. A Communist body.
OPLA	Units for the Protection of the People's Struggle. A Communist secret police and terrorist body.
PAO	Panhellenic Liberation Organization. A Republican organization, centred on Salonika, which passed on information to the British Military Authorities in Cairo during the Occupation.
PDEG	Democratic Women's Organization of Greece. A Communist body.
PEAN	Patriotic Group of Fighting Youth. A short-lived body of nationalist aims, during the Occupation.
PEEA	Political Committee of Liberation. An alternative government set up in the mountains of Greece in March 1944 by the Communists.
RAN	Initials of territory the organization would like to incorporate into Greece. A Nationalist Republican body.
SAN	League of Young Officers. An underground organization of young officers, some in the Middle East, during the Occupation.
SKE	Greek Socialist Party. Was in the EAM coalition until it broke away in January 1945.
SNOF	A Communist organization for a Southern Slav Federation, which came under Yugoslav influence.
X	An extreme right-wing organization, led by Colonel Grivas.
YIAFAKA	An underground Communist organization that supported the Democratic Army and gave intelligence, supplies and recruits.

Other sets of initials frequently used are:

AMAG	American Mission for Aid to Greece.
GNA	Greek National Army.
JUSMAPG	Joint US Military Advisory and Planning Group.
SOE (Cairo)	Special Operations Executive (Cairo).

Acknowledgements

In compiling this book I have consulted and read with pleasure and profit many works, and I would, in particular, like to make grateful acknowledgement, and to thank the authors, compilers, journalists and officers who wrote, or contributed to, the following:

Achilles and the Tortoise by J. Lincoln (Heinemann, London. 1958).

Anti-Guerrilla Struggle (The) by A. Zaphiropolou (in Greek) (Athens, 1956).

Anti-Guerrilla War in Greece (1946–49) by Lieut.-Colonel E. E. Zacharake. From *Revue Militaire Générale* (France, July, 1960).

Apple of Discord by Colonel C. M. W. Woodhouse (Hutchinson, London, 1948).

Appointment in Crete by A. M. Rendel (Wingate, London, 1953).

Battle of Greece by G. Christopoulos (Private publication, New York, 1941).

Battle of Greece, 1940–1941 *(The)* by General A. Papagos (a translation) (J. M. Skazikis 'Alpha' Editions, Athens, 1949).

Beyond Olympus by C. Jecchinis (Harrap, London, 1960).

Case Study in Guerrilla War: Greece during World War II by D. M. Condit (The American University, 1961).

Cretan Runner (The) by G. Psychoundakis (John Murray, London, 1955).

Divided Land (The) by G. Chandler (Macmillan, London, 1959).

Documents regarding the Situation in Greece Foreign Office (Comd. 6592), London, 1945.

German Attack on Greece (The) by General A. Papagos (Greek Office of Information, London, 1946).

Acknowledgements

Gods were Neutral (The) by R. Crisp (Muller, London, 1960).

Greece against the Axis by Lieut.-Colonel S. Casson (Hamilton, London, 1941).

Greece and the Great Powers 1944–47 by S. G. Xydis (Institute of Balkan Studies, Thessalonika, 1963).

Greece: A Political and Ecomomic Survey, 1939–53 by B. Sweet-Escott (Oxford University Press, 1954).

Greece Fights On by Symmachos (L. Drummond, London, 1943).

Greece: Report by the Supreme Allied Commander, Mediterranean, to the Combined Chiefs of Staff by Viscount Alexander of Tunis (HM Stationery Office, 1949).

Greece: The Whole Story by F. Noel-Baker (Hutchinson, 1946).

Greek Adventure by J. H. Gage (Unie-Volkspers, Cape Town, 1950).

Greek Entanglement by E. C. W. Myers (Hart Davis, 1955).

Greek Miracle (The) by Athenian (Chapman and Hall, 1942).

Greek Resistance Army by S. Sarafis (Birch Books, 1951).

Greek Sedition (The) by F. A. Voigt (Hollis and Carter, 1949).

Greek Tragedy by A. Heckstall-Smith and Vice-Admiral H. T. Baillie-Groman (A. Bond, London, 1961).

Greek Trilogy (The) by W. Byford-Jones (Hutchinson, 1945).

Greek White Book by Royal Greek Ministry of Foreign Affairs (1942).

Guerrilla and Counterguerrilla Warfare in Greece, 1941–45 by Hugh H. Gardner (Army Department, Washington, 1962).

Guerrilla War in Greece, 1946–49 by Lieut.-Colonel E. R. Wainhouse (Military Review USA , June 1957).

Guerrilla War the Communists Lost (The) by D. G. Kousoulas (US Naval Institute Proceedings, May 1963).

History of the Second World War: Grand Strategy (Vols. V and VI) by John Ehrman (HM Stationery Office, 1956).

I Lived with Greek Guerrillas by E. B. Turton (The Book Depot, Melbourne, 1945).

I Was in Noah's Ark by F. Reid (W. R. Chambers, 1957).

Long Road to Leros (The) by L. M. Gander (Macdonald, 1944).

Mediterranean and the Middle East (Vols. I to III) by I. S. O Playfair and Others (HM Stationery Office, 1956).

Mediterranean Front by A. Moorehead (Hamilton, 1941).

Remember Greece by D. Powell (Hodder, 1941).

Revolution and Defeat (The Story of the Greek Communist Party) by D. G. Kousoulas (Oxford University Press, 1965).

Acknowledgements

Second World War (The) by Sir Winston Churchill (Cassell, 1948) (Vols. I to V).

Short History of Greece by Edward S. Forster (Methuen, 1941).

Simiomata by R. Capell (Macdonald, 1946).

We Fell among Greeks by D. Hanson (Jonathan Cape, 1946).

When Greek Meets Greek by Sir Reginald Leeper (Chatto & Windus, 1950).

Wind of Freedom by Sir Compton MacKenzie (Chatto & Windus, 1943).

Wings over Olympus by T. H. Wisdom (Allen & Unwin, 1942).

INDEX

The words Brit(ain)(ish), Communism, Communist, Communistic, Greece, Greek and Greek Governments are not mentioned as they appear on most pages.

Index

Index

Index

Index

Index

Index

DATE DUE

APR 21 '70	OCT 2 6 76		
MAY 5 '70	OC 31 '77		
OCT 6 '70	NO 17 '77		
OCT 12 '70	DE 4 77		
DEC	NO 1 3 '80		
DEC 9 '70	SE 22 81		
DEC 9 '70	OCT 3, '88		
FEB 23 '71			
MAY 5 '71			
FEB 24 '72			
MAR 1 0 '72			
MAY 3 72			
OCT 31 72			
OCT 23 73			
FEB 25 74			
OCT 2 '74			
OCT 21 74			
OCT 27 75			